HOW TO GET
A BUSINESS LOAN

(Without Signing Your Life Away)

Joseph R. Mancuso

PRENTICE
HALL
PRESS

New York   London   Toronto   Sydney   Tokyo   Singapore

Prentice Hall Press
15 Columbus Circle
New York, New York 10023

Library of Congress Cataloging-in-Publication Data

Mancuso, Joseph.
    How to get a business loan (without signing your life away)/
Joseph R. Mancuso.—1st ed.
        p.   cm.
    Includes index.
    ISBN 0-13-407280-4
    1. Commercial loans.   I. Title.
HG1641.M25   1989
658.1'5224—dc19   89-30272
                        CIP

Designed by Irving Perkins Associates
Manufactured in the United States of America

10 9 8 7 6 5 4 3 2 1

First Edition

IT'S A BOY!

While I'm reluctant to report personal matters in this book, this bit of news is just too good to hold back. My wife, Karla, and I have been trying for five years to have children. The old-fashioned way didn't work. Neither did in vitro fertilization (though the medical bills we incurred while trying were enough to make a dent in the national debt). And adoption agencies told us we were too old to adopt a child—we're in our forties. I have three married daughters from a previous marriage.

We also looked into foreign adoptions, tried advertising in rural newspapers, telling friends, acquaintances—you name it, we tried it. Nothing seemed to work.

Then Karla, the real entrepreneur in the family, suggested we run a small ad in *USA Today*. I'd like to say that I responded by saying "Good idea," but actually I discouraged it. As happens in most partnerships, she did it anyway. The ad read "Loving couple seeking to adopt . . ." and gave our phone number.

The one-inch classified ad, which ran for a week, drew three good leads. We visited all three and decided on a young woman in Texas who was seeking a home for her baby, which was due in early March. This was November.

On February 18, 1988, Max Karl Mancuso, six pounds, thirteen ounces, was born. On February 21, 1988, we legally adopted him. He is a gift from heaven.

Hallelujah!

Contents

HOW TO GET
A BUSINESS LOAN

1. How to Write a Winning Business Plan

PREPARING YOUR PLAN

A business plan is commonly thought of as a document written to raise money for a growing company. In actuality, a business plan is a road map that gives a business direction. An entrepreneur visits his banker, or a venture capitalist, with his business plan, not his hat, in hand to attempt to raise money for his business. Attempting to raise money without a written business plan is pure folly, for your would-be backer undoubtedly will say, "Well, when your business plan is done . . . ."

The ideal business plan should really sing, so that you don't have to raise money as the plan will do it for you. The problem for most entrepreneurs, though, is we hate to write business plans. We think of them as a form of punishment or as some species of cod-liver oil—we know they are good for us, but they taste awful going down. So we write *adequate* business plans because we're too busy doing the real work of running our businesses. That work is more fun.

When you take your adequate business plan to your loan officer, what do you end up doing? You sit across from him, lean forward, and start compensating for the shortcomings of your plan with your forceful, charismatic, and persuasive personality. It's called selling.

Well, guess what? Your banker has seen this scenario a hundred times. You've acted just like everyone else he's turned down for a small-business loan in the last ten years. Everybody walks into his banker's office with an average, adequate business plan. You can easily distinguish yourself in your banker's eyes by taking the time to write a great business plan.

I'm going to show you the components of the ideal business plan, and then present to you the greatest business plan I think I've ever seen. (I've seen quite a few; in fact, I have probably the largest archive of business plans in the world).

My theory is if I show you the ideal business plan, you'll be able to compare it with your own and make some practical improvements in yours. You'll be one important step closer to getting your loan. I want you to bear two important things in mind, though.

First, most bankers and financiers don't have emotional attachments to specific kinds of businesses. They don't care if they invest in restaurants or computers, haberdasheries or medical devices. They have an emotional attachment to making money, and bankers are neurotic about the word *risk*.

Second, you cannot copy someone else's business plan, you can only learn from it. If someone tries to tell you they have a computer program that writes a perfect business plan, don't buy it! Each business plan is unique, like a work of art. In fact, it is a work of art in its own right. It expresses and personifies your company. You can no more write a business plan by following a format than you can paint the Mona Lisa using a paint-by-numbers kit.

WHY YOU NEED A PLAN

The need for a business plan is usually inversely proportional to the desire to write one. If you find you want to skip this chapter because you don't think you need to write or improve your plan, you probably need to read this chapter more carefully than any other.

Let me ask you this: Have you ever been in a situation where you're driving an automobile, but you don't know the destination and your passenger is directing you? Doesn't it make you crazy when your passenger gives you only short-term directions like "Turn left here" or "Take a right here." How many short-term directions can a human being take without knowing where he's going . . . before he blows up?

My limit is three; then I turn around and say, "Just tell me where the hell we're going and I'll get us there. I'm not stupid! Give me more than one direction at a time!"

Well, a business plan gives you your destination, and that's tremendously important, not so much for you but for everyone involved in your business—your employees and investors, your customers, and your suppliers. They don't want to just blindly follow your short-term directions, they want to know where the company is headed.

People have a great need for knowledge; in fact, many people are willing to take large risks for small amounts of information. I realized this while observing people waiting for a train at a New York City subway station. Now, I'm not a native New Yorker, so I tend to hug the wall while I wait for a train, for fear that some nut is going to shove me onto the third rail. But many people walk right up to the yellow line at the edge of the platform and lean over the third rail, placing themselves at the mercy of anyone who might be feeling a little testy—just to see if the train is coming. They aren't going to make it come faster. The motorman isn't going to get excited and speed up if they wave at him, but these people are all willing to risk their lives for a marginal level of information. They must need that bit of information badly, or feel that they do. I would like to get that information, too, but I stay glued to the back wall or a concrete pole. I choose, instead, to watch the faces of these data dummies. When they relax and smile, I move up to the yellow line.

Similarly, your employees, bankers, and investors crave every bit of information you can give them about your business. They need to know where the business is going.

DETERMINE YOUR READER

Now that I have you geared up to write your plan, there's something very basic you must decide. For whom are you writing the plan?

Reader of Plan   **Type of Plan**

Venture Source — Equity

Loan Committee (Banks) — Debt

Executive Committee (In-House) — Corporate Financing

Peer Review — Planning

You — Personal Planning

As you can see from the pyramid chart, business plans are written for different readers and for different purposes. First, there's the plan you write for yourself. That plan is useful because it will show you the bugs of your business on paper. Because if you can work them out on paper, you can save yourself some time and money. That plan doesn't receive much peer review, though, and since you worked so darn hard on it, you won't be good at catching its flaws or at criticizing it.

The second kind of plan is the one written for a corporation, such as the plan an IBM executive might write for his operating division. The peer review of these plans has a great deal to do with upper management's perception of the writer of the plan. For example, if GE's brass thinks the new president of their light bulb division is a golden boy based on the last thing he did, they are likely to be thrilled by the next plan he sends them for a project and will probably blindly approve the funding. That's why so many divisions of large companies fail to follow up their first success with another—they become enamored of a hero.

The third type of plan is the kind you write for a bank to get a loan. You give your banker the plan and tell him you want to borrow $100,000. He calls you a couple of days later and says he really likes your plan and will lend you the money if you can deposit $150,000 in CDs to secure the loan.

I've often wondered, What if he didn't like the plan? Would he ask for $350,000 in CDs? Bankers aren't initially moved by business plans to fork over cash—they're moved by collateral because all they stand to make on their deal with you is interest. Even if your business does extremely well, all the bank will get back is interest and its principal, so all the banker wants is to make sure that the bank gets that interest and principal. Period.

The most fun and valuable people to write business plans for are venture capitalists. Unlike corporations or banks, they aren't looking for heroes or collateral; rather, they are looking for exciting new enterprises in which to invest. They are looking for a dream that can become a reality with their financial assistance. The business plan you write for a venture capitalist will be the toughest one you write, because in it you will have to show exactly how you plan to realize your dream.

Even though this book is about getting money from a bank for your small business, I'm going to spend some time talking about how to write a winning business plan for venture capitalists, because if you can write a great business plan for venture capitalists, the other plans—for banks, corporations, or yourself—will be easy to write.

STRIVE FOR AN ELEVEN

One day you make the big decision. You quit your job and go home to write the great American novel, the new *Love Story* or *Godfather*. You walk over to Simon & Schuster to collect your advance. How much money could you get? A hundred thousand? How about when the book is done? Let's say the publisher loves it and gives you $2 million. That's respectable.

The great thing about a business plan is you can spend the same amount of time it would take you to write a novel and, if you write a plan as good as the one I'm going to describe . . . well, that plan attracted 250 million of today's dollars up front on day one! The sequel to the greatest movie of all time, *Gone with the Wind,* fetched $5 million up front in 1988. You can get several orders of magnitude more in up-front money by writing a business plan than by writing a novel, and, in many ways, a business plan is easier to write.

Most entrepreneurs are capable of writing a business plan that on a scale of one to ten would rate from five to nine. The problem is that to raise money from a venture capitalist or to get a loan from your bank you need an eleven. Average is not acceptable. Too many entrepreneurs shoot for a business plan that rates a five. You have to shoot for an eleven because you'll never write one accidentally. A plan has to be a ten just to attract any money. A nine is a bridesmaid who is very sweet and attractive but doesn't get married. An eight is also a bridesmaid, but she's not quite as attractive . . . and so on.

So what's an eleven? An eleven is a plan that attracts so many investors that you're up all night trying to decide who you're going to have to cut out of the deal. To be good is not enough when you dream of being great.

THE DIFFERENCES BETWEEN BUSINESS PLANS FOR BANKERS AND FOR VENTURE CAPITALISTS

The first thing to decide on before starting your business plan is what the reader needs to know. In each business plan you write, you should emphasize the figures that are important to the reader—the banker or venture capitalist.

We've already determined that a banker needs to know about collateral. He wants to know how the loan is going to be repaid. The venture capitalist, on the other hand, wants to know different things: Is the product going to sell like mad? Will customers arrive in droves? How much money am I going to make?

Another difference between bankers and venture capitalists is the way they gain control of the business's operations via their loan or investment. Bankers build negative covenants into the loan agreement. For instance, if you don't pay, they can fine you for every day the payment is late or call the loan or sell the collateral.

Venture capitalists will take seats on your board of directors to exercise control. If they're really smart, they will also give you "debt with warrants," which provides them with essentially the same checks the bankers have, i.e., negative covenants in the loan agreements.

Bankers love to run ratio analyses: They look at changes in various ratios over time. Venture capitalists like to look at the value of the stock over time.

Bankers want to see a full personal financial statement. Venture capitalists are more interested in knowing where you went to school and what your last job was. As you can see from the chart below, however, there are more similarities than differences in the business plans prepared for bankers and for venture capitalists.

BUSINESS PLAN DIFFERENCES

Bankers (Debt)	**Venture Capitalists (Equity)**
1. Emphasis on collateral	1. Emphasis on customers' need for product
2. Negative covenants in loan agreement	2. Seats on board—debt/warrants
3. Ratio analysis	3. Value of stock
4. How the bank will get its money back	4. Expected return for investors
5. Officers' financial statements	5. Officers' background

BUSINESS PLAN SIMILARITIES

1. Management Team
2. History
3. Product/Competition
4. Market
5. Industry
6. Manufacturing
7. Sales Forecast
8. Breakeven

THE GREATEST BUSINESS PLAN EVER WRITTEN

Most people collect normal things. I collect old business plans. Over twenty-five years I have built up quite an archive—not that anyone cares—of all the business plans that have launched significant companies. I have about 150 plans, including ones from Xerox, Scientific Data Systems, *Venture* magazine, Federal Express, Medical Graphics, Storage Technology, Shopsmith, and Pizzatime Theater.

See if you can guess which plan I think is the best as I describe the plan and the personality behind it to you. I mention personality because when someone reads your plan and tells you this or that is wrong with it, what they are really telling you is that you're ugly. It's very personal. They're saying, "You're ugly and corrective surgery won't help. A toupee won't do it. Losing fifty pounds won't do it. You're just basically ugly!"

And it hurts! But you're very grown up about it, of course, and you say, "Well, tell me, if I recast my financials, would I be able to be un-ugly?"

You can't separate the hero from the plan. What I like about my favorite business plan is that the hero wasn't one of those engineer or MBA types. The business wasn't high-tech or low-tech, it was no-tech. When he launched the business that raised $250 million up front (in 1989 dollars), he was twenty-nine years old. He had no business experience at all.

When he got out of school, he bummed around for about a year, and then he enlisted in the marines. He doesn't sound like much of an entrepreneurial hero yet, does he? You can't have a great plan without a hero, but a great hero can have a bad plan. That's an important concept.

In the marines he flew solo reconnaissance missions over Vietnam. He came back to the United States, bummed around some more, and couldn't figure out what he wanted to do, so he reenlisted and went back to North Vietnam! Would you invest in this guy? He sounds a little flaky.

He first wrote his business plan when he was an undergraduate at Yale, and his professor gave it a *C*. The professor wrote "Good idea. Costs too much."

Our hero's name is Fred Smith, and the business based on that plan is Federal Express.

Smith did have some money. He had about $3 million of net worth from his family, but he raised $100 million on the strength of his business plan and its opening premise: He was going to ship a package from Newark to New York— through Memphis. A package going from Fort Worth to Dallas would be shipped through Memphis, too. It sounds a little wacky. Before Federal Express, packages were delivered piggyback on passenger flight schedules. If there wasn't a passenger flight from Chicago to Des Moines on a particular day, the package wasn't delivered.

Smith planned to buy 27 airplanes and 3,000 trucks and to hire 10,000 human beings before he opened the door for business. That was a very expensive concept. He was going to strategically station the airplanes around the United States, and have them fly preassigned routes, pick up packages, and then meet in Memphis around midnight. At midnight the packages would be passed around to different airplanes and trucks to be delivered by morning. Memphis was the hub: everything came in through Memphis and everything went out through Memphis (Smith's hometown, by the way).

On day one, Federal Express delivered eleven packages, but on day two the company saw a 33 percent growth in sales!

Fred Smith changed the concept of venture capital in the United States. Before Federal Express, the largest venture capital deal had been Digital Equipment Corp. (DEC). General George F. Doriot, a professor at the Harvard Business School, gave $70,000 to Ken Olsen of Digital Equipment. Today DEC is worth billions.

The Federal Express deal was different because there was no single lead investor. Venture capital deals had been usually one on one. But Smith convinced almost every venture capitalist around to get involved in Federal Express, and the success of his company boosted the fledgling venture capital industry into maturity. The legend of Fred Smith may have already grown beyond the truth, but the stories are so colorful that few people care to separate fact from fiction, and now he is a folk hero.

Smith got those venture capitalists involved because his presentation and his business plan were so strong. He walked up to venture capitalists and said something like this: "I'm about to create an industry, not just a company. I have put all of my personal money into this project. Everybody I know has invested in this deal. I haven't got a friend or family member left who hasn't thrown his money into this deal. When the competition catches on, we're gonna kill 'em because it's going to cost them the same up-front money to catch up. I already have firm commitments for $100 million, but I know there's a chance that one or two of these commitments might fall through. One of these investors might get sick or something. It's not likely, but you never know. Someone might not show up. So I was wondering. . . . Would you come to the closing as a sort of utility player? Don't even bring your checkbook. If the deal comes up a million short, though, maybe you would step up?"

How many times did Smith tell that story? I'll let you guess. He knew this important fact: It's a lot easier to sell the last million than it is to sell the first.

If you have any qualms about the ethics of what Smith did, keep in mind that the story I just related is probably one of the most ethical ways entrepreneurs raise money. Fred Smith did what he had to do as often as he had to do it. That's why he's my favorite entrepreneur.

THE FIRST THING THEY LOOK AT

The average venture capitalist or banker can analyze your plan and decide whether he is interested in about five minutes. That sounds a little offensive, but it's true. What is the first thing a financier looks at? It's not the name of the business or the product or the size of the market. He looks at something that tells him right away whether he wants to bother to look further.

I'll give you a hint. He looks at the numbers, but not the numbers you're thinking of. He doesn't give a hoot about projected growth rate, for example, because every entrepreneur projects the greatest growth rate ever seen. For the same reason, he doesn't look at the projected market or pro forma financial statements.

The venture capitalist and the banker want to see the one thing that will tell them whether the entrepreneur is a flake or is someone with substance, i.e., money, behind him. They want to know how much money has already been invested in the plan. To find out, they look at stockholders' equity in the balance sheet—the *opening-day* balance sheet, not the projected balance sheet. A balance sheet is a snapshot, a photograph of the company at a moment in time, and one picture properly taken can be worth a thousand words (or millions of investors' dollars!)

A start-up balance sheet has only two entries: cash and stockholders' equity. Even if there has been no outside investment, the numbers under cash and stockholders' equity tell the venture capitalist and the banker how much of his own money the entrepreneur has sunk into the venture. That's important information because it proves commitment.

Did you have bacon and eggs for breakfast this morning? If you did, you ate a lesson in the difference between a contribution and a commitment. The chicken made a contribution but the pig made a commitment! After all, wasn't commitment the reason why Fred Smith's business plan was the greatest of all time?

COMMON PROBLEMS WITH BUSINESS PLANS

Dr. Edward B. Roberts, the David Sarnoff Professor of Management and Technology at MIT, did a study of twenty business plans submitted by high-tech, start-up companies to venture capitalists in the Boston area. Here are some of the results of that study:

1. While all twenty plans stated an overall objective, only fourteen had a specific strategy that appeared rational and achievable.
2. The central thrust of the plans broke down as follows:
Product   47%
Market   29%
People   24%
3. Profitability and growth were not discussed in detail in 45 percent of the plans.
4. Three-quarters of the plans failed to identify details about their competitors.
5. The marketing plan was consistently the weakest element of the twenty plans, while the R&D aspect was consistently the strongest.
6. Marketing research and selling were given very low priority in three-quarters of the plans, and little background in these areas was evidenced. (It is interesting to note that earlier research by Professor Roberts showed an inverse relationship between product success and a firm's ability to do market research. It concludes

by stating that if time exists for market research, you're already too late for the market.)

7. The financial projections offered in these plans broke down as follows:

None	10%
Data not available	5%
1–3-year income statement only	10%
4–5-year income statement only	40%
1–3-year income statement and balance sheet	15%
4–5-year income statement and balance sheet	10%
Other	10%

Roberts concluded the report on his research with the following statement: "One critical aspect of the business plan is that if you don't do it right, there is a high likelihood that you will never do anything beyond it. Business planning needs to be undertaken seriously, if for no other reason than that it is a major tangible representation of who you are, what you are, and what you want to be to the financial community. It may also even relate to later business success."

MINI–BUSINESS PLANS WON'T DO

I wish I had a dollar for every person who asked me if they could submit a "mini–business plan" to a lender or investor. Some say they want to raise $100,000, or some other small amount, so they don't need a full business plan. Some say the deal's all but done, so the plan isn't a central issue. Some say they don't have the time or money for a full-fledged business plan, or that they'll do it later. All of those excuses are cop-outs because there's no such thing as a mini–business plan!

A good business plan requires hard work. It takes months, and sometimes thousands of dollars to complete. And the one thing all of the successful business plans I've seen have in common is they're all "complete." They cover all the bases.

What Is Planning?

Planning is not something that can be done effectively in a "short form." You wouldn't ask an artist to paint a picture and then, to save time, ask him to leave out the background or the color. The picture needs all of its parts to be effective. It's the same way with a song. You wouldn't want to hear a song with just half the words. Half of a painting or a song or a business plan isn't 50 percent of the value. To have any real value at all, each has to be complete.

Telling an investor or lender that you're sending him a mini–business plan is the kiss of death to being financed. It begs the question "Where's the big plan?" and "If I don't get the big plan, who does?"

In short: "Mini–business plans" are really plans that are poorly or partially done.

Copying Business Plans

Another notion popular to business plan preparers is copying a "perfect" plan. This is a silly idea. You can't paint a masterpiece with a paint-by-numbers kit. Each business plan is an individual work of art, and while you can get new ideas by reading other plans, you can't make your plan a good one just by copying them. Reading over other business plans is like visiting many art galleries before you begin to create.

PRACTICE YOUR ANSWERS

Of all the questions a venture capitalist or banker is most likely to ask, the easiest is "What business are you in?" Even though this question is easy, you've got to practice your response. You need a crisp, sharp answer that distinguishes you from the pack. Remember Fred Smith's answer: "I'm about to create an industry, not just a company. . . ." After all, the answer to this question becomes your mission statement.

It's very important to have a mission statement and to practice it before you're asked that first question. You can find another example of a mission statement on the inside cover of the directory for the second association I founded, the Chief Executive Officers Club: "The CEO club is a nonprofit group of chief executive officers dedicated to improving the profitability and quality of their enterprises through shared experiences and personal growth." It may not be perfect, but I worked on it and I practiced saying it from the day I started the club in 1982. At least I will not fumble when someone asks, "What business are you in?" Can you say the same?

That was an easy question. Here's a tough one: "Who else have you shown the deal to?" Your answer can provide the best window through which the venture capitalist or banker looks into your business. You basically have three choices: Tell him that no one else has seen it, tell him that everyone who is anyone has seen it, or tell him that only your inner circle of family and friends has seen it. Each of these answers leaves you vulnerable to further questioning from the source about why no one else has seen it or why the people who have seen it haven't thrown all their money into it.

You might be tempted to protect yourself by saying, "Well, the people I've shown it to have asked me not to talk about it" or, simply, "I'd rather not say to whom I've shown it." The problem with these answers is they don't exactly build trust. You wouldn't start a marriage by refusing to discuss your net worth with your spouse; likewise, you shouldn't begin a five- or ten-year relationship with a banker or venture capitalist by being secretive. This question must be handled delicately. (Keep reading: The answer will follow.)

YOUR BEST CONNECTION IS ANOTHER ENTREPRENEUR

The best person to connect you to a venture capitalist or a banker is another entrepreneur in the venture or loan portfolio. This is someone to whom the venture capitalist has already given money or to whom the banker has already lent money.

Venture capitalists are extremely busy, so they rely on referrals. Dick Reardon, a major venture capitalist in Los Angeles, told me that in the history of his career as a venture source, he has never financed a deal that came in without a referral.

People prefer to invest in or lend to companies with which they are somehow familiar. The guy who financed Lotus software is likely to make his next investment in a software company.

Look in various venture capital directories for your industry to find companies like yours. Find out who has invested in those companies. Look in the portfolio of investments for that venture capitalist and find the name of an entrepreneur in whom he has invested. The same concept can be used for a banker. Look at the loan portfolio of a bank that you think might be good for you. Find an entrepreneur who has been dealing with the bank. Call him. Tell him that you are having a little trouble polishing up your business plan: You went to a Mancuso seminar and Mancuso suggested calling a successful entrepreneur in your business for some help. Ask him if he works on Saturdays (they always do!) and whether you can drop off your business plan for him to look over in the next couple of weeks.

Why would this entrepreneur be eager to help a potential competitor? Because you have just elevated him from a dumb old entrepreneur to a consultant, a fine business plan adviser. He'll love it, and he probably will be helpful because, as a successful entrepreneur, he's already demonstrated his ability to speak three foreign languages: entrepreneurese, venture capitalese, and bankese. Although you think you're multilingual (in fact, you may be able to speak bankese), learning the language of business planning is like learning a foreign language in school: You don't become fluent until you spend some time in the country.

In a couple of weeks you call your "consultant" again and ask him to take a crack at improving your business plan. A few weeks later, you invite him over to see your shop. A few weeks after that, you go to look at his shop, and a few weeks later you invite him to join your board of advisers, and so on.

During this time he's in contact with his venture sources or his banker, and you can be sure he'll drop in conversation the flattering fact that he is being consulted by another entrepreneur because he is so terrific at business planning. By this time, no doubt, he ranks his business planning acumen just under that of Fred Smith.

You can be sure that he'll keep his venture capitalist or banker posted on what's happening with your business plan. "Hey, remember that guy I helped with his plan? Well, he just got his prototype done." A few weeks later he'll report: "You know that guy I've been advising? He's got a couple of venture people flying in to see him. They're gonna close the deal."

Now, what do you think that banker or venture capitalist is going to say? He's going to say, "Why don't you give me that guy's name? I think I'll give him a call."

When he calls you, tell him this: "Preparing a business plan has been very important to me, and as I've worked on it I've given a lot of thought to which investors (or bankers) would give our business a proper fit. You've got investments in similar businesses and you've certainly got the capital to invest. You may not be the number-one choice, but you've got to be up there in the top three. I figure if you don't like it, it's likely the other investors (or bankers) won't like it because you represent the top class of possible investors (or bankers) for this kind of enterprise. I'd like you to look at it first and tell me what you think."

You've just given the best possible answer to that tough question: "Who have you shown the deal to?"

SEEK A NO (A SHORT NO IS BETTER THAN A LONG NO)

The financial officer of a fledgling computer business said to me at one of my seminars for entrepreneurs, "Joe, the CEO of my company has had about fifteen venture capitalists waste his time with about fifteen in-depth visits and meetings, but none of them has made a commitment. None of them wants to be the first into the deal, and it's just been wasting a lot of our time. How do we get them to act less like sheep and make a move?"

Venture capitalists do tend to get bunched up in herds. Bankers get up in the morning and, in front of the mirror, practice saying, "No. I don't see any way to do it. No." Entrepreneurs get up in the morning shouting, "Yes!" Venture capitalists get up in the morning saying, "I'm not sure. Maybe."

The entrepreneur's mistake is that he goes into the venture capitalist's office looking for a yes. Nobody gets a yes. Fred Smith didn't get one; Digital Equipment didn't get one.

Your strategy should be to seek a no. You seek a no because a short no is better than a long no. A long no drains your company.

Tell the venture capitalist, "I know you can't give me a yes right away, but I think it's reasonable for me to ask you to give me a no within three or four days."

After you get the no ask him, "If you can't do it, who do you think is the next best choice?" Take the no and turn it into a referral.

If he can't give you a no or a yes, say, "Look, if you can't give me an answer, at least give me something to work with so that I can move on. Why don't you agree to take, say, the last 25 percent of the deal, so I can at least keep you in the deal and go to my other prospects with that incentive and get them to move." If he says no, good, you got a no. Take it and get the referral. Maybes may feel good, but the time they take will kill you.

Fred Smith did one more very smart thing. He went to General Dynamics, the company from which he planned to buy the first airplanes for Federal Express, and he asked them to kick in some money. Fred was then able to approach venture sources with a large company having already invested, and the deal looked much more attractive.

WHAT TO DO WHEN A VENTURE CAPITALIST TURNS YOU DOWN

The following is a list of the ten questions to ask when a venture capitalist turns you down.

1. *Confirm the decision.* "That means you do not wish to participate at this time?"
2. *Sell for the future.* "Can we count you in for a second round of financing, after we've completed the first?"
3. *Find out why you were rejected.* "Why do you choose not to participate in this deal?" (Timing? Fit? All filled up?)
4. *Ask for advice.* "If you were in my position, how would you proceed?"
5. *Ask for suggestions.* "Can you suggest a source who invests in this kind of deal?"
6. *Get the name.* "Whom should I speak to when I'm there?"
7. *Find out why.* "Why do you suggest this firm, and why do you think this is the best person to speak to there?"
8. *Work on an introduction.* "Who would be the best person to introduce me?"
9. *Develop a reasonable excuse.* "Can I tell him that your decision to turn us down was based on _____?"
10. *Know your referral.* "What will you tell him when he calls?"

PUTTING TOGETHER THE PLAN: QUESTIONS AND ANSWERS

1. What is the single most important element in a business plan?
   Management
2. What two elements bring a business plan from a nine to an eleven (on a scale of 1 to 10).
   A. Answer the negatives
   B. Answer sheet (it's just like . . . , If it goes bad . . . , the other guys have deep pockets)
3. List the five questions a venture source needs answered. Circle the easiest and toughest question.
   A. What business are you in?
   B. How much money?
   C. For what percentage of the business?
   D. Who is in the deal?
   E. What's unique about this deal?
4. How is a business plan read in five minutes? Rank the six things for which a financial source looks.
   A. To determine the characteristics of the company and the industry
   B. Terms of the deal
   C. Balance sheet
   D. Caliber of the people
   E. To find the USP (unique selling proposition)
   F. Once over lightly
5. Rank, in order of importance, the following linkage methods of introducing your deal to a venture capital source.
   1   A. Entrepreneur in the venture portfolio
   2   B. Another venture capitalist
   6   C. Accountant familiar with the venture source
   7   D. Lawyer familiar with the venture source
   5   E. Banker familiar with the venture source
   3   F. Social friend of the venture source
   10 G. Letter to the venture source followed by phone call
   8   H. Customer of a company familiar with the venture source
   4   I. Investor in the venture capitalist's portfolio
   9   J. Direct visit to the venture capitalist
6. Identify the nine players who make up the entrepreneurial baseball team. Circle the pitcher.
   A. Partners
   B. Lawyers
   C. Accountants

      D. Consultants

      E. Advertising agencies

      F. Bankers

      G. Board of directors

      H. Manufacturers' agents

      I. Controller

7. What information must appear on the summary page outline?

      A. Percentage of company being sold

      B. Price/share vs. last price/share

      C. Minimum investment (number of investors)

      D. Total valuation (after placement)

      E. Terms of placement

8. List the six-step sequence of events for presenting a business plan.

      A. Prospecting

      B. Approach

      C. Qualifying the source

      D. Presenting the plan

      E. Handling objections

      F. Gaining commitment

2. The Components of a Successful Business Plan

HOW TO PRICE YOUR DEAL

In chapter 1 I said that each business plan is a unique work of art. I advised against copying someone else's business plan, but I encouraged you to look at other plans. Artists haunt galleries, studying the works of other artists to get ideas. You should do the same thing. Study the example in appendix IV and in my other books to get your own creative juices flowing and to learn the basic components of various business plans.

All business plans contain information that shows the return on an investment in the business. The rule of thumb is that venture capitalists want six times their money back over a five-year period. That works out to about a 45 percent return on investment (ROI). That's a lot of return, but that's what they demand. Maybe we should call them vulture capitalists! A banker will expect to see similar information in her version of the business plan.

Since venture capitalists often seek to tie their investments in your company to equity, I will show you how to use the earnings curve to figure out how much an investment is worth in equity. If someone gives you $1 million to start your company, for example, how much of the company should you give up based on that earnings curve? (Bear in mind that we entrepreneurs are not smart enough to work in the per-share universe. There was only one man who was smart enough: Einstein. Always figure the price of a deal in total value, not in per share.)

If you look at the example in the figure on page 18, you will observe that the company is worth $20 million in the fifth year because the profit during the fifth year is $2 million and the price-to-earnings ratio (P/E) is 10. Multiply the net profit by the P/E to calculate the total value of the business—$20 million. Capitalization times earnings equals the worth of the company.

How much of the stock do you have to give up on day one to attract $1

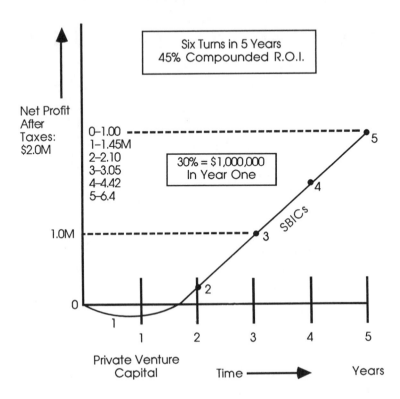

$P/E = 10$
Value in 5th Year = $20M

Net Profit After Taxes: $2.0M

0–1.00
1–1.45M
2–2.10
3–3.05
4–4.42
5–6.4

Six Turns in 5 Years
45% Compounded R.O.I.

30% = $1,000,000
In Year One

SBICs

1.0M

Private Venture Capital

Time ➡ Years

How to Price a Venture Deal: A venture source wants to earn about 45 percent compounded annual return on all funds invested. Offer them much below 40 percent and they're usually not interested. If your projections are much over 60 percent, they'll become very skeptical. So in order to get financed, business plans should offer a 45 percent compounded return on investment (ROI). This figure is a sample of how that works on a $1 million investment.

million of investment? What's fair? We know the venture capitalist wants her investment of $1 million to be worth $6 million in five years, so we can figure out how much equity to give her on the day she hands over the $1 million. She wants $6 million worth of stock in five years. We have figured the value of the company to be $20 million in five years. Divide $6 million by $20 million to find out what percentage of the company $6 million represents. It's about 30 percent; therefore, in exchange for the $1 million the venture capitalist should receive 30 percent of the stock of the company on day one. If you follow the same procedure for a $200,000 investment, you'll find that the venture source should receive about 6 percent of the stock on day one, given the earnings curve in the figure on page 18.

All successful business plans end up projecting about a 40 percent to 50 percent ROI. Consequently, all the projected ROI graphs for successful businesses look very similar. The actual return experienced by the venture capitalist usually turns out to be 20 percent to 30 percent for all ventures because many plans produce a zero return.

PREPARING YOUR FINANCIALS

Most business plan financials are very hard to read because most entrepreneurs or their accountants come up with their own formats. What's more, we all keep different kinds of accounts. I suggest you use a standardized form. The best is probably the Robert Morris form. Robert Morris is the predominant training arm of the commercial lending and banking industry. The firm also provides valuable industry statistics and financial ratios for industries. When bankers are trained to become commercial lenders, they are often trained on Robert Morris forms.

Robert Morris forms allow the venture capitalist or banker to see all three financial statements of a company in one fell swoop. You can have the detailed balance sheet, cash flow, and income statement in the appendix, but bring old Robert Morris along and show it to your banker. Her eye will pivot to line 34 and line 35—where the cash figures are. The Robert Morris "Projection of Financial Statements" form is widely used by entrepreneurs in preparing financials for business plans. Contact:

> Robert Morris Associates
> 1616 Philadelphia National Bank Bldg.
> Philadelphia, PA 19107
> (215) 665-2858

Or you can purchase them by mail from:

> Bankers Systems Inc.
> P.O. Box 1457
> St. Cloud, MN 56302
> (612) 251-3060

On the back of the Robert Morris forms are sixty carefully worded assumptions. Bankers and venture capitalists love to fool around with your assumptions, but using the Robert Morris form offers some protection. If you say that you've based your assumptions on receivables or paybacks on experience, you're leaving yourself wide open to contention.

Use old Robert Morris to your advantage when you're asked how you made

PROJECTION OF FINANCIAL STATEMENTS

SUBMITTED BY _____

	ACTUAL	PROJECTIONS →								

SPREAD IN HUNDREDS ☐ DATE
SPREAD IN THOUSANDS ☐ PERIOD

PROFIT and LOSS

1	NET SALES	1
2		2
3		3
4	Less: Materials Used	4
5	COST OF GOODS SOLD	5
6	GROSS PROFIT	6
7	Less: Sales Expense	7
8	General & Administrative Expense	8
9	Depreciation	9
10		10
11	OPERATING PROFIT	11
12	Less: Other Expense	12
13	Add: Other Income	13
14	PRE-TAX PROFIT	14
15	Income Tax Provision	15
16	NET PROFIT	16

CASH PROJECTION

17	CASH BALANCE (Opening)	17
18	Add: Receipts: Cash Sales & Other Income	18
19	Cash Sales Plus Receivable Collections	19
20		20
21		21
22	Bank Loan Proceeds	22
23	Other Loan Proceeds	23
24	TOTAL CASH AND RECEIPTS	24
25	Less: Disbursements: Trade Payables	25
26	Direct Labor	26
27	OPERATING & OTHER EXPENSES	27
28		28
29	Capital Expenditures	29
30	Income Taxes	30
31	Dividends or Withdrawals	31
32	Bank Loan Repayment	32
33	Other Loan Repayment	33
34	TOTAL CASH DISBURSEMENTS	34
35	CASH BALANCE (Closing)	35

BALANCE SHEET

36	ASSETS: Cash and Equivalents	36
37	Receivables	37
38	Inventory (Net)	38
39		39
40	CURRENT ASSETS	40
41	Fixed Assets (Net)	41
42		42
43		43
44		44
45	TOTAL ASSETS	45
46	LIABILITIES: Notes Payable-Banks	46
47	Notes Payable-Others	47
48	Trade Payables	48
49	Income Tax Payable	49
50	Current Portion L.T.D.	50
51		51
52	CURRENT LIABILITIES	52
53	Long-Term Liabilities:	53
54		54
55		55
56	TOTAL LIABILITIES	56
57	NET WORTH: Capital Stock	57
58	Retained Earnings	58
59		59
60	TOTAL LIABILITIES AND NET WORTH	60

Sample Robert Morris Projection of Financial Statements

Sample Robert Morris Projection of Financial Statements (*cont.*)

Sample Robert Morris Projection of Financial Statements (*cont.*)

HOW TO USE THIS FORM

RMA's Projection of Financial Statements, Form C-117, may be completed by the banker, the customer, or both working together. It is designed to be flexible and may be used as a:

1) Projection tool to provide a picture of the customer's present and future financial condition. Actual and estimated financial data form the basis of the calculations.
2) Tool for analysis of the customer's borrowing needs and debt repayment ability.
3) Budget to aid in planning for the customer's financial requirements and repaying the banker's credit accommodation.

INSTRUCTIONS: In the first column, enter the actual PROFIT AND LOSS STATEMENT and BALANCE SHEET of the date immediately prior to projection period. Then, in each subsequent column, covering a projection period (e.g., month, quarter, annual):

- Enter on the "date" line, the ending date of each projection period (e.g., 1/31, 3/31, 19____)
- Enter on the "period" line the length of each projection period (e.g., 1 mo., 3 mos., 12 mos.)
- Then, follow the line-by-line instructions below:

Line No.	Title	Instructions
PROFIT AND LOSS STATEMENT		
1	NET SALES	Enter actual or beginning net sales figure in the first vertical column. We suggest you project future net sales based upon a % sales increase or decrease. Estimate acceptable % figure and record here _____%. (This % is generally calculated based on historical changes in net sales. However, consideration must also be given to factors, such as general business conditions, new products and services, and competition.)
2 through 5	COST OF GOODS SOLD	Enter all relevant components of customer's cost of goods sold calculation. Project future cost of goods sold based upon % increase or decrease. Estimate acceptable percentage figure and insert here _____%. (This figure is generally estimated as a percentage of sales based on prior years.)
6	GROSS PROFIT	Line 1 minus line 5.
7 through 10	Sales Expense; General and Administrative Expenses; Other	Enter all items. Project future expenses based on an increase or decrease. Estimate acceptable percentage figure and insert here _____%. (This figure is generally estimated as a percentage of sales based on prior years. Anticipated increases in major expenses, such as lease, officers' salaries, etc., should also be considered.)
11	OPERATING PROFIT	Line 6 minus the sum of lines 7 through 10.
12 through 13	Various adjustments to Operating Profit	Enter all items and estimate future adjustments.
14	PRE-TAX PROFIT	Line 11 minus the sum of lines 12 through 13.
15	Income Tax Provision	Common methods used for calculating Income Tax Provision include the most current year's tax as a % of the Pre-Tax Profit.
16	NET PROFIT	Line 11 minus the sum of lines 12 through 15.
CASH PROJECTION CALCULATION		
17	CASH BALANCE	Enter opening cash balance. For subsequent periods, enter the closing cash balance (Line 35) from previous period. Or enter an adjusted amount to reflect a desired cash balance.
18 through 21	Receipts	Enter total cash sales & other income plus receivables collected. Receivable collections must be calculated separately. This requires an analysis of the customer's sales and collection patterns:

       (1) Estimate the portion of each month's sales collected in that month and subsequent months.

       (2) From the sales figure last month and the previous month(s), calculate how much of the existing receivable figure will be collected in the current month.

       (3) Deduct the collected receivables balance calculated in (2) above from the month-end balance of accounts receivables.

       (4) Add this month's sales figure to the remainder of receivables calculated in (3) above. This figure is the new accounts receivable figure for the end of the current month.

EXAMPLE   Assumptions:
Projection calculation - monthly

Monthly Net Sales:
      9/30 - $250M
      10/31 - $300M
      11/30 - $150M

Accounts Receivable balance:
      9/30 - $250M
      10/31 - $367M

The average collection period is 45 days. This means that 66.7% (30 days ÷ 45 days) of each month's sales will be collected the following month and the remaining 33.3% in the second month.

To determine receivable collections for November --

Accounts Receivable balance, 10/31		$367M
Deduct: 66% of 10/31 sales	200M	
33% of 9/30 sales	83M	283M
		84M
Add: 11/30 sales		150M
Accounts Receivable Balance, 11/30		$234M

Line No.	Title	Instructions
22 through 23	Bank Loan Proceeds/ Other	Enter actual or projected bank loan proceeds on line 22. Enter any other receipts on line 23.
24	TOTAL CASH AND RECEIPTS	Enter sum of lines 17 through 23.
25 through 33	Disbursements	Enter actual or estimated cash disbursements on these lines.
34	TOTAL DISBURSEMENTS	Enter sum of lines 25 through 33.
35	CASH BALANCE (Closing)	Line 24 minus line 34. Note: The closing cash balance on line 35 may be entered on line 17 in the next column. However, if the closing cash balance is negative, or below the desired opening cash balance, then bank loans (line 22) may be needed to raise the closing cash balance to zero, or to the desired opening cash balance. The bank loan necessitates planning for repayment (line 31 and 32) in subsequent columns.

Sample Robert Morris Projection of Financial Statements (*cont.*)

<u>BALANCE SHEET</u>

(36 through 44)	ASSETS	
36	Cash and Equivalents	Enter cash and readily marketable securities--current year only. For subsequent years use the closing cash balance (line 35).
37	Receivables	Enter actual receivables in the first column. To project, use previous receivables figure plus projected net sales (line 1), minus projected cash sales and receivables collections (line 19).
38	Inventory	Enter actual inventory in the first column. To project, add purchases to beginning inventory. Then, subtract materials used to calculate the ending inventory amount (lines 2 through 4). If the inventory purchase figure is not available, balances can be calculated based on historic turnover ratios.
40	Current Assets	Enter sum of lines 36 through 39.
41	Fixed Assets (Net)	Enter fixed assets. To project, add previous year's fixed assets and any fixed asset additions. Then, deduct estimated accumulated depreciation.
42 through 44		Enter other non-current assets (stockholder's receivables, intangibles, etc.).
45	TOTAL ASSETS	Add lines 40 through 44.
(46 through 56)	LIABILITIES	
46	Notes Payable-Banks	Prior period balance plus loan proceeds (line 22), less repayments (line 32).
47	Notes Payable-Others	Prior period balance plus note proceeds (line 23), less repayments (line 32).
48	Trade Payables	Prior period balance plus purchases less payments (line 25). If the inventory purchase figure is not available, balances can be projected based on historic payables turnover.
49	Income Tax Payable	Add prior period balance to income tax provision (line 14) and deduct income taxes paid (line 30).
50	Current Portion Long-Term Debt	Estimate current maturities by entering the sum of prior period debt's maturities and additional bank loan proceeds scheduled repayments.
51		Enter the sum of any other current liabilities.
52	CURRENT LIABILITIES	Enter the sum of lines 46 through 51.
53 through 55	Long-Term Liabilities	Enter long-term liabilities here. Calculate long-term debt by adding previous period long-term debt (line 53) to loan proceeds (lines 22 & 23), and subtracting current maturities (line 50).
56	TOTAL LIABILITIES	Enter sum of lines 52 through 55.
(57 through 59)	NET WORTH	
57	Capital Stock	Enter current capital stock figure. An increase will occur if capital stock is sold; a decrease will occur if existing stock is repurchased or retired.
58	Retained Earnings	Add prior period retained earnings to projected net profit (line 16), and deduct dividends or withdrawals (line 31).
59		Enter other equity items.
60	TOTAL LIABILITIES AND NET WORTH	Enter sum of lines 56 through 59.

Practice turning negatives into opportunities. Remember, practice doesn't make perfect. Perfect practice makes perfect.

I knew a terrific entrepreneur in Boston whose previous company went bankrupt. On the front page of his new business plan, he stated that his past company went bankrupt.

When the inevitable question came about the bankruptcy, he didn't excuse his way out of it. Instead, he said, "You know, I did go belly up one time, but I've started five businesses and I probably learned more from that one mistake than from all the rest put together." You have to take the negative and make it a positive or you'll get creamed.

After you've practiced the ten toughest questions, integrate the questions and answers into your business plan. Now we have a ten. The risk is zero, and when the risk is zero money will flow.

One more thing: Always seek advice from your banker or venture source. Don't worry, money always follows advice—and when risk is zero, advice acts like a superconductor for money.

THE ANSWER SHEET

To make a ten into an eleven you need a magical element called "The Answer Sheet." Every business plan should contain an answer sheet that summarizes the key aspect of the plan. This is an elusive concept, so the best way to illustrate it is with examples. Here are three. Each one shows the reader a key aspect of the plan that should convince the reader that it represents a no-risk deal for her.

1. It's Just Like . . .

If your company is just like Apple or Amway or some other supersuccessful company, say so right up front. There is always a venture capitalist or banker out there who turned down such a company and wants a second chance.

Let's take a venture capitalist I knew in Boston who heads one of the New England venture capital companies. We'll call him Peter. Peter is the dean of venture capital in New England. Over the past twenty years, his average rate of return on invested capital has been 46 percent. But two deals he missed (both in his own backyard, Massachusetts) are Digital Equipment (DEC) and Data General (DG), two of the biggest venture deals in history. When Peter goes home at night, his wife says, "How are you, sweetheart? Nice to see you. Did any deals come along today that look like Digital or Data General?" If the front end of your plan looks like DEC or DG, Peter is immediately interested.

Now, the guy who did invest in a company like Apple Computers might not need to make any money, but thousands of people made millions investing along with "Mr. Apple." When he goes out socially, his friends always pester him: "Hey, have you seen any more young Apple Computers . . . ?" If a key aspect of your business is how much it looks like another very successful venture, highlight that feature early on. I call that an answer sheet.

2. The Other Guys Have Deep Pockets

This is the story of In-Line Technology, a company located in New Bedford, Massachusetts, operated by Gene St. Onge and Hank Bok. Gene and Hank went to see a famous New York venture capitalist in his Fifth Avenue apartment. During breakfast, the venture capitalist spent an hour and a half discussing a new painting his wife had just purchased, and then discussed the business for a half hour. At the end of breakfast, the venture source agreed to put up half of the $200,000 they were trying to raise.

His condition was that they shouldn't call him if they ran out of money—he wouldn't invest any more. Now, just because the venture source said he wouldn't invest any more didn't mean the other investors had to know. They naturally assumed that the deal was safe because the first investor was known to have deep pockets. Having secured a promise of $100,000 from a well-known venture capitalist, Gene and Hank had no problem raising the second $100,000. The deal was oversubscribed (an eleven), in fact, and they had to cut some investors back.

When a Rockefeller or General Electric backs your deal, lower-level investors jump in. Fred Smith claims the early commitment from General Dynamics was crucial to launching Federal Express because everyone knows General Dynamics has deep pockets. Watch out, though, because by some strange quirk of fate everyone born with deep pockets seems to have short arms.

3. If It Goes Bad . . .

The third example of an answer sheet should be a contingency plan. In other words, if it goes bad. . . .

After about six months, In-Line Technology did run out of money. And, although Gene and Hank remembered the venture capitalist's instructions not to call him for help, they also knew this: Your best investors are your current investors. Underline that concept! *It may be the most important one in this section on business plans.* Gene and Hank didn't hesitate. They called their venture source and told him they needed another $200,000 to keep going.

Well, the venture capitalist didn't get to be so wealthy by being a fool. Before he made the initial investment, he sent the business plan to a West Coast portfolio company where he was a director. This company needed the technology that In-Line had developed, and the venture manager and executive vice president had both said, "Gee, this business plan looks interesting." The venture capitalist had his backside well covered because one of his portfolio companies was willing, able, and even anxious to pick up the company if it ever went bad. The West Coast company bought In-Line within thirty days and all investors ended up with a healthy ROI.

When preparing your answer sheet, don't limit yourself to the answers illustrated in these three examples. Think up your own answers. What special key element would make your plan a sure thing for an investor or banker? The answer sheet should provide a compelling motivation for someone to want to be part of your deal. That's what makes an eleven.

THE APPROACH

Believe it or not, the first thing you do when you arrive at your banker's office or at a meeting with a venture capitalist is hide your plan. Some entrepreneurs walk in and lay their business plan on the desk. Then they sit down and wait to play whatever game the banker or venture capitalist wants to play.

The problem with this approach is that both bankers and venture capitalists like to play very tiring games. Bankers like to play "go fetch," as in, "The plan looks good, but I need more information about this and that." You have no choice but to go fetch the information, and when you return, she'll send you out again.

Here is a list of working documents that are often forgotten by entrepreneurs:

1. Leases
2. Patents, licenses
3. Employment contracts
4. Distribution agreements
5. Firm price quotations
6. Insurance contracts (key man)
7. Authorization by the board of directors—certified by the secretary of state, for you to negotiate and conclude loan agreements
8. Certificate to do business—in the state of good standing
9. Evidence of current payment of taxes and rent
10. Legal opinions on pending litigation

Venture capitalists are a little meaner. They like to play dodgeball, with you in the center. If you walk into a venture source's office and put your plan on her desk, she'll pick it up, look it over quickly, and start the conversation with tough, sometimes impossible questions. She does all the initial talking, and you're on the defensive. Even though you've practiced answers to a lot of mean questions, she'll throw you some you never thought of. This is not a good way to start off.

The game you want to play with bankers and venture capitalists is not go fetch or dodgeball. You want to play catch. The person in control is the person asking the questions. Ask questions, and kill two birds with one stone by using the questions to find the investor's hot button. Once you've found it, push it. These questions will help to draw her out, and you'll find out the color of her hot button, what makes her nervous. For example, if you ask a venture capitalist why a particular investment went bad, and she begins to list the problems with genuine regret, you could then concentrate on telling her how your company is set up to avoid those problems. You could also ask her advice on how to avoid problems of that nature. Remember, money follows advice.

FEEL, FELT, FOUND

After you hand over your plan, expect an avalanche of objections and criticism. Bear in mind that Digital Equipment Corporation was turned down by everyone before American Research & Development (AR&D) in Boston decided to take a $70,000 chance on it. And Fred Adler didn't put $25,000 into Data General until many other established venture capitalists had turned down the deal. These are two of the best venture capital deals of all time, and they almost didn't happen, so expect objections.

The secret to your success is in how you handle those objections. Answer each question carefully: the goal is to reduce the risk to zero. To do this you need to learn to take an objection and turn it around so that it works for you. I recommend the "Feel, Felt, Found" technique.

When your banker objects to the fact that you've made a former engineer your marketing director, the first thing you should do is agree: "I know exactly how you *feel*. It's very uncommon for an engineer to also be skilled in marketing. I *felt* the same way initially, but. . . ." Then you must supply the missing piece of information. I like to say that the banker or venture source is never wrong, she's only partially informed. It's your job to totally inform her.

Tell her, "But, John's been on the team for six months now, and just listen to what we've *found* out he's accomplished. He already has a purchase order from Intel; we couldn't get one for two years. Not only that, he's written a purchase order from General Mills with advance payment in full. He's also instituted the first sales/cost control system in our history. And what we've *found* is . . ." Take the objection and spin it around in your favor. You've not only changed an objection into a winning point but also shown your banker how well you think on your feet.

GAINING THE COMMITMENT

We've discussed what not to talk about first, i.e., the business plan. What do you lead off with, then, when you enter the office of your banker or a venture source for that important meeting? Resist the urge to start waxing poetic about your product. They want to talk about money. Show them the first thing we discussed in this chapter—how much money is already in the plan. Then tell them about the management, especially about the chief financial officer. She is the most important player on your team as far as they are concerned. They will not lend money to or invest in a company with a weak financial officer.

Now you can present the plan. You are prepared with techniques for handling objections and with questions of your own. You are going to play catch, not dodgeball or go fetch. They throw a question at you, you put a spin on it and throw it right back. And remember, you are seeking yes or no answers, not maybes that will take up the next six months of your life. Don't be tempted by maybes that sound like "maybe so" to you; it's more likely that they mean "probably not."

Despite all this preparation, you may still find yourself sitting at a table in endless negotiations with a potential investor. Believe it or not, there are seven simple words that will close that unclosable financial deal. If that sucker is closable, bang!, it will close when you recite these seven magic words. If it's not closable, you can feel very good about getting up from the table and moving on because you've given it your best shot. Any further time is wasted.

What are those seven words? I'll give you a hint: "What do you still need to close?" is not the phrase. That phrase will have you running around for yet more data for that lender or investor, and you've already wasted enough time.

Don't spend any more time on trying to sell your dream. Getting your business off the ground may be your dream, but the art of raising capital isn't the art of selling dreams. It's the art of reducing risk! The closing phrase for financial deals.

Eighteen months ago I bought a gorgeous piece of oceanfront property in Yarmouth, Nova Scotia. If you take the ferry up from Portland, Maine, you can walk to it from the dock. Eighteen months ago, I paid $100,000 for these 100 acres, but a few months later I needed some cash, so I decided to sell off a piece. I divided the land into two parcels of equal value, and I put one of them on the market. Guess how much the asking price was for the one parcel? Remember,

struggle with the ethical question of what I would do if someone actually guesses correctly: Would I eat one jelly bean or give away a stranger's car?). I announced a second round of guesses, with the car going to the person who came the closest.

In the first round, both the bankers and the entrepreneurs made guesses that formed a bell-shaped curve. In the second round, though, things changed dramatically. The bankers' curve narrowed until it formed an almost straight vertical line around the mean, which was 1,000. The entrepreneurs' curve, on the other hand, spread out horizontally until it was almost flat.

In the second round, the bankers bunched up their guesses around the mean of the original distribution. Because there were no hard data to work with, they chose to create data, and they bunched their answers around an imputed norm, where it was safe and warm.

The entrepreneurs made second guesses that ranged from 300 to 2,000. They each grabbed for their own share of turf, figuring that way they'd have a better chance of being the closest to the unknown figure.

The natural tension between bankers and entrepreneurs comes from the fact that they are different psychological types. The entrepreneur is driven by his nature to strike out on his own, away from the pack, while the banker is driven to play it safe and minimize his losses. Each is in a different business because each is a different kind of person.

Acknowledging this fundamental difference is the best first step you can take toward improving your relationship with your banker. Your business plan, for example, should be written with your reader in mind. By the way, I've found that Mancuso's Jelly Bean Principle applies to venture capitalists, too. They also tend to bunch, although not quite as severely as bankers do.

One way to compensate for your lack of understanding of bankers is to hire one. Royal Little, the ninety-year-old founder of Textron Corp., Indian Head Mills, and Narragansett Capital, told me that his secret as an entrepreneur was to hire ex-bankers as his company presidents. (Mr. Little is from Rhode Island and is widely recognized as the father of the conglomerate.) Bankers were no good at managing or motivating employees, he said, but "they can make sense out of all the dumb things I do and explain to other bankers that the latest disaster was actually part of our business plan." That, Roy said, was worth millions. Two of Roy's presidents, in fact, went on to fill the shoes of the nation's number-one banker; they each served as United States Secretary of the Treasury.

You may not be in a position to run out and hire a couple of ex-bankers, but don't worry, with a little effort you can learn to deal with your banker almost as well as an ex-banker could. You'll have to, if you want to avoid personal loan guarantees.

IT JUST AIN'T FAIR

There is nothing hostile about my approach to getting off personal loan guarantees. It's really a negotiating ploy between the small-business owner and the lender. There are all types of lenders—commercial credit corporations and equipment leasing companies, for example. They all jump on the bandwagon and require personal loan guarantees from small-business owners. When you go to lease a computer for your office, the leasing company may ask you to sign personally for the equipment.

When I started a business twenty-five years ago, I went to lease a $5,000 office copier through my corporation. The copier leasing company required a twenty-four-year-old to personally guarantee the lease payments. The copier leasing company required my personal guarantee that all payments would be made on the lease. No personal signature, no copy machine. It didn't occur to me that I had a choice. I signed because I needed the copier—maybe that's why I'm writing this book a quarter of a century later.

Personal guarantees defeat the purpose of having a corporation in the first place. One of the key reasons a small business is incorporated is to protect the stockholders and officers from liabilities incurred by the corporation. The corporation gives the individuals some level of protection from having to sell their houses, cars, and personal belongings to pay the corporation's debts should the business fail.

What lenders have done very systematically and rather forcefully over the last twenty years is to penalize the small-business owner for taking out debt. As a result, a president of a small corporation can very seldom borrow from a lender without personally "autographing" the back of the bank note.

I would like to pose a philosophical question to lenders. Look at all the small businesses in the United States that have personally guaranteed debt; then look at Third World borrowers, such as Brazil and Argentina, that have borrowed enormous sums from American banks. Who is going to pay back their debt? The thousands of small U.S. businesses or Brazil and Argentina? I haven't even mentioned Mexico!

As a matter of fact, the debts of Third World countries are being rolled consistently, that is, the lenders extend the debts by allowing them to be paid with new debt. When a small company can't pay its debt, though, the banks aren't so willing to roll it, are they?

For that matter, when Chrysler, Penn Central, Lockheed, and other large corporations got into trouble, the government stepped in to guarantee their debt so that lenders would advance the money needed to resuscitate these businesses.

Sure, Chrysler got itself out of trouble and everything worked out, but what if Chrysler had been a thousand little companies? Those companies would have sunk at the moment they needed to borrow additional funds to get out of trouble, and a thousand entrepreneurs behind a thousand personal guarantees would have lost their houses and cars, and jeopardized their families. The situation reminds me of the plight of the American farmer. He is a victim of being a small independent businessman instead of a huge corporation like Continental Illinois. It seems the government will only bail out the big guys, not a big group of little guys. The little guys are allowed to drown, even if their demise could have an enormous impact on the country's economy. We can't count on the government to help us, so we have to help ourselves. Someday, perhaps, the small-business owner will have the privilege of playing on a level playing field.

This brings me to the three great entrepreneurial lies (the clean version):

1. It's free.
2. The check is in the mail.
3. I'm from the government and I'm here to help you.

I can't do much about this inconsistent system and neither can you, but I can show you how to be the best customer the bank ever had so that you and your entire family can sleep well at night, knowing your "autograph" isn't on the back of your company's bank note.

WHAT YOU SHOULD KNOW ABOUT YOUR BANKER

I recommend that you make your banker your best friend; in fact, start to think of him as the key person in your company. When you think about it, you will realize that your banker is really the key to building a good company, but too many of us do a poor job of cultivating this crucial relationship.

One of two nonprofit membership associations I head is the Chief Executive Officers (CEO) Club. The average size of the member companies is about $17 million in annual sales, and we have about 310 CEO club members, with offices in eight U.S. cities. One of the most important meetings we have annually is "Banker's Day." It's probably the best annual event; we host it at posh private clubs in all eight chapters.

On Banker's Day, all the CEOs take their bankers to lunch, and they don't ask them for any money—that's a rule (at least until after cocktails). If you're not taking your banker to lunch at least once a year without asking for money, you're not doing your job as a CEO. It's a key responsibility of the CEO to develop this bond with his banker.

The theme of Banker's Day is "how to be the best customer the bank ever had," and each banker has to give each CEO one good tip on how to win that award. We've learned from this experience that being the best customer the bank ever had means understanding exactly how the bank functions. You should be prepared to do the banker's job, or at least half his job.

I should take a moment here to note that all bankers are not men. In fact, I'd say about one-third of all commercial lenders today are women. This is a terrific development for women entrepreneurs, who have too often been confronted with hostile male bankers.

I also head an association of small-company presidents called the Center for Entrepreneurial Management (CEM), which has about 3,000 members in the United States. When I first started the group in 1978, there were about ten or twelve female members. In the last year or so about one-third of our new members have been women. There has probably been no stronger movement in this country, in fact, than that of women adopting the entrepreneurial lifestyle.

Bearing this in mind, I would still like to offer these definitions:

> A *banker* is a man who knows a great deal about very little, and who goes along learning more and more about less and less until he finally knows practically everything about nothing.
>
> An *entrepreneur* is a man who knows very little about many things and keeps learning less and less about more and more until he knows practically nothing about everything.
>
> A *loan committee* starts out knowing everything about everything but through its association with entrepreneurs and bankers ends up knowing nothing about anything.

Here's another thing to remember about banks: the people who write the advertisements for the bank don't work for the bank. They work at the advertising agency down the block. The banker is not a charming actor, he is a hard-nosed businessperson who wants detailed information from you about numbers and paybacks.

To see how far along you already are toward being the best customer your bank ever had, take the following quiz.

BANKERS QUIZ

Test your score on this quiz and compare your knowledge with that of the 310 members of the CEO Club who scored an average of 175 points out of a possible 330 points.

1. Can you draw an organization chart of the bank with your banker in the chart?

Yes   No   25 Points

2. Did you give your banker a small Christmas present under twenty-five dollars last year?

Yes   No   20 Points

3. Can you tell me where your banker went to school?

Yes   No   10 Points

4. Can you tell me your banker's spouse's first name?

Yes   No   10 Points

5. Can you tell me your banker's boss's first and last name?

Yes   No   15 Points

6. Can you tell me the names and backgrounds of at least two other members of the loan committee? (20 points each)

Yes   No   40 Points

7. Can you tell me your banker's hometown?

Yes   No   10 Points

8. Can you tell me your banker's birthday?

Yes   No   15 Points

9. Have you taken your banker and/or his boss on a tour of your facilities in the last six months?

Yes   No   25 Points

10. Have you gone out socially with your banker and his spouse (not as part of a loan request) in the last six months?

Yes   No   30 Points

11. Did you refer a good customer (depositor) to the bank in the last year?

Yes   No   50 Points

12. Did you send your banker's secretary one red rose on Secretary's Day last year?

Yes   No   20 Points

13. Did you sign your banker's name to the secretary's gift in question 12 above, rather than your own name?

Yes   No   20 Points

14. Did you invite your banker to your Christmas party or company picnic last year?

Yes   No   20 Points

15. Does your banker know your lawyer and accountant on a first-name basis? (10 points each)

Yes   No   20 Points

The correct answer to every question is yes. To be your bank's best customer, you need to score 200 points or better on this quiz. Here's why:

SCORING ON THE BANKERS QUIZ

1. Today, so much of banking is branch banking that you need to know where the decision making power is and where your banker fits into it.

2. When I say a small gift, I mean something like a book—if you know he's got a hobby, like boating, give him a book that relates to that. It lets him know that you think of him as a human being.

3. One of the first things two people do when they get to know each other is to look for some common ground. Knowing what school your banker went to will not only tell you something about him, it can often provide an opener like "We played you in football" or "My brother did his undergraduate work there."

4. Again, people tend to trust familiarity, so it helps if you know your banker's spouse's name, and ask after him or her once in a while.

5. It's the nature of the banking business that bankers tend to move up quickly in their jobs—either changing banks or bouncing from one branch to another. If you know your banker's boss (and he knows you), then it's possible that when your banker moves, your account will be passed *up* to the boss rather than down to the new loan officer. And the higher the person you're dealing with, the better off you are.

6. Ninety percent of the time, your loan officer will make the decision on your loan, but he still has to get it approved by the loan committee. If you know who's on the committee (and, again, if they know you), then that will smooth the process, not to mention speed it up.

7. Again, familiarity and common ground are the keys to a good relationship. And the more you know about your banker, the easier it is to strengthen and develop those ties.

8. Whenever I mention that it's a good idea to give your banker a quick phone call on his birthday, people laugh and tell me that that's just a little too corny. They laugh, that is, 364 days a year, but on *their* birthday they get a kick out of the fact that someone remembers. (Also, calling your banker on his birthday tells him that you have a good memory for dates and will remember the date that your loan payments come due.)

9. A banker has an amazing change in attitude when he actually sees a product being produced, sold, and shipped. (If you're in a service business, like real estate, more important than showing your banker your office is driving him or her past houses you've sold in the past, as well as houses you currently have listed.)

10. When I say you should take your banker out socially (for instance, for dinner), I mean socially. No business. And don't make the mistake of asking an especially touchy question after a pleasant meal. (Something like "My wife is a little worried about the fact that you want her signature on a loan, and she thinks it would be a good idea to discuss it with you while your wife is here" is a definite no no.) And let your banker do 90 percent of the talking. The more you let him talk about his interests, the better impression you'll make.

PROTECTION FROM BANKING'S HIGH TURNOVER

There is one chink in this "befriend your banker" strategy, and that is the high rate of turnover in the banking industry. I estimate that bankers change jobs every six months. If you scored more than 200 points on the bankers quiz or you work up to it and your banker leaves the bank or is promoted within the bank, it can be very frustrating—unless you take the following precaution.

March into your banker's office tomorrow and tell him this: "You know, Frank, it's so obvious to me that you're the shining star of this bank that at night I worry because you're a crucial part of my business. You know we couldn't have built this business without you. It's obvious to me that you're either going to be promoted soon at this bank or you're going to go to a higher position at another bank. I worry about this because my company rests on your shoulders. I couldn't have built it without you (it's okay to say this twice). Now, Frank, I understand that when some bankers get promoted, they take a few clients with them. I know we're just a small part of your clientele, but I would sure sleep better at night knowing that you would consider taking us along with you."

Protect your business from the current high turnover in banking by talking to your banker and letting him know how important he is to the continued success of your business. If you don't talk to him when he's a small potato, you'll never have a chance with him when he's a big potato, and you walk into his big, shiny new office with your little applecart and say, "Remember me?"

Further protect your business from turnover turmoil by becoming acquainted with your banker's boss. One of two people is going to pick up your banker's clients when he leaves—his boss or his subordinate. Who would you rather have handle your account? The boss, obviously, but if you don't know the boss, who is going to handle the account? That's right, the subordinate. Take the time to investigate the organizational chart of your bank and get acquainted with your banker's boss. While you're at it, get to know everybody at the bank. You never know who will end up on your next loan committee.

BANKERS ARE PEOPLE, TOO

When you start your friendship with your banker, keep in mind that old caveat about never having a second chance to make a first impression. That's why preparation is so important. Remember, practice does not make perfect, only perfect practice makes perfect.

Dress is important, too. Bankers like to flock. It wouldn't hurt you to dress like another conservative bird. Remember to dress up for your banker and down for your lawyer. It's an old axiom that happens to be true.

Also keep in mind that bankers are people, too, and your relationship with your banker is a human one. Human beings like other human beings to be interested in them. Believe it or not, bankers like to make loans!

In this chapter I advocated learning about your banker's spouse, boss, and birthday, and developing points of interest common to both of you. You should also get to know some members of the loan committee.

As banks continue to fail in the 1980s, bankers have begun to lean more heavily than ever before on their loan committees. If a camel is a horse designed by committee, a kangaroo is a horse designed by a loan committee! The loan committee allows your banker to spread the risk of making a bad call on your loan by giving him three or four other people with whom to share the blame. As a result, banks are taking longer than ever to answer the typical small-business owner's request for a loan. The loan usually gets stuck in the loan committee. The best way for you to speed up the loan committee's decision-making and improve it is for you to get to know some members. Give them a known entity to deal with—you.

How do you meet them? Well, have you ever been to one of those seminars your bank sponsors? I'm not saying they are valuable sources of information; actually, most of them are pretty bad, but attending a few is part of doing business. Don't spend the whole day. Usually, the commercial lenders will run over just before lunch to hunt for customers. Stand by the door and let one of them grab you for lunch. You've just met a new banker who probably serves on someone's loan committee.

The American Bankers Association, the banking industry's trade association, holds seminars for bankers and offers some publications that tell bankers how to analyze small-business loans. Attending some of these seminars and reading these publications are good ways to learn how bankers think. Contact:

American Bankers Association
1120 Connecticut Ave., N.W.
Washington, DC 20036
(202) 663-5000

I recommend that you buy a share of bank stock to get on the mailing list for all the latest financial reports and news. It also entitles you to attend the annual stockholders' meeting. This is a wonderful opportunity for you to meet key bank officers! Wear a hat and a big carnation and get to the stockholders' meeting early so that you can grab the middle seat in the first row. For the first hour or so, the bank's vice president in charge of numbers will stand up in front of the stockholders and explain why the bank's stock has lost value for the umpteenth consecutive quarter. When he's finished he will be bombarded with hostile questions from little old ladies who've had stock in the bank since 1903. It's your job to wait until there's an ebb in the flow of bile and then raise your hand.

"Gee," you'll say, "how is it that despite excessive government meddling and all this destabilizing deregulation and the infringement on your business by the securities industry, you guys managed to perform so well this quarter on behalf of the stockholders of the bank and the citizens of this community?" You may want to photocopy this section of the book—I'll allow it without permission—so that you won't forget this all-important question. After the vice president and the chairman have recovered from shock, you can be sure they'll ask around after the meeting: "Who was that nice gentleman with the broad-brimmed hat and the carnation sitting up front?" Your banker will say with pride, "That was my client, Mr. Jones. He has this very interesting new business. . . ." Scratch their backs and they'll scratch yours.

Do you send your banker letters inviting him to your CEO luncheon, reminding him to come, and thanking him for having attended? Do you send him a note after you've taken him to lunch (and not asked him for money)? Do you send him little success bulletins about your company's progress? The bank's best customers do!

Bankers keep these notes. They file everything, and a thick file full of friendly notes is another point in your favor. You are laying groundwork for the moment when your banker decides to leave that bank or is promoted. Leave a friendly letter audit trail for him to follow to his best customer.

When a new banker is assigned to your account (remember, this can happen about every six months in the turbulent banking world), where do you think he goes first to start learning about your company?

That's right! He goes to your file, and what does your new banker find? A file full of friendly letters and invitations and progress updates. He'll feel as if he already knows you and your company after reading your file.

MANCUSO'S TEN RULES FOR BANKING

1. It's technically impossible to give a banker too much information.
2. Seek advice: money follows advice.

3. The only time to raise capital is when you don't need it.
4. Dress up for your banker and down for your lawyer.
5. A short no is better than a long no.
6. Money flows only when risk is zero. Fully answer all the negatives.
7. Always pick a banker, never a bank.
8. Practice answering the single most important banking question: How will the bank get its money back?
9. The best thing to do for your banker is to refer a good depositor.
10. Bankers hate surprises. There is no such thing as good news and bad news. There is only good news and better news.

4. Investigate Your Bank and Your Banker

HOW STRONG IS YOUR BANKER?

Besides the facts you'll learn about your banker by following through on the recommendations of the bankers quiz in chapter 3, you should also find out how much power she has. What are her secured and unsecured lending limits? At what level does she need a second signature? What size loan can she approve without going to the loan committee? The answers to these questions tell you something about the strength of that individual, and you should have that information before you begin to negotiate. A successful negotiator knows more about the other person than the other person knows about her, and, believe me, your banker will know a lot about you.

Before loan negotiations even begin, the banker and the loan committee will analyze your detailed business plan, visit your company, talk to your customers and suppliers, and talk to your other bankers. They will also investigate your personal and business creditworthiness. How much time do you plan to spend on investigating your banker? If you're like most small-business owners, only about 25 percent of the time and effort your banker spends on investigating you. Is it really any surprise that your banker out-negotiates you?

Let's talk about your banker's investigation of you, focusing on your creditworthiness.

CHECK YOUR OWN CREDIT

It is imperative that you know what your credit history looks like before your banker runs a credit check on you, so you can make any necessary repairs. It's very simple—sometimes credit agencies make mistakes, and it's your responsibility to correct those mistakes before your banker sees them. At the very least, you can avoid being put on the defensive when your banker brings up derogatory comments about your credit that you had no idea existed.

A banker first asks you to provide the following information on a loan application: your full name and, if applicable, maiden name; date of birth; social security number; places of residence for the last three to five years; and places of employment for the last three to five years. The answers to these questions allow the banker to run a credit check on you.

The principal credit reporting agency for individuals is TRW Inc. Your business is probably covered by Dun & Bradstreet, an older agency that covers established businesses. However, the D&B rating is used mostly by suppliers, not by bankers, to determine credit for trade. Another common source of credit reports on businesses is NCR Corp. It's important to find out which agencies your bank will use to determine your creditworthiness. Don't be shy—ask!

The first thing you should understand is that agencies such as D&B and TRW merely receive and record information given to them voluntarily by suppliers, bankers, etc., who have had credit dealings with their customers. These agencies do not investigate the reported information for accuracy, nor do they evaluate it. They merely supply it on a standard form.

All your banker sees are "the facts," and if they look bad, your chances of getting a loan, not to mention getting off personal loan guarantees, are nil. It's your job to check on these reports periodically and make sure they are clean.

If your loan application is rejected because of derogatory information in your credit reports, your banker is required by law to tell you so and to tell you where to obtain exact copies of the offensive reports. Believe me, though, you do not want to wait until that embarrassing moment to see your reports. Contact TRW and D&B to determine whether they are covering you. If they are, you can order their reports for a modest fee (currently thirty-five dollars). The local yellow pages are your best source for the addresses and phone numbers of the regional bureaus of these agencies.

What if your credit check is unfavorable? Well, there are four possibilities. First, the information in the report is wrong or misleading. If that's the case, contact the creditor who made the report and ask to have it withdrawn. If the creditor won't, send copies of your correspondence to your banker, the credit-reporting agency, and the creditor.

A second possibility is that the information in the report is correct, but really isn't as bad as it looks. Let's say, for example, that you never paid a certain bill because you moved and it was never forwarded. This is the time to clear that up and have it erased from the reports. A third possibility is that you had a legitimate reason for not paying a bill on time. Few bankers will hold late payment of a huge medical bill against you, for example, if you can document that you missed a lot of work because of an illness. Perhaps you're having a dispute with a department store

Dun & Bradstreet

a company of
The Dun & Bradstreet Corporation

INFORMATION FURNISHED

As a Basis for Credit, Insurance, Marketing and other business decisions by its customers

NOTE: Transmittal of financial statements on this particular form is optional. The full report of your accountant is preferred. Financial statements on your own stationery or on that of your accountant will be equally useful.

Business Name
Used for Buying.. Other Name or
Style Used, if any...

Street Address.. Mail Address...

City...State.................ZIP.............. County...

Line of Business..Telephone (include Area Code)...............................

FINANCIAL CONDITION AT .... 19...   ☐ Fiscal   ☐ Interim

ASSETS				LIABILITIES			
CASH .... $				**DUE BANKS**			
GOVERNMENT SECURITIES				Unsecured ....$			
MARKETABLE SECURITIES				Secured			
NOTES RECEIVABLE (Customers)				**NOTES PAYABLE-TRADE ACCEPTANCES**			
ACCOUNTS RECEIVABLE (Customers)				Merchandise ....$			
Not Due ....$				Machinery & Equipment.			
Past Due				....			
Less Reserves				**ACCOUNTS PAYABLE**			
INVENTORY				Not Due ....$			
Finished Goods ....$				Past Due			
In Process				**ACCRUALS**			
Raw Materials				Salaries & Wages ......$			
....				**TAXES (Except Federal Income)**			
OTHER CURRENT ASSETS				**FEDERAL INCOME TAXES**			
......................$				**DUE RELATED CONCERNS**			
....				Loans & Advances ......$			
TOTAL CURRENT				Merchandise			
FIXED ASSETS				**LOANS & ADVANCES**			
Land ....$				From Officers ....$			
Buildings				....			
Machinery & Equipment..				**LONG TERM LIABILITIES—DUE WITHIN 1 YEAR**			
Furniture & Fixtures				Real Estate Mortgages...$			
Less Depreciation ..				....			
INVESTMENTS—RELATED CONCERNS							
Stocks & Bonds ....$				**TOTAL CURRENT**			
Loans & Advances				**LONG TERM LIABILITIES—DUE AFTER 1 YEAR**			
Accounts Receivable				Real Estate Mortgages...$			
INVESTMENTS—OTHER				....			
......................$				**PREFERRED STOCK**			
MISCELLANEOUS RECEIVABLES				**COMMON STOCK**			
Officers & Employees ...$				**ADDITIONAL PAID IN CAPITAL**			
DEPOSITS				**EARNED SURPLUS—RETAINED EARNINGS**.			
SUPPLIES							
....				**NET WORTH (Proprietor or Partners)**			
TOTAL .... $				**TOTAL** .... $			

BASIS OF INVENTORY VALUATION_____

RECEIVABLES PLEDGED OR DISCOUNTED....................YES ☐ ....NO ☐

CONTINGENT LIABILITIES $_____(SEE OVER)

ABOVE FIGURES PREPARED BY_____
          Name   Independent Accountant Yes ☐ No ☐

SUMMARY STATEMENT OF INCOME

NET SALES $_____FROM_____TO_____

FINAL NET INCOME (LOSS) $_____

DIVIDENDS OR WITHDRAWALS $_____

BUSINESS NAME_____

SIGNED BY_____

TITLE_____DATE_____

5G-10(791213)

Sample Dun & Bradstreet Statement Form C

Sample Dun & Bradstreet Statement Form C (*cont.*)

STATEMENT OF INCOME   NET WORTH RECONCILIATION

From_____ 19___ TO_____ 19___

NET SALES . . . .$		
COST OF GOODS SOLD		
GROSS PROFIT (LOSS) ON SALES		
EXPENSES		
Selling . . . .$		
General		
Administrative		
. . . .		
. . . .		
. . . .		
NET INCOME (LOSS) ON SALES		
OTHER INCOME		
. . . .$		
. . . .		
. . . .		
. . . .		
OTHER EXPENSES		
. . . .$		
. . . .		
. . . .		
NET INCOME (LOSS) BEFORE TAXES		
Federal Income Tax . . . . .$		
Other Taxes on Income. .		
. . . .		
FINAL NET INCOME (LOSS) . . . .$		

NET WORTH RECONCILIATION

NET WORTH AT START . . . .$		
ADDITIONS		
Final Net Income . . . .$		
. . . .		
. . . .		
DEDUCTIONS		
Final Net Loss . . . .$		
Dividends		
Withdrawals		
. . . .		
. . . .		
NET WORTH AT END . . . .$		

When financial statements prepared or certified to by independent accountants are transcribed to this form, indicate whether the statements transcribed are identical with the accountant's statement(s) Yes ☐ No ☐. If No, please describe adjustments. Attach copy of accountant's certificate.

THE FOREGOING STATEMENTS, IF CONSOLIDATED, INCLUDE THE FIGURES OF WHAT OTHER CONCERNS? . . . .
. . . .
. . . .
. . . .

MONTHLY RENT $ . . . . **LEASE EXPIRES** . . . . 19. . . . **FIRE INSURANCE ON: Merchandise $** . . . .**Machinery & Equipment $** . . . .**Furniture & Fixtures $** . . . .**Bldgs. $** . . . . **IS EXTENDED COVERAGE CARRIED?** . . . .
IS BUSINESS INTERRUPTION (Use & Occupancy) INSURANCE CARRIED? . . . . . .**ARE OFFICERS AND EMPLOYEES BONDED?** . . . . .
BASIS OF VALUATION OF: Fixed Assets . . . . **Marketable Securities—Investments** . . . .
. . . .
ARE LIABILITIES SECURED IN ANY MANNER? Yes ☐ No ☐ If Yes, describe the security and the manner of payment . . . .
. . . .
STATE AMOUNT OF EACH CONTINGENT LIABILITY: (Describe) . . . .
. . . .

REAL ESTATE—LOCATION	Title—In Name Of	Value Mkt. ☐ Cost ☐	Mortgage	Due Date	Net Income—R. E.
. . . .	. . . .	$.	$.	. . . .	$. . . . .
. . . .	. . . .				
. . . .	. . . .				

NUMBER OF EMPLOYEES	FULL TIME	PART TIME	COMMISSION SALESMEN
HEADQUARTERS_____			
BRANCH AT_____			
BRANCH AT			

IF THERE ARE ADDITIONAL BRANCHES, PLEASE ATTACH LIST GIVING LOCATIONS AND NUMBER OF EMPLOYEES.

Full Names of all Officers, Directors, Partners or Proprietor. If Partners, state if General, Special or Limited

FULL NAMES AND TITLES	% of Ownership	Year of Birth	Marital Status	Amount of Life Insurance Carried for the Benefit of the Business
A._____				$
B._____				
C._____				
D._____				
E._____				

Printed in U.S.A.

48

Updated Credit Profile

INQUIRY INFORMATION

RTS 3122250XIJ CONSUMER ROBERT QS.,10655 B 91502,
P-6613 S 92807,235 F 12401,S-548603388,Y-1944,T-18010005,
E-AJAX HARDWARE/2035 BROADWAY/LOS ANGELES CA 90019

PAGE	DATE	TIME	PORT	H/V			
1	04-15-88	11:14:45	HP26	A60	CONSUMER		TCA1

2-88 ROBERT Q CONSUMER   10-87 AJAX HARDWARE   SS# 548603388
    10655 BIRCH ST   2035 BROADWAY
    BURBANK CA 91502   LOS ANGELES CA 90019

ACCOUNT PROFILE POS/NON/NEG	SUBSCRIBER NAME / STATUS COMMENT	STATUS DATE	DATE OPENED	SUBSCRIBER # / TYPE	ASSN. CODE / TERMS	AMOUNT	BALANCE	ACCOUNT NUMBER / BALANCE DATE	AMOUNT PAST DUE	PAYMENT PROFILE 1 2 3 4 5 6 7 8 9 10 11 12
A	MOUNTAIN BANK			1139999	2	ORIGL		3562401973		
	CURWAS30-2	8-87	3-85	SEC	60	$43000	$22227	3-26-88		CCCCCCC1C1CC
	SCH MONTH PAY						$717	LASTPAY 02-28-88		
A	HILLSIDE BANK			3149999	5	ORIGL		29144508119		
	CURR ACCT	3-88	6-87	AUT	48	$6300	$5148	3-15-88		CCCCC-CCC
	SCH MONTH PAY						$132	LASTPAY 02-25-88		
A	HEMLOCKS			3319999	2	HIBAL		986543184026		
	TOO NEW RT	4-88	2-88	CHG	REV	$600	$440	4-05-88		CC
	EST MONTH PAY						$44			
A	BAY COMPANY			3339999	1	LIMIT		46812391013		
	CUR WAS 60	10-87	10-Y	CHG	REV	$1500	$0	3-21-88		CCCCC21CCCCC
								LASTPAY 10-15-87		
M	BOWERS			3369999	2	C/OAM		212250		
	CHARGE OFF	10-86	1-81	CHG	REV	$200				
A	GARDEN FINANCE			3509999	2	ORIGL		24187010		
	DELINQ 120	3-88	3-87	UNS	24	$2200	$1400	3-17-88	$425	321CCCCCCCC
	EST MONTH PAY						$100	LASTPAY 11-05-87		
A	HILLSIDE BANK			3149999						
	INQUIRY	5-18-87		AUT	48	$6300				

------ *ATTN* FILE VARIATION:STREET INIT IS M, ZIP IS 85207
ROBERT Q CONSUMER
7157 E MAIN
PHOENIX AZ 85207

A	WISTERIA FINANCE			8549999	4			5238610		
	PD WAS 30	5-87	4-86	SEC	12	$500				CCC1CCCCCCCC
M	PHOENIX JUSTICE COURT			8019999				07505853		
	JUDGMENT	4-19-86					$1200	ALLIED COMPANY		

>>>>> CHECKPOINT >>>>> *** NICKNAME SEARCH *** 1ST NAME IS BOB
BOB Q CONSUMER
10655 BIRCH ST
BURBANK CA 91502

A	WYATT FINANCE			3519999	1			29416413		
	REPO	7-85	1-83	AUT	36	$7500				

***** MORE

780 WC (Rev 4 85)
7061-625

Confidential

©TRW Inc. 1971, 1978
TRW is the name and
mark of TRW Inc.

Sample TRW Credit Profile

Updated Credit Profile

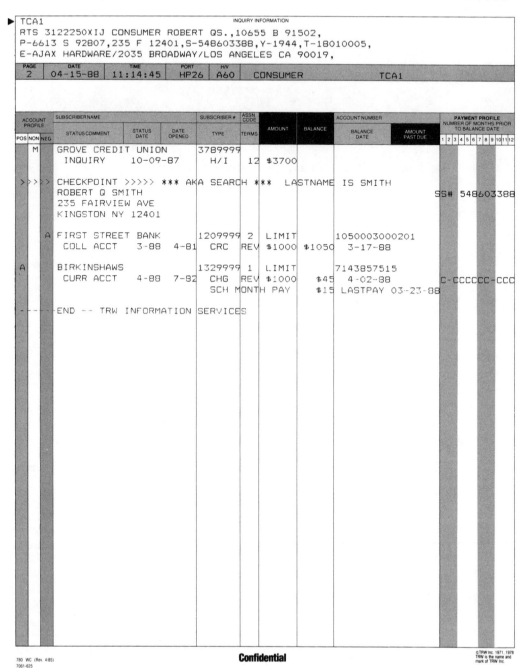

TCA1
INQUIRY INFORMATION
RTS 3122250XIJ CONSUMER ROBERT QS.,10655 B 91502,
P-6613 S 92807,235 F 12401,S-548603388,Y-1944,T-18010005,
E-AJAX HARDWARE/2035 BROADWAY/LOS ANGELES CA 90019,

PAGE	DATE	TIME	PORT	H/V			
2	04-15-88	11:14:45	HP26	A60	CONSUMER		TCA1

ACCOUNT PROFILE			SUBSCRIBER NAME			SUBSCRIBER #	ASSN CODE	AMOUNT	BALANCE	ACCOUNT NUMBER		PAYMENT PROFILE NUMBER OF MONTHS PRIOR TO BALANCE DATE
POS	NON	NEG	STATUS COMMENT	STATUS DATE	DATE OPENED	TYPE	TERMS			BALANCE DATE	AMOUNT PAST DUE	1 2 3 4 5 6 7 8 9 10 11 12
	M		GROVE CREDIT UNION			3789999						
			INQUIRY	10-09-87		H/I	12	$3700				
>>>>			CHECKPOINT >>>>> *** AKA SEARCH *** LASTNAME IS SMITH									
			ROBERT Q SMITH									SS# 548603388
			235 FAIRVIEW AVE									
			KINGSTON NY 12401									
		A	FIRST STREET BANK			1209999	2	LIMIT		1050003000201		
			COLL ACCT	3-88	4-81	CRC	REV	$1000	$1050	3-17-88		
A			BIRKINSHAWS			1329999	1	LIMIT		7143857515		
			CURR ACCT	4-88	7-92	CHG	REV	$1000	$45	4-02-88		C-CCCCCC-CCC
						SCH MONTH PAY			$15	LASTPAY 03-23-88		
-----			END -- TRW INFORMATION SERVICES									

780 WC (Rev. 4-85)
7061-625

Confidential

©TRW Inc. 1971, 1978
TRW is the name and
mark of TRW Inc.

50

Glossary of National Status Comments – Alpha

Report Abbrev.	Pos	Non	Neg	Status Code	Explanation
BK ADJ PLN		X		69	Debt included in or completed through Bankruptcy Chapter 13.
BK LIQ REO			X	67	Debt included in or discharged through Bankruptcy Chapter 7, 11, or 12.
CHARGE OFF			X	97	Unpaid balance reported as a loss by credit grantor.
CLOS INAC		X		04	Closed inactive account.
CLOS NP AA			X	90	Credit line closed/not paying as agreed.
COLL ACCT			X	93	Account seriously past due/account assigned to attorney, collection agency or credit grantor's internal collection department.
CO NOW PAY			X	86	Now paying, was a charge-off.
CR CD LOST		X		03	Credit card lost or stolen.
CR LN CLOS		X		20	Credit line closed/reason unknown or by consumer request/there may be a balance due.
CR LN RNST		X		44	Account now available for use and is in good standing. Was a closed account.
CURR ACCT	X			11	This is either an open or closed account in good standing. If the account is a credit card or charge account, it should be available for use and there may be a balance due. If the account is closed, there were no past due amounts reported and it was paid.
CUR WASCOL		X		43	Current account was a collection account.
CUR WAS DL		X		30	Current account was past due.
CUR WASFOR		X		45	Current account. Foreclosure was started.
CUR WAS 30		X		31	Current account was 30 days past due date.
CURWAS30-2		X		32	Current account was 30 days past due date twice.
CURWAS30-3		X		33	Current account was 30 days past due date three times.
CURWAS30-4		X		34	Current account was 30 days past due date four times.
CURWAS30-5		X		35	Current account was 30 days past due date five times.
CURWAS30+6		X		36	Current account was 30 days past due date six times or more.
CUR WAS 60		X		37	Current account was 60 days past due date delinquent.
CUR WAS 90		X		38	Current account was 90 days past due date delinquent.
CUR WAS120		X		39	Current account was 120 days past due date delinquent.
CUR WAS150		X		40	Current account was 150 days past due date delinquent.
CUR WAS180		X		41	Current account was 180 days past due date or more delinquent.
DECEASED		X		21	Consumer reported as deceased.
DEEDINLIEU			X	89	Credit grantor received deed for collateral in lieu of foreclosure on a defaulted mortgage.
DELINQ 60		X		78	Account delinquent 60 days past due date.
DELINQ 90			X	80	Account delinquent 90 days past due date.
DELINQ 120			X	82	Account delinquent 120 days past due date.
DELINQ 150			X	83	Account delinquent 150 days past due date.
DELINQ 180			X	84	Account delinquent 180 days past due date.
DEL WAS 90		X		79	Account was delinquent 90 days past due date/now 30 or 60 days.
DEL WAS120		X		81	Account was delinquent 120 days past due date/now 30, 60 or 90 days.
FORCLOSURE			X	94	Credit grantor sold collateral to settle defaulted mortgage.
FORE PROC			X	87	Foreclosure proceeding started.
GOV CLAIM			X	88	Claim filed with government for insured portion of balance on a loan.
INQUIRY		X		01	A copy of the Profile report has been sent to this credit grantor at their request.
INS CLAIM		X		92	Claim filed for payment of insured portion of balance.
NOT PAY AA		X		70	Account not being paid as agreed.
PAID ACCT		X		13	Closed account/zero balance/not rated by credit grantor.
PAID SATIS	X			12	Closed account/paid satisfactorily.
PD BY DLER		X		66	Credit grantor paid by company who originally sold the merchandise.
PD CHG OFF			X	64	Paid account/was a charge-off.
PD COLL AC			X	62	Paid account/was a collection account, insurance claim or government claim.
PD FORECLO			X	65	Paid account. A foreclosure was started.
PD NOT PAY		X		50	Paid account. Some payments were made past the agreed due dates.
PD REPO			X	63	Paid account/was a repossession.
PD VOL SUR		X		61	Paid/was a voluntary surrender.
PD WAS 30		X		51	Paid account/was past due date 30 days.
PD WAS30-2		X		52	Paid account/was past due date 30 days 2 or 3 times.
PD WAS30-4		X		53	Paid account/was past due date 30 days 4 times.
PD WAS30-5		X		54	Paid account/was past due date 30 days 5 times.
PD WAS30+6		X		55	Paid account/was past due date 30 days 6 times or more.
PD WAS 60		X		56	Paid account was delinquent 60 days past due date.

Report Abbrev.	Pos	Non	Neg	Status Code	Explanation
PD WAS 90		X		57	Paid account was delinquent 90 days past due date.
PD WAS 120		X		58	Paid account was delinquent 120 days past due date.
PD WAS 150		X		59	Paid account was delinquent 150 days past due date.
PD WAS 180		X		60	Paid account was delinquent 180 days past due date or more.
REDMD REPO		X		42	Account was a repossession/now redeemed.
REFINANCED		X		10	Account renewed or refinanced.
REPO			X	96	Merchandise was taken back by credit grantor; there may be a balance due.
SCNL			X	98	Credit grantor cannot locate consumer.
SCNL NWLOC		X		85	Credit grantor could not locate consumer/consumer now located.
SETTLED		X		68	Account legally paid in full for less than the full balance.
TERM DFALT			X	91	Early termination by default of original terms of lease or sales contract.
TRANSFERED		X		05	Account transferred to another office.
VOLUN SURR		X		95	Voluntary surrender.
30 DAY DEL		X		71	Account past due date 30 days.
30 2 TIMES		X		72	Account past due date 30 days 2 times.
30 3 TIMES		X		73	Account past due date 30 days 3 times.
30 4 TIMES		X		74	Account past due date 30 days 4 times.
30 5 TIMES		X		75	Account past due date 30 days 5 times.
30 6+TIMES		X		76	Account past due date 30 days 6 times or more.
30 WAS 60		X		77	Account was delinquent 60 days past due date/now 30 days.

Items of Public Record

Report Abbrev.	Pos	Non	Neg	Explanation
BK 7-FILE			X	Voluntary or Involuntary Petition in Bankruptcy Chapter 7 (Liquidation) filed.
BK 7-DISC			X	Voluntary or Involuntary Petition in Bankruptcy Chapter 7 (Liquidation) discharged.
BK 7-DISM		X		Voluntary or Involuntary Petition in Bankruptcy Chapter 7 (Liquidation) dismissed.
BK 11-FILE			X	Voluntary or Involuntary Petition in Bankruptcy Chapter 11 (Reorganization) filed.
BK 11-DISC			X	Voluntary or Involuntary Petition in Bankruptcy Chapter 11 (Reorganization) discharged.
BK 11-DISM		X		Voluntary or Involuntary Petition in Bankruptcy Chapter 11 (Reorganization) dismissed.
BK 12-FILE			X	Petition in Bankruptcy Chapter 12 (Adjustment of Debt-Family Farmer) filed.
BK 12-DISC			X	Petition in Bankruptcy Chapter 12 (Adjustment of Debt-Family Farmer) discharged after completion.
BK 12-DISM		X		Petition in Bankruptcy Chapter 12 (Adjustment of Debt-Family Farmer) dismissed.
BK 13-FILE			X	Petition in Bankruptcy Chapter 13 (Adjustment of Debt) filed.
BK 13-DISM		X		Petition in Bankruptcy Chapter 13 (Adjustment of Debt) dismissed.
BK 13-COMP		X		Petition in Bankruptcy Chapter 13 (Adjustment of Debt) completed.
CITY TX LN			X	City Tax Lien.
CITY TX REL		X		City Tax Lien Released.
CO TAX LN			X	County Tax Lien.
CO TAX REL		X		County Tax Lien Released.
FED TAX LN			X	Federal Tax Lien.
FED TX REL		X		Federal Tax Lien Released.
JUDGMENT			X	Judgment.
JUDGMT SAT		X		Judgment Satisfied.
JUDGSATVAC		X		Judgment Satisfied and Vacated.
MECH LIEN			X	Mechanic's Lien.
MECH RELE		X		Mechanic's Lien Released.
MN MTG FIL		X		Manual Mortgage Report (contact your local TRW Information Services Office).
NT RESPON		X		Not Responsible Notice, e.g., husband or wife claims not responsible for debts incurred by the spouse.
STAT TX LN			X	State Tax Lien.
STA TX REL		X		State Tax Lien Released.
SUIT		X		Suit.
SUIT DISMD		X		Suit Dismissed or Discontinued.
WAGE ASIGN			X	Wage Assignment.
W/A RELEASE		X		Wage Assignment Released.
AKA		X		Also Known As.

Note: "Negative" subscriber and Public Record items become "Non-Evaluated" when they appear in the file with certain special comments.

Sample TRW Glossary of Credit Profile Terms

Sample TRW Glossary of Credit Profile Terms (*cont.*)

The first digit represents the region in which subscriber is located.	The Code Number		The second digit represents the subscriber's industry.
1 Eastern Region 2 Midwestern Region 3 Western Region 4 Inquiries from Broker Customers 6 Eastern Region 7 Western Region 8 Western Region	Example [3] 234567	0 Public Record 1 Bank 2 Bank Credit Card 3 Retail 4 Credit Card 5 Loan Finance 6 Sales Finance 7 Credit Union 8 Savings & Loan 9 Service & Professional	Example 3 [2] 34567

Type of Account

Type	Abbrev.	Explanation	Type	Abbrev.	Explanation	Type	Abbrev.	Explanation
*24	ASL	Auto	74	GMD	Govt. Miscellaneous Debt	27	R/O	Real Estate Mortgage – with or without collateral. Usually a second mortgage – terms are in months. Amount shown in $100.00 increments.
00	AUT	Auto	70	GOP	Govt. Overpayment			
10	BUS	Business	*23	H+0	Secured by Household Goods & Other Collateral			
15	C/C	Check Credit or Line of Credit				25	R/V	VA Real Estate Mortgage – terms are in years
37	CCP	Combined Credit Plan	04	H/I	Home Improvement			
07	CHG	Charge Account	*22	HHG	Secured by Household Goods			
47	CLS	Credit Line Secured	78	I/L	Installment Loan	77	RCK	Returned Check
48	COL	Collection Attorney	49	INS	Insurance Claims	11	REC	Recreational Merchandise
14	COM	Co-Maker (not borrower)	06	ISC	Installment Sales Contract	29	REN	Rental Agreement
18	CRC	Credit Card	13	LEA	Lease	03	SCO	Secured by Co-Signer
43	D/C	Debit Card	17	M/H	Mobile Home	68	SDL	Govt. Secured Direct Loan
34	DCS	Debt Counseling Service	*21	NCM	Note Loan with Co-Maker	02	SEC	Secured
12	EDU	Educational	*20	NTE	Note Loan	66	SGL	Govt. Secured Guaranteed Loan
35	EMP	Employment	03	P/S	Partially Secured	*28	SLC	Co-Maker (not borrower)
16	F/C	FHA Co-Maker (not borrower)	83	PPI	Post Prescreen/Extract Prescreen Inquiry	30	SUM	Summary of Accounts with same status
50	F/S	Family Support	26	R/C	Conventional Real Estate Mortgage – terms are in years	67	UDL	Govt. Unsecured Direct Loan
05	FHA	FHA Home Improvement				65	UGL	Govt. Unsecured Guaranteed Loan
75	G/B	Govt. Benefit	08	R/E	Real Estate Specific Type Unknown – terms are in years	31	UNK	Unknown
71	G/F	Govt. Fine				01	UNS	Unsecured
69	G/G	Govt. Grant	19	R/F	FHA Real Estate Mortgage – terms are in years			*Small Loan Company Loans Only
73	GEA	Govt. Employee Advance						
72	GFS	Govt. Fee for Service						

Association With Account Currently Active	Association Codes With Definitions	Association Terminated As Of Date Reported	24-Month Payment Profile		
0	**Undesignated:** Reported by TRW Information Services only.	A	Shown below are the definitions of the coding that will display in the 24-month Payment Profile.		
1	**Individual:** This is the only person associated with this account (Termination code H to be used only in cases of mortgage loans being assumed by others.)	H			
2	**Joint Account – Contractual Responsibility:** This individual is expressly obligated to repay all debts arising on this account by reason of having signed an agreement to that effect. There are others associated with this account who may or may not have contractual responsibility.	B	C	Current	
			N	Zero balance reported/current account	
			1	30 days past due	
3	**Authorized User – Joint Account:** This individual has use of this joint account for which another individual has contractual responsibility.	C	2	60 days past due	
			3	90 days past due	
4	**Joint Account:** This individual participates in this account. The association cannot be distinguished between Joint Account – Contractual Responsibility or Authorized User.	D	4	120 days past due	
			5	150 days past due	
			6	180 days past due	
5	**Co-Maker:** This individual has guaranteed this account and assumes responsibility should maker default. This code only to be used in conjunction with Code 7 Maker.	E	– (Dash)	No history has been reported for that particular month.	
			Blank	No history maintained, see status comment.	
6	**On Behalf Of:** This individual has signed an application for the purpose of securing credit for another individual, other than spouse.	F			
7	**Maker:** This individual is responsible for this account, which is guaranteed by a co-maker. To be used in lieu of Code 2 and 3 when there is a Code 5 Co-Maker.	G			

Your subscriber code number _____

Your local telephone number _____

Your TRW marketing representative _____

over a washing machine and you won't pay the bill until it's fixed. Have the debt moved from the late ninety-day column to the disputed column.

Finally, what if the credit information is correct and unfavorable and you have no good explanation? First, pay the offending debts immediately and have proof of payment with you when you see your banker. In fact, you should have a full explanation *in writing* of all of the blots we've just discussed, to show your banker how on top of things you are. That way, when she receives the actual printout from the agencies, she'll be prepared.

Your banker may also receive unfavorable reports about you from another bank or a creditor. You have the right to see these negative reports, too, and you should respond to them. For an annual fee of thirty-five dollars, TRW will inform you every time someone accesses your credit report. It's a good value, in my opinion.

If you find that you are not being reported on by TRW or any other credit agency, file a report with one yourself. They will usually supply you with questionnaires, and you can also give them additional information to make your credit report stronger.

EVALUATING YOUR BANK

Most people never even consider evaluating their banks, even though the banks put them through the most intense scrutiny. It must have something to do with the quasi-religious character of most bank buildings and the somber attitudes and dress of most bankers. The high ceilings, the imposing columns, the churchlike quiet—it all adds up to one thing: intimidation.

The bottom line, though, is that you are a customer of a bank, and you should be as informed before you "buy" a bank as you would be before you buy a car. After all, you buy money from the bank like you buy water from a water company.

How healthy is the bank? Take a look at its financial statements. Is the bank planning a merger with another bank in the near future (aren't they all!)? Ask your banker; I'm sure it will be on her mind if it is a possibility. Does the bank have its own venture capital company, a small business investment company (SBIC)? About two hundred banks in the United States do. If your bank has one and you are turned down for a loan, you might be able to turn to the venture capital company (SBIC) and do a joint loan/venture capital transaction instead.

What is your bank's loan-to-deposit ratio? This will tell you how much room for lending the bank has at a given time. The typical rate is 75 percent, so a bank with a 95 percent rate might not be in a position to do further lending. A rural bank might run a loan-to-deposit ratio of 65 percent. Find out this information by asking the banker or by looking at the bank's balance sheet and income statement. How active is the bank, and in what areas? What are its liquidity and capital ratios? They typically average 30 percent and 60 percent, respectively.

The loan-to-deposit ratio, the liquidity ratio, and the capital ratio combined give you a distinct picture of whether your bank is in a position to lend you money. Know the ratios so that you won't be artificially discouraged. You might be turned down by First Republic Bank in Dallas because your banker is staring at a loan-to-deposit ratio of 110 percent, a liquidity ratio of only 10 percent, and a capital ratio of 3 percent—hell, that bank is looking to borrow money itself! If you leave it up to your banker, of course, she'll just let you believe that you didn't get the loan because your business plan was not up to snuff or your suit needed a good cleaning. These ratios can change dramatically from quarter to quarter.

In addition, you have to develop a feel for what's hot and what's not at the bank. If the bank just had a real estate/condominium deal go bad, the bankers are likely to be biased against your real estate deal. Your deal may be a winner, but for a bank with a recent bad experience, it will be a turnoff. You have to have a sense of whether your deal was turned down after an honest evaluation or because of some current crisis or fad within the bank.

To stay current and, as a result, to seek loans from your banker at the best possible time (for example, when the bank's loan-to-deposit ratio is low, they are looking to make new loans to put their deposits to work), you should do two things. First, become a shareholder of the bank. Buying just one share will entitle you to all the stockholders' reports, which are full of all the bank's balance sheet information. You should also subscribe to a service like the ones provided by Veribanc, Inc., and by Sheshunoff Information Services Inc. For seventy-five dollars Sheshunoff will send you a report analyzing your bank's capital strength and income performance. With a credit card and a Federal Express number you can have this report in your hands by the next morning. It can be an invaluable negotiating tool in developing relationships with a lender. Contact:

> Sheshunoff Information Services
> One Texas Center
> 505 Barton Springs Rd.
> Austin, TX 78704
> (512) 472-2244

The Veribanc report basically does an equity test and an income test on the bank. You can obtain the bank's financial statement by asking your banker for it and then running the equity and income tests yourself, if you like.

The equity test is used by federal bank regulators to indicate a bank's overall health. To run it, check near the end of the bank's financial statement for an entry for "equity," "surplus," or "net worth." Divide the amount by the figure given for "total assets" and express it as a percent. This is the equity ratio.

BOSTON SAFE DEPOSIT & TR CO   BOSTON   MA

EXECUTIVE SUMMARY

SHESHUNOFF RATING GUIDELINES

Percentile Ranking (PCT) 99 PCT = Best   0 PCT = Worst

WEIGHTING: A+ = 90-99   A = 70-89   B+ = 50-69   B = 30-49   C+ = 20-29   C = 10-19   NR = 0-9

	Total Assets $(000)	Asset Size Peer Group	Bank President's Weighting — All Banks in State	All Banks in Nation	Asset Peer Group	Equal Weighting — Asset Peer Group	Capital — Primary Capital Assets / PCT	Asset Quality — Nonperform. Loans Assets / PCT	Mgmt.	Earnings — Return on Avg. Assets (R.O.A.) / PCT	Liquidity — S/T Assets less Large Liabilities Assets / PCT	Loan Quality — Net Charge Offs Avg. Loans	Loan Growth	Nonperforming Loans Primary Capital
DEC 87	17247021	1	64/B+	58/B+	79/A	60/B+	6.66/22	0.14/98		1.36/92	-44.05/16	0.61	54.0	2.2
SEP 87	10734777	1	57/B+	57/B+	70/A	52/B+	5.89/3	0.12/98		1.42/93	-45.61/17	0.41	64.6	1.9
JUN 87	10298151	1	59/B+	59/B+	74/A	53/B+	6.15/6	0.11/98		1.45/95	-41.43/22	0.32	83.6	2.2
MAR 87	8255386	1	53/B+	59/B+	77/A	60/B+	6.07/7	0.13/98		1.63/97	-43.70/18	0.15	103.6	2.2
DEC 86	7825930	1	66/B+	64/B+	78/A	58/B+	6.18/10	0.12/97		2.08/96	-41.64/20	0.62	116.7	2.2
SEP 86	6234723	1	73/A	64/B+	79/A	66/B+	6.24/16	0.14/96		2.07/97	-37.00/28	0.37	****	2.6
JUN 86	5851598	1	71/A	66/B+	82/A	71/A	6.26/10	0.10/97		2.10/98	-26.47/47	0.20	****	1.5
MAR 86	4920020	2	76/A	68/B+	83/A	68/B+	6.61/25	0.10/97		2.36/97	-26.43/15	0.08	****	1.4
DEC 85	3468799	2	81/A	65/B+	80/A	68/B+	6.46/22	0.09/96		1.72/95	-20.16/24	0.18	173.2	1.4

EXCEPTION ANALYSIS AS OF 12/31/87

PERCENTILE RANGE: OVER 75 | 25 TO 75 | UNDER 25

PROFITABILITY

	OVER 75	25 TO 75	UNDER 25
RETURN ON AVERAGE ASSETS = 1.36%	92		
RETURN ON AVERAGE EQUITY = 24.82%	94		
NET INTEREST SPREAD/AVERAGE EARNING ASSETS = 2.20%			5
NET OVERHEAD EXPENSE/AVERAGE EARNING ASSETS = 0.35%	96		
OPER. INC. (EXCL. PROVISION, SEC. G/L) PER SALARY = 1.48%	85		

ASSET QUALITY (DOMESTIC)

	OVER 75	25 TO 75	UNDER 25
NET CHARGE-OFFS/AVERAGE LOANS = 0.61%		59	
LOAN LOSS RESERVE/TOTAL LOANS = 0.43%			2
NONPERFORMING LOANS/GROSS LOANS = 0.35%	98		

LIQUIDITY & FUNDS MANAGEMENT

	OVER 75	25 TO 75	UNDER 25
S/T MONEY MKT. ASSET LESS LG. LIAB./ASSETS = -44.05%			16
LARGE LIABILITY DEPENDENCE RATIO = 66.56%			15
$100M+ TIME DEPOSITS/TOTAL DEPOSITS = 52.84%			2
PUBLIC FUNDS/TOTAL DEPOSITS = 5.44%			15
TOTAL LOANS/DEPOSITS - PUBLIC FUNDS = 45.54%	97		
CUMULATIVE 6 MONTH GAP/ASSETS = -53.31%			2

CAPITAL ADEQUACY

	OVER 75	25 TO 75	UNDER 25
PRIMARY CAPITAL/ADJ. ASSETS = 6.66%			22
TOTAL CAPITAL/ADJ. ASSETS = 6.66%			11
NONPERFORMING LOANS/PRIMARY CAPITAL = 2.24%	98		
DEBT + LIMITED-LIFE PREF. STOCK/TOT CAPITAL = 0.00%	84		
DIVIDEND PAYOUT = 0.00%	84		

CONTINGENT LIABILITIES

	OVER 75	25 TO 75	UNDER 25
CONTINGENT LIABILITIES/TOTAL ASSETS = 6.81%	96		
TOTAL CAPITAL/ASSETS PLUS CONTINGENT LIAB. = 5.63%		69	

FIVE YEAR COMPOUND GROWTH

	OVER 75	25 TO 75	UNDER 25
5 YEAR COMPOUND GROWTH IN TOTAL ASSETS = 80.35%	97		
5 YEAR COMPOUND GROWTH IN IPC DEPOSITS = 92.24%	97		
5 YEAR COMPOUND GROWTH IN TOTAL LOANS = 245.41%	97		
5 YEAR COMPOUND GROWTH IN C&I LOANS = *******%			
5 YEAR COMPOUND GROWTH IN COMM'L RE LOANS = ******%			
5 YEAR COMPOUND GROWTH IN NET OVERHEAD EXP. = 24.10%			6

Sample Sheshunoff Bank Analysis Report

Courtesy Sheshunoff Information Services Inc.

BOSTON SAFE DEPOSIT & TR CO BOSTON MA

EXECUTIVE SUMMARY

OVERVIEW Year	ASSETS Total $(000)	ASSETS % Change	DEPOSITS Total $(000)	DEPOSITS % Change	LOANS Total $(000)	Nonper- forming $(000)	% Change	Net Charge-Offs for Period $(000)	Loan Loss Reserve $(000)	PROFITS Income Before Extra. Items $(000)	% Change	Divi- dends $(000)	CAPITAL Total Equity $(000)	% Change
DEC 87	12747021	62.9	11445040	67.6	4928307	17214	54.0	23881	21142	135725	15.2	0	745695	80.97
SEP 87	10734777	72.2	9517993	73.2	4166928	12623	64.9	15252	24440	98688	24.1	0	584359	62.46
JUN 87	10298151	76.0	8990290	76.6	3863449	10919	83.6	11175	26360	63667	27.7	0	541644	66.49
MAR 87	8255386	67.8	7266179	70.1	3480049	10557	103.6	4941	28564	32797	32.6	0	450415	56.73
DEC 86	7825930	125.6	6830142	127.1	3200440	9560	116.7	13624	29520	117789	151.3	0	412047	104.35
SEP 86	6234723	****	5496850	****	2526722	8556	****	7248	24235	79546	****	0	359698	****
JUN 86	5851598	****	5092137	****	2104756	5646	****	3584	19905	49874	****	0	325326	****
MAR 86	4920020	****	4272408	****	1713075	4695	****	1263	16882	24737	****	0	287390	****
DEC 85	3468799	74.0	3008186	81.7	1476985	2979	173.2	1865	14333	46870	253.5	0	201634	75.31
DEC 84	1993899	33.2	1655459	26.4	540628	254	401.4	406	688	13259	91.9	0	115017	40.85
DEC 83	1497136	124.3	1310131	204.9	107828	338	975.7	59	174	6910	-2.1	0	81658	228.30

PEER GROUP COMPARISONS

(PCT = Percentile Rank within National Asset Size Peer Group)

	12/87	9/87	6/87	3/87	12/86	12/85	12/84	12/83
PROFITABILITY								
Return on Average Assets (R.O.A.)	1.36/92	1.42/93	1.45/95	1.63/97	2.08/96	1.72/95	0.76/35	0.64/33
Return on Average Equity (R.O.E.)	24.48/95	26.48/95	27.21/95	30.42/98	37.13/97	29.60/99	13.48/40	12.97/45
Net Interest Spread (Tax Adj.)	2.20/5	2.37/9	2.50/13	2.82/20	3.03/19	2.75/4	1.60/1	1.73/3
Noninterest Income/Average Assets	1.11/26	1.17/29	1.13/32	1.04/24	1.36/54	2.18/90	3.82/96	3.32/96
Overhead/Average Assets	1.57/96	1.65/96	1.65/96	1.72/93	2.07/89	2.86/93	4.51/12	4.51/12
Net Overhead Expense/Avg. Assets	0.33/96	0.46/96	0.53/92	0.67/91	0.74/91	0.66/93	0.39/97	1.19/91
ASSET QUALITY								
Nonperforming Loans/Total Assets	0.14/98	0.12/98	0.11/98	0.13/98	0.12/97	0.09/96	0.01/98	0.02/96
Nonperforming Loans/Gross Loans	0.35/98	0.30/98	0.28/98	0.30/98	0.30/98	0.20/96	0.05/98	0.31/93
Nonperforming Loans/Primary Capital	2.24/98	2.07/98	1.92/98	2.20/98	2.17/97	1.38/96	0.22/98	0.41/96
Earnings Coverage: Net Charge-Offs	5.69/79	6.30/69	5.92/66	6.22/72	5.41/70	19.33/85	23.14/91	-26.90/0
Net Charge-Offs/Average Loans	0.61/59	0.41/51	0.32/40	0.15/39	0.62/49	0.18/79	0.13/85	0.10/89
Loan Reserve/Total Loans	0.43/2	0.59/1	0.68/1	0.82/2	0.92/2	0.97/17	0.13/0	0.16/0
LIQUIDITY								
S/T Money Mkt Assets - Lg. Liab./Assets	-44.05/16	-45.61/17	-41.43/22	-43.70/18	-41.64/20	-20.16/24	21.66/99	26.15/99
$100M+ Time Deposits/Total Loans	122.97/16	123.17/1	117.48/1	113.47/1	111.46/41	71.20/2	30.51/25	136.57/1
Borrowings & Foreign Dep/Total Loans	122.36/40	25.73/36	21.36/42	16.81/49	21.46/41	13.12/14	2.79/45	0.84/74
Net Fed. Funds Purch (Sold)/Tot. Loans	-1.59/90	-4.02/95	-0.86/92	-1.18/95	5.94/80	-2.33/83	-15.63/97	-81.46/99
Brokered Deposits/Total Loans	0.00/**	0.00/**	2.62/34	2.21/39	7.18/10	3.47/0	61.36/0	349.95/0
Total Loans/Deposits - Public Funds	45.54/97	46.70/97	46.59/97	50.81/96	50.53/96	55.98/94	39.73/98	9.00/99
CAPITAL								
Primary Capital/Assets	6.66/22	5.89/3	6.15/6	6.07/7	6.18/10	6.46/22	5.80/14	5.47/11
Total Capital/Assets	6.66/11	5.89/3	6.15/6	6.07/4	6.18/10	6.46/13	5.80/7	5.47/7
Total Capital/Total Loans	15.56/91	14.61/86	14.70/85	13.73/82	13.80/86	14.62/84	21.40/97	75.89/99
% Change: Primary Capital	73.66/97	58.57/97	64.53/96	57.42/96	104.46/97	86.65/99	41.39/97	228.34/98
% Change: Total Assets	62.88/97	72.18/97	75.99/96	67.79/96	125.00/89	73.00/86	33.18/95	124.28/97
Dividend Payout	0.00/84	0.00/85	0.00/81	0.00/84	0.00/89	0.00/86	0.00/89	0.00/89

Sample Sheshunoff Bank Analysis Report (*cont.*)

Courtesy Sheshunoff Information Services Inc.

Most commercial banks are required to have an equity ratio of 5 percent and most fall between 5 percent and 10 percent. The loan limit of this ratio is going to be gradually increased over the next few years, and 7 percent will probably be the new floor by the time this book is published.

For the income test, look on the bank's statement for "net income" and see whether net income was a profit or a loss. Losses are enclosed by parentheses (yes, banks have losses, too). Compare the most recent loss to equity (or surplus or net worth, whichever appears on the statement). If the loss represents a large piece of equity, the bank may be shaky.

You Can Figure for Yourself How Safe Your Bank Is

Assets		Liabilities	
Cash & due from banks	$ 74,621	Deposits	$480,555
Federal funds sold	9,460	Federal funds purchased	12,186
U.S. Government securities	106,450	Other liabilities	19,452
State & municipal securities	21,610	Capital stock	33,302
Other securities	9,569	Surplus	25,422
Loans	341,682	Undivided profits	14,221
Other assets	21,746	TOTAL LIABILITIES	$585,138
TOTAL ASSETS	$585,138		

- *Liquidity ratio.* This ratio measures the amount of liquid assets, or assets easily convertible into cash, that stand behind each dollar of deposits.

    First, add Cash on Hand, Federal Funds Sold and U.S. Government Securities. Next, add to that 70% of State and Municipal Securities. Then subtract Federal Funds Purchased from the total.

    Finally, to obtain the liquidity ratio, divide your final total by Deposits. In the case of the Neighborhood Bank, the liquidity ratio would be $193,470 ÷ $480,555 for a ratio of 40.3%.

    In other words, the Neighborhood Bank has just over 40 cents in liquid assets standing in back of each dollar of deposits. Again, that's fairly conservative. A typical 1989 liquidity ratio for a commercial bank would be in the 25 percent to 35 percent range.
- *Loan-to-deposit ratio.* The loan-to-deposit ratio is easily obtained by dividing deposits into loans. In the case of the Neighborhood Bank, the ratio stands at 71 percent ($341,682 ÷ $480,555). By today's standard, that's rather stolidly conservative. The norm is around 75 percent these days, compared to a typical 50–60 percent in the 1960s.
- *Capital ratio.* This ratio measures the amount of capital assets behind each dollar of deposits. Merely add together capital, surplus, and undivided profits. Then divide the total by deposits. For the Neighborhood Bank, the capital ratio would be 15.1 percent or $74,495 ÷ $480,555. Relatively few commercial banks maintain a capital ratio beyond 10 percent, with most falling in the 5–7 percent range.

If you don't have the time or inclination to perform your own calculations, Veribanc provides a "Short Form Report" that simplifies the equity and income tests into a color code. Each bank included in Veribanc's computerized data base (containing federal government data on more than 34,000 institutions) is classified green, yellow, or red. Veribanc can provide, at a cost of fifty dollars, a report on any of these institutions. For more information, contact:

> Veribanc
> P.O. Box 2963
> Woburn, MA 01888
> (617) 245-8370

You want to know how healthy your bank is for basically two reasons. Remember "go fetch," that game bankers love to play? When you walk into your banker's office armed with your own questions, it'll be easier to play your game, "catch." Ask her how the loan-to-deposit ratio is holding up or whether the bank is thinking of merging. Get a dialogue going.

You also want to investigate the health of your bank for a more obvious reason: to avoid being the customer of a failing bank. Sure, your money is insured, but that doesn't tell you how long it will take for you to retrieve your money if your bank fails. Did you know that it can take as long as nine weeks? Where are your employees going to go when it takes you nine weeks to make payroll? Across the street to work for your competitor, that's where! Remember, 187 banks failed in 1987, and the entire banking industry is in turmoil. Bank of America (California), Continental Illinois (Chicago), and First Republic (Dallas) were all very big important banks, but for all their size and churchlike trappings, they got into big trouble.

OBTAINING INSIDE INFORMATION

I want you to obtain two more pieces of information from your bank before you go into your next loan negotiation: a copy of the bank's analysis of your account and the spread sheet for your account.

As more and more banks failed in the 1980s, bankers began to develop account analyses in an effort to avoid failure by dropping accounts that weren't making them money. Remember what I said about bankers hating risk? Well, account analysis stems from that hatred. Account analyses are basically profit and loss statements for your account. Banks now run computer programs that take all the data about your account and work it into account analyses. If your account is showing a loss, the banker will consider dropping it when times are tight at the bank. Account analysis is an effort on the part of bankers to foist some of the decision-making risk (there's that word again) about accounts onto a computer. It includes your balances at the bank, lines of credit, and outstanding loans. About three-quarters of the banks in the United States now use account analysis.

The account analysis clearly shows whether or not you are making money for the bank—whether or not you are a good customer. A banker is a person who gladly lends you her umbrella when it's sunny and wants it back when it rains. You should keep your copies of account analyses in a drawer in case there's a storm at the bank. Pull it out when your banker gets nervous about your loan renewal and remind her that in 1981 you made $23,000 for the bank, and that she'd better think twice about not lending you any more money just because it's raining at the moment.

Have you read Lee Iacocca's autobiography yet? He tells a great story about going around the country to line up the financing deal that's going to turn Chrysler around. He's got the president of the United States backing him, the Congress of the United States, the Office of Management and Budget, Chase Manhattan, Manufacturers Hanover, and Chemical Bank all lined up to support him in his effort to turn this giant company around and save America. At the last minute, though, some sleepy banker in Kansas wouldn't go along with the deal for his $75,000. This banker had been a participant in all the Chrysler loans for forty-two years and he looked the deal over and said, "It ain't gonna work. I don't wanna be in the deal. I'm out." Iacocca's big house of cards was about to come tumbling down because this goddamn (I'm quoting) sleepy Kansas banker was withholding his $75,000. So Iacocca flies out ninety-seven Chrysler executives to see the farmer banker and tell him, "Do you realize that for forty-two years you've participated in Chrysler's debt packages? Not once in forty-two years have we ever been late or skipped a payment. Not once in forty-two years! We're not even asking you to take an adjustment; we're just saying step up with the president of the United States and Congress!"

Wouldn't it have been nice if those executives could have come in with a truckload of forty-two years worth of account analyses? They could have shown the Kansas banker: "Look, in 1936 your bank made $7,400 on a loan to Chrysler, in 1937 you made $8,300. . . ." and so on. That would have been a very concrete way to have dealt with that sleepy banker.

Keep a copy of your account analyses both to help you deal with your banker and to back you up should you ever change banks. A bank will do business with you for one reason—to make money. Your account analysis says exactly how much money you are making for your bank. Keep copies of it in your desk.

Quarterly, or sometimes monthly, you submit your business's financial data to the bank. The banker takes that information and puts it on a spread sheet to understand it better. Most banks use a similar style of spread sheet, often called the green sheets. Green sheets usually show about ten years of balance sheet and profit and loss information in an easy-to-read format. Banks use spread sheets to keep track of your business's performance and to make transitions between bankers easier. It's easier for them to interpret the spread sheets than your submitted accounting data.

When you look at the spread sheet you may discover that certain numbers are starred, while others are circled or erased. A close look at the spread sheet will tell you a lot about what is important to your bank's evaluation of your business. You're going to be the best customer of the bank because you're going to be an informed customer. You're not going to walk into the bank and say, "Gee, this ceiling is awfully high, I wonder if they've got any loan officers in here."

As I stated earlier, banks are like religious institutions: the colossal brick structures, the formal trappings, the hints of secrecy. . . . Banks and bankers are intimidating. This intimidation is designed to make it difficult for you to negotiate with them. After all, how comfortable would you feel negotiating with your priest or rabbi or minister? How do you get in a power position when you negotiate with God?

So, what do you do when your banker says you can't see your account analysis or spread sheet? Try the following negotiating ploy.

The first principle of the art of obtaining inside information is never trap your banker. Be persistent but be nice. If she says no, ask why. If she says because it's bank policy, ask who made the policy. If she says the chairman made the policy, ask to speak to the chairman. If she says you can't speak to the chairman, ask to write to the chairman (send a copy to the banker). If she says no, ask her to ask her boss if you can write to the chairman.

Explain to her that you would like to see what ratios the bank tracks on the spread sheets so that you can keep track of them, too: "Joan, let me see if I understand exactly what the spread sheet is. You simply lift my numbers out of the accounting information I supply you and transfer them to your spread sheets, right? In other words, there's no data on the spread sheet that I haven't seen in another format, is there? It's basically just my financial numbers in a standard accounting format, right?" Gently suggest that you can't see the harm in seeing your own numbers. Tell her you'll be happy to give her as much time as she needs to get the answer for you ("Shall I check back with you on the twenty-second, Joan?"). Ask her for things she feels relatively comfortable saying yes to. If you apply steady, even pressure in this manner, you will eventually see the account analysis and the spread sheets. The underlying negotiating principle is: Never trap your banker. Always give her two or three ways out at each stage. Persist, but persist slowly and steadily.

NO BANKER IS AN ISLAND

Each of the steps I have outlined thus far—preparing to answer questions about your business, getting to know your banker, investigating your bank, looking at your bank records—are steps toward the final goal of getting off personal loan guarantees. But don't forget that your banker is not an island. Hold meetings with your banker, lawyer, accountant, and key people from your company. Give your banker lots of information. (I don't believe it's humanly possible for an entrepreneur to give a banker too much information.) In all my travels and in all my work with entrepreneurs and bankers, I have never heard a banker tell an entrepreneur, "Stop! You're giving me too much information!" Information, especially sales figures and other growth statistics that they can write down, makes bankers feel secure. (They can file it.)

Here's a tip: When you have a banker and are negotiating a loan, don't use your corporate lawyer. Find a lawyer who represents a competing bank and retain that law firm for your negotiations. That firm's lawyers will obviously be familiar with banks, and your negotiating power will increase perceptibly when you use a competitor's legal counsel. Your bank may already have used this law firm, or may do so in the future. Either way, you're in good shape if your lawyer has some knowledge of the kinds of deals competing banks are offering to entrepreneurs. When you go into negotiations, she'll assist you with evaluating your requests in terms of whether competing banks are offering what you are asking for. (Letting your banker know that you know that other banks are willing to do what you're asking for should put you in a stronger bargaining position.) Your lawyer will be able to help you to avoid making a fool of yourself by asking for something no bank is willing to give. To find such counsel, simply call your bank's competitors and ask what law firm they use. Simple enough!

Your accountant is your most crucial link to your banker. If they don't like or trust each other, your chances of successful borrowing are greatly reduced. Use common sense: The best way to hire an accountant your banker likes is to ask her to recommend one to you.

You will want to have your banker involved on many levels with your business because you need her advice. Don't forget, money always follows advice. Your advisers are your team, and your banker is easily the most important part—the heart—of that team. Lawyers and accountants are hired help; your banker has to be courted. It's a relationship that demands tender, loving care.

5. Dealing with Your Banker

THINK LIKE A BANKER

As an entrepreneur, when you go to your banker's office to request a loan, it is your duty to be thoroughly prepared to show him that a loan to you is a low-risk proposition because every banker has been burned at some point in his career, and no banker wants to experience that pain again. Show him how well prepared you are to answer every doubtful question he has. You've learned a lot so far about bankers as people—the way they think, the way they tend to act. Now use that information to improve your negotiating abilities. This combination of information and preparation is the most powerful negotiating tool in the world.

Bankers like to be safe, so they tend to flock, like turkeys. It's hard to soar with the eagles when you work with a bunch of turkeys. I once did a little experiment at a seminar I held for bankers. I placed eight pieces of string on a table. Seven of the pieces were twenty-two inches long, but the eighth piece was only eighteen inches long. The strings were laid out on the table with their ends justified, not ragged, so that everyone could clearly see that all of the strings except the last one were the same length. I then planted six stooges in the room—actually, they were entrepreneurs, but I made them wear nice three-piece suits like the bankers did. I brought the stooges into the room and had them stand in a row in front of the table; then I called one of the real bankers into the room. The poor slob didn't know he was the subject of an experiment. I told him, "Take a look at the strings on the table and decide whether they are all the same length." While he was thinking, I asked each stooge whether he thought the strings were all the same length. Of course, I had already told them all to say yes. So what do you think our poor banker said after hearing his "peers" agree that the strings were the same length? Naturally, being a banker, he concurred.

No matter how I did it, the results of the experiment were always the same. I tried it on a bunch of different bankers at the seminar and tried varying the number of stooges from two to eight. It didn't matter. When a banker heard more than one other person he thought was a banker say the strings were the same length, he agreed.

The findings were fascinating, but the experiment was getting a little boring, so I devised a variation. I told one of the stooges to say that he thought the eighth string was shorter. What do you know? Our banker suddenly became a hero, now that he had an ally! He said, "Hey, there's a short piece of string there!" In the land of the blind, the one-eyed banker is king.

Bankers don't want to make high-risk loans regardless of the profit prospects for your business. They are bankers, not venture capitalists or entrepreneurs. Bank lending is the process by which someone lets you borrow money and expects that money to be paid back with interest. It is not an equity process. There is no "up side." Even if you turn your high-risk business into an immensely profitable one, all your banker gets out of it is his principal and interest. Bankers prefer to lend to low-risk, low-profit ventures than to high-risk businesses with exciting profit prospects because they want their money back. Avoiding failure earns your banker his promotion, not hitting a home run!

At the beginning of this section I told you that bankers resemble turkeys. Well, they also resemble elephants: They have very long memories. You can go to your banker's office confident about your strong, healthy business, but if he remembers that six years ago you had to sign personally for a loan, he'll want you to sign again.

"But I paid that loan off perfectly on schedule," you protest. "Doesn't that count for something?" (Note that in chapter 6 I strongly suggest borrowing and paying back a loan when you don't need it just to establish credibility.) Most small-business borrowers do in fact pay their loans back conscientiously, so you really don't distinguish yourself from the crowd by doing so. You've proven you're a good customer of the bank, but you have to prove you're the best to get off personal loan guarantees.

HOW TO ANSWER CRUCIAL QUESTIONS YOUR BANKER WILL ASK

You can distinguish yourself by being prepared. I think you'll be surprised to learn that a thoroughly prepared borrower has a four times greater chance of having his loan approved than a borrower who waltzes into the bank without knowing the answers to the questions we've discussed in previous chapters. That's a significant advantage.

You should also know the answers to the following five questions. Your banker will ask them, and you should have the answers on the tip of your tongue.

WHAT A BANKER WANTS TO KNOW ABOUT YOUR LOAN REQUEST

1. How much money do you need?
2. How long do you need it for?
3. What are you going to do with it?
4. When and how will you repay it?
5. What will you do if you don't get the loan?

You know how much money you need and you would probably love to keep it for ten years, but most commercial banks have a policy of lending for less than twelve months. A banker usually feels comfortable offering a maximum maturity of ninety days to a small-business owner, but you can get a six-month loan. My advice is to ask for a six-month loan with an automatic renewal to be given by the bank if all conditions remain satisfactory, i.e., if you make prompt payments and the bank is happy with the interest structure. In this way, you secure for yourself a loan of one year, which is the longest loan you can possibly get from a bank today.

The question of what you are going to do with the money should be thoroughly answered by your business plan. If it isn't, go back to chapters 1 and 2 and review the sections on use of funds.

WHAT TWO ELEMENTS A BANKER RELIES ON FOR REPAYMENT OF A LOAN

1. Collateral
2. Cash flow generated by the business (pays the loan 99 percent of the time)

Ninety-nine percent of small-business loans are repaid from cash flow generated by the business. Please reread that sentence—it's important. Thank you! Your business plan should clearly show how you plan to generate enough cash to pay back the loan. Your banker will still want collateral. He'll want to know the worth of the assets of your business. If he says your assets aren't enough, and he wants your summer home and your spouse's car, you might remind him that more collateral does not turn a bad loan into a good loan. A good loan is paid back from the cash flow of the business. So when your banker talks about collateral, you should talk about cash flow! Remind him that 99 percent of loans are paid out of cash flow, and show him your strong cash flow. Whenever he says *collateral,* you respond by saying *cash flow.*

FOUR WAYS YOU ACTUALLY REPAY A LOAN

1. Cash flow generated by the business (99 percent of the time)
2. Get an investor (equity infusion pays off some debt)

    3. Sell an asset or the business
    4. Borrow somewhere else

TWO REASONS FOR RENEWING A LOAN

    1. It didn't happen!
    2. It happened but you used the money for something else.

Many entrepreneurs have renewed a loan for one of the two reasons mentioned above. We get stuck with frequent renewals that we constantly have to explain to our banker ("It didn't happen because . . ." or "I used the money for something else because . . ."). If you are constantly in your banker's office to renew your ninety-day note because the time frame is too short, you will be constantly giving him excuses that make you look bad. Within ninety days, it's pretty unlikely that your business is going to "happen" in such a big way that you're not going to need to renew the note. Also, it's pretty likely that a more pressing need (for example, payroll) than the one you told him you needed the money for will come up. For an entrepreneur, this is just part of running a business. You had to be flexible, so you did what you had to do. Bankers don't admire flexibility, and they hate surprises. For bankers there is no such thing as good news and bad news. There is only good news and better news. That's why I talked earlier about going for a six-month loan with an automatic renewal if all conditions remain satisfactory. That's a good option; it avoids surprises.

Prepare yourself for your meeting with your banker by knowing the answers to the questions he will ask. Another way to prepare yourself is to listen to tapes or to read a book on banking before making a presentation to a banker. I recommend *How to Plan and Negotiate a Loan* by Kenneth W. Spanks (hardcover, 188 pages, $20; available from Walker & Co., 720 Fifth Ave., New York, NY 10019); the *Loan Officer Handbook* by the American Bankers Association; and the audiotape on which this book was based, "How to Get a Business Loan Without Signing Your Life Away" by Joseph Mancuso ($60; available from the Center for Entrepreneurial Management, 180 Varick St., 17th floor, New York, NY 10014; 212-633-0060). Also consider *Get That Business Loan: Convince Your Banker to Say Yes* by Harley A. Rennhoff (hardcover, 163 pages, Pelican Publishing Co., $14.95), available from Books of the Unusual, 110 Second St., Lakewood, NJ 08701; (201) 370-4422, (800) 843-9646, or (800) 345-4422.

WHAT IF HE'S JUST PLAIN MEAN?

A doctor comes into a heart transplant patient's room to tell him about the available heart donors. "We've got three donors for you," the doctor says, "a thirty-six-year-old steamfitter—real healthy guy, a forty-six-year-old marathon runner, and a fifty-six-year-old banker." Which heart do you think the patient decides to take a chance on?

The patient says, "I'll take the banker's heart."

The doctor, astonished, says, "Why do you want the oldest heart when you could have these younger, much healthier hearts?"

The patient answers, "Because I know that the banker's heart has never been used!"

Many entrepreneurs can relate to that story, but, as I've stressed from the beginning, your banker is the key to the growth of your business, and your relationship with him should be a friendly and helpful one.

But what if you've really tried to get along with your banker and the relationship is just not working? You feel that your requests for a loan are being arbitrarily turned down. Should you go over his head?

Probably not, because even if you do it is likely that the same banker will sit on your loan committee or be contacted by the new loan officer. You'll be in negotiations with a banker you made look bad. This is not a win-win negotiating situation, it's a win-lose situation, and guess who's going to lose. The guy with the money or the guy with the idea? Mancuso's golden rule is "Those that have the gold make the rules." The guy with the idea is going to lose.

My advice to you is to get another banker at another bank. If you really have a personality conflict with your banker, don't borrow money from his bank. He may decide to make trouble for you at every turn. That advice is 99 percent infallible, so take note.

If you're very happy with your bank, but not your banker, and don't want to change banks in order to change bankers, try speaking with your banker's boss. Politely request to change to a different banker. Be prepared to describe the problem as simply "poor communication" and take most of the blame yourself. Do not attempt to crucify your banker. His boss will know what you are getting at and will appreciate your tact. You will get what you wanted—a different banker—without alienating a possible member of your loan committee. Generally, though, never pick a bank, always pick a banker. The individual you work with is usually more important than the institution you choose.

If you do decide to change bankers and banks, there are a couple of good ways to improve your position. The best way to find a good banker is to ask for a referral from a successful entrepreneur. (Bankers tell me that the nicest thing a customer can do for them is to offer a good referral; in fact, the single best thing you can do for your banker is to refer a good depositor.) This is probably the most valuable piece of information in this book. You see, most entrepreneurs approach a bank directly. They try to determine who they should talk to about a loan by starting at the front desk. Little do they know that banks have a secret system for placing their employees. Everyone who applies for employment at a bank must take an IQ test, and the people who score the lowest man the front desks or the phones.

Entrepreneurs are natural phone people—we do our best wheeling and dealing on the phone. We make the mistake of approaching a banker the way we would another entrepreneur—on the phone. Bankers hate phones. Phones make them feel insecure. They like to write letters and send memos. They like communications they can file. You may hate to pin yourself down by putting all your communications with your banker in writing, but that's too bad. You're in the business of becoming your banker's best friend, and that includes humoring his formal tendencies. Choose a banker who was recommended to you by a successful entrepreneur and approach him in writing. Don't phone!

The best source of listings of banks and of bank information is Polk's World Bank Directory. Contact:

> R. L. Polk & Co.
> 2001 Elm Hill Pike
> P.O. Box 1340
> Nashville, TN 37202
> (615) 889-9350

TEN TIPS FOR COMMUNICATING EFFECTIVELY WITH BANKS

1. When calling a bank, it's always best to ask for the president's office. Unlike small companies, banks always seem to put their lowest-level employees on the phones. But the secretary in the president's office is always knowledgeable and can actually answer questions.

2. Banks will generally lose your call and about one call in four always seems to result in being cut off. Your call will always be transferred at least twice—the average is about four times. (One of our calls was actually transferred twelve times.) Also, the bigger the bank, the longer you'll spend on hold.

3. Never call and say you want to send a letter of complaint to the bank. Most large banks have a person in charge of complaints, and your phone calls or letters produce fewer results when you write to the complaint person. Complaints should be sent to the president, with copies to others, to have any hope for results.

4. Trying to locate a commercial loan officer is very difficult in most banks. Calling a branch to find out who to approach for a commercial loan is much less effective than calling the president's office to ask the same question.

5. Banks change loan officers and organizational charts about as frequently as O'Hare Airport changes air traffic controllers. Consequently, the bank telephone directory, if you happen to have one, is always out of date and is effectively useless. Throw it away.

6. A bank's personnel department is totally useless for finding out who to speak to on any subject. Don't waste your time calling them.

7. Letters are always better than phone calls because banks will eventually forward letters to the appropriate people. And while phone calls are frequently cut off, letters are almost never thrown away. Letters work well, but responses take weeks. Plan ahead.

8. Letters sent to bank employees are most effective when they are sent to several people. It is better to send a letter and follow it up with a phone call than it is to call blind. The most effective letter-writing technique is to get copies to people at the branch, the asset lending group, the main office, and the loan department because these people seldom talk to one another, and the copies force them to talk a little.

9. A referral from a good customer of the bank is invaluable. If you say on the phone or by letter, "So-and-so referred me," it puts you into a new category. The best way to approach a bank—through a customer referral.

10. Loan officers don't get promoted for the loans they make (or don't make). They get promoted for the deposits they bring the bank. It is, therefore, better to talk or write about deposits, not loans. The nicest favor you can do for a bank or a banker is to refer a good depositor to the bank. It's invaluable.

11. While I promised you only ten points, I couldn't resist this bonus point. The average salary of the average commercial loan officer is about $45,000 annually. These lesser-paid people are making decisions about the well-being of your multimillion-dollar business. Your life-style may be significantly different from theirs and it must be factored into your relationship.

Twenty Ways to Improve Your Banking Ability

Today, the equity markets have become tighter and the debt markets looser. There is less venture capital available since the market crash, and the banks have more money to lend. Hence, it's not surprising to find entrepreneurs now seeking to raise capital from their friendly banker. Here are a few techniques and tips for being more successful in locating a good bank and a great banker.

1. Never pick a bank, always pick a banker. The individual you work with is usually more important than the institution you choose.

2. The best way to find a good banker is to ask for a referral from a successful entrepreneur. The nicest thing a customer can do for a banker is to offer a good referral.

3. After you have a banker and are negotiating a loan, don't use your corporate lawyer. Find a lawyer who represents a competing bank and retain that law firm for your negotiations. Obviously, they'll be familiar with the bank, and your negotiating power will increase perceivably when you use a competitor's legal counsel.

4. Try not to fill in the bank's forms for personal finances. Rather, substitute a signed and notarized form that you have prepared ahead of time, which gives the same level of information. Do not inflate personal financial statements, as false statements can come back to haunt you.

5. In addition to knowing your loan officer and his background, become familiar with the bank. Know what's hot and what's not. Real estate? The middle market? What is the bank seeking to specialize in? From annual reports or quarterly statements, you can usually find out where the problem loans are: it's very likely that the bank will be timid about lending in that area for a few years. This can be vital information.

6. From the bank's financial information, determine its loan-to-deposit ratio, a key indicator of its lending aggressiveness. If it's climbing, the bank is lending, and if it's shrinking, the bank isn't lending. The ratio usually runs about 60 to 70 percent. (At urban banks, the ratio may be higher.)

7. Banks typically claim that for every one dollar they have in assets, they like to lend out 60 cents and keep 20 cents in cash and 20 cents in secondary resources, which can be made liquid in one or two days. How does your bank check out on these ratios?

8. A banking rating service can supply you with a report on any bank, analyzing its strength. It can give you details not commonly accessible, because its information comes from regulatory agencies that monitor banks. For instance, it can tell you the level of Third World debt or insider loans. For more information, see "How Safe is Your Bank?" *Entrepreneural Managers Newsletter,* (Vol. 9, #5, February 1988) or contact Veribanc Inc., P.O. Box 2963, Woburn, MA 01888; (617) 245-8370.

9. The Harvard Business School has an excellent case analysis of the New Venture Group at the Bank of Boston. Contact: Publishing Division, Harvard Business School, Soldier's Field, Boston, MA 02163. Ask for case #9-286-070, by W. A. Sahlman. The cost is $10 for this twenty-three-page case; it's a best buy.

10. Don't forget that a good bet might be an SBA-guaranteed loan: as much as $750,000 for a term of seven years. Call the SBA field office nearest you or call the SBA Answer Desk at (800) 368-5855.

11. Banks are in the business of lending money and are not hostile to small-business owners who are knowledgeable and fully prepared. Submitting a written business plan to your loan request is crucial. It shows that you are an above-average candidate for a loan.

12. It is usually helpful to listen to tapes or to read a book on banking before making a presentation to a banker. I recommend the following:
• *How to Plan and Negotiate a Loan* by Kenneth W. Spanks (hardcover, 188 pages, $20; available from Walker & Co., 720 Fifth Ave., New York, NY 10019)
• *How to Get a Business Loan Without Signing Your Life Away* by Joseph R. Mancuso. A four-hour audiotape, with a 116-page workbook ($60; available from the Center for Entrepreneurial Management, 180 Varick St., 17th Floor, New York, NY 10014; (212) 633-0060)
• Material on borrowing is also available from banking consultant and former bank president Somers White, Somers White Co., 4736 N. 44th St., Phoenix, AZ 85018; (602) 952-9292.

13. The best source of listings of banks and bank information is Polk's World Bank Directory. Contact:

> R. L. Polk & Co.
> 2001 Elm Hill Pike
> P.O. Box 1340
> Nashville, TN 37202
> (615) 889-3350.

14. The best source of commercial lending training materials for banking officers is Robert Morris Associates, which offers a wealth of information on how to become an effective loan officer and supplies accepted financial forms for business plans. Contact:

> Robert Morris Associates
> 1616 Philadelphia National Bank Bldg.
> Philadelphia, PA 19107
> (215) 665-2858

For Robert Morris Forms, contact:

> Bankers Systems, Inc.
> P.O. Box 1457
> St. Cloud, MN 56302
> (612) 251-3060

15. The American Bankers Association (ABA) is the banking industry's trade association. They hold seminars for banks and offer publications telling banks how to analyze small-business loans.

For example, the ABA sponsors a two-day conference for banks seeking to specialize in small-business activity. The fee is $575, and it is an excellent method of learning how bankers think.

Two useful publications offered by the ABA are *Analyzing Financial Statements* (#054601), $25.00, workbook (#054602), $7.50, and *Asset Based Lending,* student handbook (#621600), $19.50, lender's guide (#621601), $18.00. Contact:

American Bankers Association
1120 Connecticut Ave., N.W.,
Washington, DC 20036
(202) 663-5000.

16. Two good general pamphlets describing SBA loan functions are "Business Loans from the SBA" and "Your Business and the SBA." Published by the Office of Public Communications, they are available from regional SBA field offices, or call the SBA Answer Desk at (800) 368-5855.

17. A good source of seminars and publications for the banking industry is Executive Enterprises, 22 W. 21st Street, New York, NY 10010; (212) 645-7880.

18. Your accountant is your most crucial link to your banker. That's not to say that other professionals are not also good contacts, but if your banker and your accountant don't like or trust each other, your chances of successful borrowing are greatly reduced.

19. Not everyone has to personally guarantee corporate bank debt, but banks will tell you that everyone does. Your task is to find small-business owners who borrow without personal guarantees, and then determine what they have that you don't.

20. The only time to raise capital is when you don't need it. Bankers prefer to lend money to borrowers who have borrowed money at least once and have paid back at least one loan on time. It's a psychological factor like preferring to lend to a business that already has an account at their bank. This encourages entrepreneurs to have accounts at multiple banks and relationships with multiple bank officers.

6. How to Stay Off Personal Loan Guarantees and Get Off Them If You're Already On (Ditto for Your Spouse)

IS IT WORTH IT TO YOU?

If you've followed the strategy mapped out in this book so far, you are well on your way to becoming the best customer your banker ever had. By now you may have thought I forgot to deliver what the title of the book promised. The title isn't *How to Be Your Banker's Best Friend,* it's *How to Get a Business Loan (Without Signing Your Life Away).* I haven't forgotten—in fact, all of our work so far has been leading up to this chapter's important discussion of how you and your spouse can get off and stay off personal loan guarantees. By a personal loan guarantee I mean any form of loan under which, if your business is unable to make the payments, you, as its guarantor, are personally responsible for doing so.

Bankers, being the orderly people they are, like to do a two-step negotiation—first the loan and then the guarantee. After the loan is negotiated, they like to say, "By the way, with all loans we require borrowers to fill out these personal financial statements. . . ." You should seek a one-step negotiation with the guarantee negotiated as part of the loan application. When your banker says, "I'm sorry, that's not negotiable," you should say innocently, "Gosh, isn't everything negotiable?"

Think of the negotiation as a pyramid.

We've talked about every step of the pyramid but the tip—the personal loan guarantee.

If you are currently on a personal loan guarantee, write down how much it would be worth to you to get off the personal loan guarantee. Do this before you

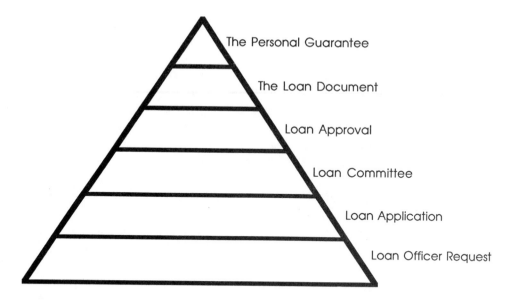

The Personal Loan Guarantee

begin negotiating. When negotiating such a sensitive issue, you don't want to win the battle just to find out that you've lost the war.

1. Write a dollar amount.
2. Consider interest rates. Would you pay a higher rate if you didn't have to sign personally for the loan?
3. Would you be willing to borrow less money in exchange for not having to sign a personal guarantee?
4. Would you be willing to put up a higher compensating balance for the money you've borrowed?
5. Would you settle for a shorter maturity on your loan?

This step is crucial because it will prevent you from allowing the banker to take advantage of your emotional desire to get off the personal loan guarantee. Over time personal loan guarantees have become an emotional issue between entrepreneurs and lenders: Entrepreneurs today are overzealous about their value and the need to get off the guarantees.

Between you and me, I have been on a few personal guarantees. In a few select cases, when it came down to getting the money but not getting off the personal loan guarantee, I took the money because the money was doing me enough good to offset the potential harm of the guarantee.

Set limits for yourself before negotiations begin. Know how much it is really worth to you (and to your spouse) to get off the personal loan guarantee *before* you step into the banker's office for negotiations. When it gets to the short strokes, the value of getting off personal loan guarantees suddenly gets bigger and bigger, and you end up losing everything.

At first glance, a higher compensating balance might seem to be the most painless offer to make for release from a personal loan guarantee. After all, you have to keep your cash somewhere—why not keep it at the bank in the form of a compensating balance? Your banker will encourage you to do this. Bankers love compensating balances because, as a rule of thumb, banks only have a capital base of 5 percent. This means that they can take your compensating balance of, say, $150 and potentially turn it into $3,000 (20 × $150) in interest-earning loans. By now you're probably thinking: Compensating balances won't cost me anything—after all, I've got to keep some cash at the bank anyway, and it'll make my banker happy.

This reasoning is problematic because it overlooks one thing: Compensating balances raise the actual rate of interest on your loan. It works like this: You borrow $1,000 from the bank at 12 percent interest, but you are asked to leave $150 in the bank as a compensating balance. This seems relatively painless because it leaves you with $850 to use. Your actual rate of interest now, though, is not 12 percent. It is 12 percent divided by 0.85, or 14.1 percent. If you are not willing to pay that rate of interest, do not agree to leave that compensating balance. If 14 percent is a better interest rate than the banker is willing to offer if you don't leave a compensating balance then, of course, you'll want to reconsider.

Understanding the role of compensating balances and idle balances is part of cash management, a subject too large to be covered in this book. I would like you to note, though, that a study by the Caruth Institute of Owner-Managed Business at Southern Methodist University in Dallas, Texas, showed that a major bank's pretax earnings on small-business loans were 2.7 percentage points higher than its earnings on loans to large firms, in spite of the higher administrative costs and the greater risks of small-business loans.

This finding indicates that the small businesses were paying an average of 17.7 percent interest instead of the 15.0 percent interest averaged by large businesses.

The study revealed further that the reason for this was that small businesses did not manage their idle cash as well as the large firms did. They left more of their funds in idle cash balances that the bank could lend. If your financial officer and accountant are not well versed in cash management, you may have a weak catcher and center fielder.

ASK AND YE SHALL RECEIVE

The next important step is simply to ask to get off the personal loan guarantee and to keep asking until you get closer to your goal. *You've got to ask your way off.*

Learn a lesson from the following anecdote.

The president of a small company was sitting on the toilet in a men's room when he noticed that there was no toilet paper. He saw feet in the stall next to his, so he tapped on the wall partition.

"Excuse me," he said, "do you have any toilet paper in your stall that you could pass to me?"

"Nope," the other guy said.

The entrepreneur thought for a moment, then he tapped again.

"Excuse me, again, but you don't happen to have a copy of the *Wall Street Journal* or the *New York Times* over there, do you?"

"Nope," his neighbor said.

By now the CEO was really in a pickle, so he tapped again and asked the question he should have asked originally, "How about change for a twenty-dollar bill?"

To get out of your personal-loan-guarantee pickle, you are also going to have to ask a sequence of questions. First, ask your banker if everybody who borrows from her bank signs personally for corporate debt. If she says yes, say, "Come on, I'm sure some of the bigger companies don't sign." Find out how "big" you have to be to avoid signing. You want to know where your bank draws the line. You should also seek out small-business owners who are borrowing without personal guarantees. Determine what they have that you don't have and keep in mind the arguments about public companies and Lee Iacocca that I present later in this section. Second, ask your banker, politely, what those larger businesses have that you don't have in terms of ability to pay back their loans.

By now your banker will have asked you the big guilt question: "Why don't you want to sign personally—aren't you going to pay back the loan?" Bankers practice this question in front of their mirrors at home. They love how it puts you on the spot. You should practice your answer to it just as often.

Throw her a curve with this answer: "Of course I'm going to pay it back, Joan. You've seen my business plan, the loan is well accounted for. Besides, I've paid back all my other loans, but this isn't that simple. Life is more complicated than sets of numbers would have us believe. It may not be all that logical, but for me this is a big issue. I lose sleep over it. It's like my wife, Matilda, was saying the other day. She asked me why we couldn't just pay off the mortgage on our beautiful quarter-million-dollar house in Cape Cod. I explained to her that the 6 percent interest on the mortgage is the least expensive borrowed money we've got and that it would be foolish to pay it off. Do you know what she told me? She said, 'I know the numbers and the facts, but I've always wanted to live in a house that was all mine, with no mortgage.' You know, Joan, I guess I feel the same way about the personal loan guarantee. The loan will be paid back with or without the guarantee, but I'll sure sleep better without it. I'll even perform better at work without the extra worry, and we both want me to perform at my best, don't we? Joan, can you relate to my wife's feeling?"

Give your banker this second reason: "With the present turmoil in the banking industry, I am very uneasy about personally guaranteeing corporate debt because that decreases my flexibility. If your bank gets in trouble, like Bank of America, Continental Illinois, or Republic did, the personal guarantee could hinder my flexibility while the regulators are undoing the mess at your bank. My only choice in such a predicament might be to borrow elsewhere personally for my business. The guarantee would prevent me from being able to keep my business going. I think you'll agree that in these times bank failure is not a remote possibility, and that it's unhealthy for both of us to put a ball and chain around the foot of the one person who could bail out the company if the bank gets in trouble."

Now you can see why you've laid such careful groundwork for a warm, friendly relationship with your banker. You want her to understand how you feel about signing that loan guarantee, not just to look at the numbers. When she throws you that hard logical question, you can use it as a launching pad for your own "Matilda" story. Then you can get logical again by telling her that, quite frankly, the worry over the guarantee is adversely affecting your performance.

ASK FOR THE FUTURE, NOT FOR NOW

A person's willingness to do something for you depends not only on what you are asking for but also on how much lead time you are giving her.

For example, a representative from your alma mater calls you on Friday and asks if you'll participate in a telephone fund-raising drive on Monday. Chances are you'll beg off. But what if the same person calls you on Friday and asks if you might be willing to help out with the fund-raising drive coming up in a couple of months. You'll probably say yes or maybe—not no. Use your understanding of this human tendency to say yes to future commitments on your banker. Her willingness to do something for you is partially a function of the amount of time you give her to do it. If you come in close and tight about wanting to get off the guarantee next week, she won't do it.

Try this approach: "On my $100,000 loan, of which I've paid back $50,000, would it be unreasonable for me to ask if I could be released from the personal loan guarantee when I've paid back $75,000? I know I'll sleep better."

If she says no, ask her: "If I came in here after I'd paid off $99,990 of that loan, and I told you that the personal guarantee was still causing me sleepless nights, wouldn't you let me off the guarantee?" Of course she'll say, "I don't see why not," and then you've got something to work with. At least you've established in your banker's mind the possibility of letting you off the guarantee. *The best way to get off a personal loan guarantee is to ask and to continue to ask and bargain after you have shown some sign of your ability to pay back the loan.* Ask for the future, not for now. It may be a slow and tedious process, and it is even possible that your banker won't let you off until you've paid off nine-tenths of the loan, but remember that you are taking on the enormous task of reprogramming her elephant-like memory. That memory will work in your favor on the next loan, when she remembers that letting you off the personal guarantee did not ruin her career.

HELP YOUR BANKER BE A HERO—GIVE HER A GOOD STORY

What if you have no track record of previous loans to show your banker? All is not lost. Not having a track record is better than having a bad track record, and you can make your case stronger with a good story. A good story can be even better than an average track record.

It's your job to provide your banker with a very neatly bundled, coherent, exciting, and colorful story. Your banker would love to go home to her husband and tell him how she single-handedly saved your terrific new company and made the world a better place.

She would be even happier to have a wonderful story to tell to the loan committee. Remember, your banker will have to go to the loan committee with your request to be released from the personal loan guarantee. She would much rather go to the loan committee with a wonderful story than with just a loan-guarantee-release request.

Let's say your company is producing a newly invented monitoring device for babies that will eliminate crib deaths—Sudden Infant Death Syndrome (SIDS). Do you go into your banker's office and ask her for a loan for the production of an electronic oscilloscope? No! You tell her the story of how her loan to you will protect the children of the community. Make the banker a hero for lending you the money.

It's your responsibility as an entrepreneur to do that for your banker. Maybe you'll even get her promoted. Don't forget to take her to lunch or to a ball game because she's your company's best friend. You'll have a great time, and eventually the efforts you've put in to be her best customer will pay off, and her need for your personal loan guarantee will be a thing of the past.

ASK FOR MONEY WHEN YOU DON'T NEED IT

Since we're talking about timing, I'd like to introduce at this point Mancuso's Law: *The only time to raise capital is when you don't need it.* Banks prefer to lend money to borrowers ~~who have borrowed at least once~~ and have paid back at least one loan on time. It's a psychological factor, just as they prefer to lend to a business that already has an account at their bank. Take advantage of your banker's methodical nature. Remember all those audit trail letters in your file? Bankers remember everything; they're like elephants with file cabinets instead of trunks.

Bankers like to hear from you frequently because it makes them feel more secure about their loan to you. I recommend monthly payments on a loan over payment every six months. Get in the habit of keeping your banker up-to-date on your business.

If you expect to need to request a new loan in six months, mention to your banker now that you are working on an exciting expansion that might require more credit. When you actually make your request three months later, she will be pleased. It will confirm her expectations and your reliability. If, on the other hand, you just walk in and tell her that you are out of money and need more for expansion, she will treat what is basically an identical request with suspicion and mistrust.

Don't forget to invite your banker to your facilities to see the results of your latest loan. Bankers love an excuse to get out of their offices, and they need to fully understand your business and see it in operation to be totally comfortable.

IF YOU CAN'T GET OFF IT, CHIP AT IT

You can chip away at the guarantee at several negotiation points if asking to get off doesn't work. Don't give up just because the banker didn't give in after a couple of tries. No banker likes to give up personal loan guarantees. Start chipping away at the guarantee by negotiating with your banker about different aspects of it.

First, let's talk about the form of the guarantee. There are two basic types of guarantees: joint and several and payment versus collection (indemnity versus guarantee).

Are you guaranteeing the payment of the debt or the collection of the debt? In other words, if the business fails, can the bank sue you and the business simultaneously and proceed against both entities aggressively until it gets paid (joint and several guarantee) or does it have to sue the business first and, if it fails to get the money from the business, then go after you (payment versus collection guarantee)? The bank would obviously prefer the joint and several guarantee—it would rather sue both you and the company simultaneously rather than have to wait until it finds out it can't get the money from the company to go after you. This is a negotiating point. If you can get an indemnification guarantee instead of a joint and several guarantee, you are one step closer to establishing yourself as a customer who does not sign personal guarantees. Just knowing that there are different kinds of guarantees will help you to negotiate. For example, you could give up your push for an indemnification guarantee late in the negotiations and ask your banker to give up something in return.

These are legal points, and I certainly advise you to consult with your lawyer, but I frown on letting your lawyer negotiate for you. Do it yourself, even though you'll probably have to consult your lawyer continuously during the negotiations.

There is a second negotiating point concerning the form of the guarantee. If your company has multiple stockholders, you can negotiate for limited guarantees. Try to share the personal guarantee liability with the other major stockholders of your company. For example, if you have five equal stockholders, the bank will seek to have each of you sign for 100 percent of the loan. During negotiations, ask your banker if each of you can sign for 20 percent of the loan, for a total guarantee of 100 percent.

I handled a negotiation like this for a surveying and mapping company in Massachusetts. The company had five major stockholders, and the bank wanted a 100 percent personal guarantee on a $100,000 loan from each stockholder. Technically, the bank could collect $500,000 on a $100,000 loan by having each partner sign. If you and your four partners sign and the loan goes bad, the bank may decide to go after you because you've got the most assets or the deepest pockets. You will then have to sue your partners to have them take responsibility for their share of the loan. That could turn into a long legal mess, and it's not some remote possibility—it happens all the time.

When I went into negotiations for the Massachusetts company, we asked that the personal guarantee be split five ways, so that each stockholder was responsible for $20,000. The bank didn't want to do it because it's much more expensive for the bank to have to sue five people for $20,000 each than it is to sue one person for $100,000. Depending on how the loan guarantee is written, there is often a jury trial, and in most states today it takes about six years just to get a jury trial. Also, the contract statute of limitations is usually for six years. You should know the facts about personal loan guarantees before you start negotiations. Ask your lawyer to brief you so that you can negotiate intelligently. State laws vary, and you really need good legal advice (and remember, I'm not a lawyer).

Although we didn't come out of the negotiations with a 20 percent guarantee for each stockholder, we did get 50 percent. That's still quite an improvement over 100 percent. Don't hesitate to negotiate. The bank wants to lend you the money and you need the money—both parties ought to be able to find some middle ground on all the issues. In the case of the Massachusetts surveying and mapping company, the bank was happy. It had a $250,000 guarantee. The stockholders would have been happier with only 20 percent liability, but they were pleased to have gotten their guarantees halved.

Another negotiable aspect of the guarantee is when it goes into effect. For example, tell your banker that you don't want to sign the personal guarantee, but if your company is late on more than three consecutive loan payments, the personal guarantee will go into effect. With your banker, arrange a scenario that will trigger when the guarantee will go into effect; in this way, you are not guaranteeing the debt unless certain unlikely events occur. Here are a few conditions:

1. You miss three consecutive loan payments.
2. Working capital falls below a specified amount.
3. Net worth falls below a specified amount.

One more thing: Avoid the entrepreneur's innate tendency to act like a blow-fish when it comes to filling out the personal financial statement required by the bank. Do not exaggerate the value of your assets; this tactic will only come back to haunt you. Your best bet is not to inflate your net worth, but to show the truth (or a little less than the truth). Keep in mind that the personal loan guarantee and the personal financial statement act as a directory for the bank's lawyer to find where you keep attachable assets (typically real estate) in case your company defaults on the loan.

NEGOTIATING THE LOAN AGREEMENT

All of the negotiation points we've just discussed are ways to chip away at the personal loan guarantee, but the principles of give-and-take negotiation involved should also be applied when you negotiate the loan itself. Remember, the game is catch, not go fetch. The concept of chipping away is useful in both situations. Bankers negotiate with entrepreneurs three times a day, but entrepreneurs negotiate with bankers once every few years.

It's common for bankers to work some fairly troublesome loan provisions into a loan agreement. You may find them unfair or too strict, but don't just complain to your banker about them, chip away at them. There is no such thing as boilerplate; every item in a loan agreement is negotiable, depending on your situation.

The following is a list of some troublesome loan provisions.

1. Five days to advise you of infraction: via Federal Express—fifteen days.
2. One week to cure a default—substitute fifteen *business* days.
3. The word *material* should modify declaration of default. For example, leasing capital equipment prevents renting a photocopier.
4. Inequitable Provisions:
   A. Bank mistakes against you to which you fail to call attention within thirty days are forfeited.
   B. Bank mistakes in your favor that you don't catch can be corrected by the bank at any time (no time limit).
5. Exceptions for restrictions, such as working capital, thirty-day exception for seasonality, etc.

For example, if the bank wants a notice period of five days to advise you of an infraction of the loan contract, ask your banker for ten business days. That's quite a difference, isn't it? Or, if your loan agreement offers you a grace period of one week to cure a default, ask to substitute fifteen business days to assure that you'll have enough time after written notice of the default is received.

Also watch for a list of petty technical violations that would put the loan into default. Your loan agreement may prevent you from leasing "capital equipment." Does that include an office copier? You may not think so, but, technically, it does, and if your loan officer comes under pressure to trim his loan portfolio, he could use this technicality to keep you playing go fetch. Often the loan officer is overridden by bank regulators, and the letter and the spirit of the "law" can be quite opposite. Make sure the word *material* is used to modify a declaration of default.

Watch for inequitable provisions in the loan agreement and don't hesitate to challenge your banker on them. If you look carefully, you might find that bank mistakes against you to which you fail to call attention within thirty days are forfeited while bank mistakes in your favor that you don't catch can be corrected by the bank at any time. Ask your banker to delete or modify such an imbalanced provision. You can also negotiate exceptions for restrictions placed by the loan agreement on your working capital. Let's say the agreement requires you to maintain net working capital of $250,000 at all times, but your business experiences a slump in inventory every April. Ask your banker for a thirty-day suspension of the provision during that time.

If you practice these examples of how to use the principle of chipping away on your loan agreement, you'll be an expert negotiator by the time you reach the personal loan guarantee!

One more thing: don't *offer* to fill out your bank's preprinted personal financial statement. If you do, you are tacitly agreeing to sign the personal loan guarantee. Let your banker raise the subject. When he does, remind him of the value of the assets already included in your business plan. I suggest not filling in the bank's forms for personal finances. Substitute a signed and notarized form that you have prepared ahead of time, which gives the same level of information. (See the sample personal financial statement).

Talk to your lawyer before filling out the financial statement. You pay your lawyer high fees: Use him for advice early on because the fees become higher if you get into trouble. Find out from your lawyer how much information you can withhold while staying within the bounds of generally accepted legal procedure. Lawyers, bless their little hearts, are all well versed in handling this delicate subject. If putting down that expensive second home bothers you, maybe it's time to sell it and put the money into your business.

HOW TO KEEP OFF PERSONAL GUARANTEES IN THE FIRST PLACE

If you are new to getting loans for your business and you've never signed a personal loan guarantee, read this section slowly and carefully. The best thing you can do for your future is to avoid signing for your loans from the very start. Remember your banker's long, elephantlike memory? No banker has ever said to a customer who has been on personal loan guarantees, "Gee, you're such a good customer of the bank, I don't think we need to bother with these silly guarantees any more." No matter how hard you work at becoming your banker's best friend and customer, if you signed personal loan guarantees in the beginning, she'll never forget it. She'll expect you to sign them from now until you die, no matter how successful you become. (In practice, most CEO's get off personal loan guarantees by switching banks. The entrepreneur walks into the new bank across the street and says, "I'll bring my business to your bank—same terms and conditions—but no personal guarantees. What do you say?" According to my research, that's how about half of all guarantees are released in the real world.)

The first step is the same as that for getting off a personal loan guarantee: Decide what it's worth to you to avoid signing.

Early in the history of your business ask your board of directors to vote on this resolution: "Officers and shareholders of this corporation will not be allowed to sign personally for any debt. Any debt for which they sign personally will not be honored by this corporation." Have this resolution signed, dated, notarized, and put in your minutes book. Renew it by voting on it at every annual meeting.

When you are asked by your banker to personally guarantee your first loan, you can moan and pull out your minutes book. Show her what a tremendous hassle it's going to be for you to go to the board of directors and change company

Personal Financial Statement

To: **BARCLAYS**

Barclays Bank of New York, N.A.

As at _____ 19 _____

Name _____

Address _____ Telephone _____ Branch

Employer _____ Address _____ Telephone _____

Social Security Number _____

" Notice: Do not give information regarding co-applicant or other party unless you are relying on income derived from another party. Income from alimony, child support or separate maintenance payments need not be revealed if you do not wish them to be considered as a basis for repayment."

ASSETS	OMIT CENTS			LIABILITIES	OMIT CENTS		
Cash (Sched. 1)				Accounts Payable			
Collectible Accounts Due Me				Installment Contracts payable (Sched. 2)			
Good Notes Receivable & Mortgages Owed (Sched. 3)				Notes Payable to Bank (Sched. 2)			
Other Receivables				Notes Payable to Others (Sched. 2)			
Readily Marketable Receivables (Sched. 4)				Income Taxes Payable			
Other Investments (Shed. 4)				Other Taxes Payable			
Cash Surrender Value of Life Insurance (Sched. 5)				Loans On Life Insurance (Sched. 5)			
Real Estate Owned (Sched. 6)				Real Estate Mortgages (Sched. 7)			
Other Assets (describe)				Other Liabilities (describe)			
TOTAL ASSETS				TOTAL LIABILITIES			
				NET WORTH (Total Assets Less Total Liabilities)			

ANNUAL INCOME				PLEASE ANSWER THE FOLLOWING	CONTINGENT LIABILITIES		
Salary				Have you ever gone through bankruptcy or compromised a dept? ☐ Yes ☐ No	As Endorser		
Dividends					As Guarantor		
Fees or Commissions				If this is a statement of you and your spouse are any assets spouse's separate property? ☐ Yes ☐ No	On Damage Claims		
Rentals					For Taxes		
Other				Are any assets pledged or debts secured except as shown? ☐ Yes ☐ No	Other		
TOTAL					Total (indicate if none)		

Schedule 1 CASH

Svgs.	Coml.	CASH BALANCE ON ABOVE DATE	WHERE CARRIED (NAME OF FINANCIAL INSTITUTION)
☐	☐		Barclays Bank of New York, N.A.
☐	☐		
☐	☐		
☐	☐		
☐	☐		
☐	☐		Total on this statement

Schedule 2 NOTES AND CONTRACTS PAYABLE TO BANK AND OTHERS

AMOUNT OWED ON ABOVE DATE	INT RATE	HOW PAYABLE	STATE HOW LOAN IS GUARANTEED OR SECURED

Schedule 3 NOTES, MORTGAGES, AND TRUST DEEDS OWNED

NAME OF DEBTOR	Total Amount Due	Maturity Date	How Payable	Description of Security
			$ per	
			$ per	
			$ per	
			$ per	
			$ per	

F00720 (4/85)

Please complete all applicable schedules and sign on reverse side.

Sample Barclays Personal Financial Statement

Sample Barclays Personal Financial Statement (*cont.*)

Schedule 4 READILY MARKETABLE SECURITIES AND OTHER INVESTMENTS

DESCRIPTION	No. of Shares or Par Value Bonds	READILY MARKETABLE SECURITIES–VALUE NOW		OTHER INVESTMENTS VALUE NOW		Yearly Dividend	Year Acquired	REGISTERED OWNER
		Price	Extension	Price	Extension			
TOTAL								

Schedule 5 LIFE INSURANCE

INSURED	PRIMARY BENEFICIARY	FACE AMOUNT	CASH VALUE	LOAN ON POLICY
TOTAL				

Schedule 6 REAL ESTATE OWNED

Parcel No.	LOCATION AND TYPE OF PROPERTY	TITLE IN NAME OF	COST	Year Acquired	VALUATION ON THIS STATEMENT	
					LAND	IMPROVEMENTS
1						
2						
3						
4						
5						
6						
	TOTAL BEFORE DEPRECIATION					
	LESS RESERVE FOR DEPRECIATION					
	TOTAL					

Schedule 7 REAL ESTATE MORTGAGES

Show No. of Parcels from Schedule 6	TO WHOM PAYABLE	HOW PAYABLE		INT RATE	FINAL MATURITY DATE	ORIGINAL AMOUNT	PRESENT BALANCE
		$	per				
		$	per				
		$	per				
		$	per				
		$	per				
		$	per				
	TOTAL						

To induce Barclays Bank of New York, N.A., to give or continue accommodation to, or at the request of, the undersigned from time to time, and in consideration of any such accommodation, the undersigned represents and warrents that the foregoing is a true statement of the financial condition of the undersigned as of the date indicated; and agrees (1) that said Bank may rely upon it as continuing to be true until notified in writing to the contrary by the undersigned; (2) that if it be not true in any material respect, or if the undersigned should die, become insolvent, make an asignment for the benefit of creditors, be the subject of any bankruptcy, reorganization, arrangement, insolvency, receivership, liquidation or dissolution proceedings, or if any property of the undersigned be attached, garnished or subjected to any other legal process, or if an adverse change occurs in the financial condition of the undersigned, then at the election of said Bank all indebtedness and obligations, direct and contingent, of the undersigned to said Bank shall become immediately due and payable without demand or notice.

It is the practice of Barclays Bank of New York, N.A., to request a credit report in connection with all loan applications, both for borrowers and guarantors, and for updates, renewals, or any extension of credit. Upon request, the Bank will inform you if a report has been obtained and will give you the name and address of the agency furnishing the report.

DATE SIGNED ———————————————————— By ————————————————————

Personal Information On

Work Phone:

Owns—lived there 8 years

Education: BSME University of Wisconsin, MBA, Texas Tech
Married 27 years, wife (Kay), three boys—ages 18, 16, and 9
SS#:
Date of Birth:

Employed by
Chairman & CEO, employed by   for 11 years, annual salary $150,000
National Manufacturing Company throughout USA
Headquarters

Other Income: Misc. Rental Income from land and real estate . . . approx 3,500
               Income from Federal CRP program on farm in W. Texas 4,850

Liabilities (excluding real estate) and credit references
1. American Express Centurion Bank, Account #   , P.O. Box 15325,
   Wilmington, DE. Current balance as of 10-20-89: $4,833. Monthly payment of
   approx. $275.
2. American Express Green Card, Account #   , P.O. Box 1270, Newark,
   NJ 07101, member since 1967. Current balance: $0.
3. American Express Platinum Card, Account #   , 777 American Ex-
   pressway, Ft. Lauderdale, FL 33337. Current balance: $?.
4. First Chicago Bank VISA, Account #   , P.O. Box 8991, Wilmington, DE.
   Current balance: $1,250. Monthly payment of approx. $100.
5. M Bank VISA, Account #   , P.O. Box 35001, Wilmington, DE. Current
   balance: $2,600. Monthly payment of approx. $150.
6. Citibank VISA, Account #   , P.O. Box 6062, Sioux Falls, SD 57117.
   Current balance: $850. Monthly payment of approx. $50.
7. Associates National Bank VISA, Account #   , Pleasanton, CA 94582.
   Current balance: $280.
8. Sears, Account #   , 1099 S. Sherman, Richardson, TX 75081. Current
   balance: $575.

Statements:
1. I am not liable for alimony, child support, or maintenance payments.
2. I have no lease obligations.
3. I am not an endorsee, guarantor, or comaker on any loans or obligations.
4. I have never been a subject of a bankruptcy proceeding.
5. There have never been any judgments against me.
6. I am not involved in a lawsuit.
7. I am a U.S. citizen.
The above information is true to the best of my knowledge as of 10-21-89.

Sample Personal Financial Statement Information

Sample Personal Financial Statement Information (*cont.*)

BANKING REFERENCES:

   Texas 76201
Checking Account #
Approximate balance as of 10-20-89: $8,500

Provident Bank
2220 San Jacinto
P.O. Box 50599

Checking Account #   (commercial account for   )
Approximate balance as of 10-20-89: $20,000

Merrill Lynch
Cash Management Account
Account #
13355 Noel Road, 7th Floor
Dallas, TX 75240
Approximate balance as of 10-20-89: $10,500

PERSONAL FINANCIAL STATEMENT:

ASSETS:

1. Cash and silver on hand: $35,000
2. Cash in checking accounts: $39,000
3. Accounts, loans, and notes receivable: $28,000
4. Automobiles, furniture, and misc.: $125,000
5. Real estate (see attached schedule): $5,018,063

Total Assets: $5,245,063

LIABILITIES:

1. No taxes due
2. No notes payable (except construction note on home)
3. No rents or interest due
4. Liens on real estate (see attached schedule): $462,000 (includes money owed on home)
5. Other liabilities (credit cards as shown on first page): approx. $10,400

Total Liabilities: $472,400

Net Worth: $4,772,663

I certify that the above information is correct to the best of my knowledge.
Date: 10-21-89.

---

policy. Bankers love to tell you, "It's our policy." Fight policy with policy.

One of our CEO Club members, Dr. Charles Feldman of Cardio-Data in Sudbury, Massachusetts, heard me give this advice ten years ago. He was buying a large piece of medical equipment for his business and the supplier wanted him to sign a personal loan guarantee. The delivery man waltzed into Charles's office with the personal guarantee for him to sign. Charles said, "Gee, I never knew when I ordered the CAT scan machine that you were going to require a personal guarantee. That wasn't even discussed."

Of course the delivery man said, "Well, I can't just leave it here. This piece of equipment is worth three times your whole company. You have to be responsible for it."

Charles pulled out his minutes book and showed him nine years of annual corporate minutes to the effect that no officer of the corporation may sign personal guarantees on corporate purchases.

"Do you know what I would have to do to undo this?" Charles said. "I'd have to call a meeting of the stockholders. The stockholders will have to elect new directors. I don't know what they're going to do—this could take nine months! I can't sign that thing. If I do, I could be criminally prosecuted for going against the rules of the board of directors."

Now, between you and me, that statement in the minutes book would hold up in court for about five seconds, but it is a useful and often convincing negotiating tool. In Charles's case, it worked on the truck driver. Every little "policy" helps.

After you show your minutes book to your loan officer and moan about company policy, ask her if everyone signs personally for loans at her bank. Even if all you do is ask this question, you're ahead. You're showing that you're no dummy.

Finally, try offering another piece of collateral as a means of staying off a personal loan guarantee. If you have a second home, offer it as collateral: An assignment on your second home is better than a personal blanket guarantee on everything you own. By doing this you protect your primary homestead.

Don't hesitate to mention Lee Iacocca. Try this approach: "When Chrysler found itself in trouble and borrowed all that money, Lee Iacocca didn't have to sign a personal guarantee for the money, did he? Did any members of Chrysler's team have to guarantee the debt? Why should I? I'm not borrowing as much money as they did, and my company certainly is not in as bad shape as Chrysler was at that time. The likelihood that Iacocca was going to turn Chrysler around was a lot less than the likelihood that I'm going to keep my profitable business profitable. Why should I have to sign personally for my small loan for my solid company?"

Don't be afraid to get indignant! "It's not fair! Banks pick on little guys like me and let the big guys like Iaccoca off the hook! It's discrimination against the backbone of the U.S. economy—the entrepreneur—and if you don't believe me, just think of the millions of small farmers in the Midwest who are being discriminated against by an unfair double standard!"

Your banker will probably say something like this: "Well, Chrysler is a public company, and public companies are not controlled by their officers."

Here's a comeback: "Public company, oh yeah? Tell me, what was Lee Iaccoca's salary for the year he got that debt package. That's right, it was $1.00. And what was his salary the year he saved the business? It was $20.6 million! Public company, baloney! That sure sounds like an entrepreneurial company to me! I tell you, the damn banking system is just plain unfair to the little guy."

From the policy in your company minutes and your "Matilda" story to this tirade against injustice, your banker will get the picture: You don't take personal guarantees lightly.

HOW TO KEEP YOUR SPOUSE OFF THE GUARANTEE

Do not let your nonworking spouse cosign your loan (by nonworking I mean not working with you in the business). It used to be common procedure for a businessman to take his loan agreement home to his wife for her to sign somewhere between cooking dinner and putting the kids to bed. Nowadays, though, more and more women are bringing home loan agreements for their husbands to cosign (male spouses are being asked to autograph the dotted line even more than wives these days). The days of automatic signing of a personal loan guarantee by a spouse are over. Nonetheless, your banker will probably hand the loan agreement to you and say, "Okay, just take it home and have your wife (or husband) sign it and bring it back tomorrow and we'll give you the money."

Don't do it. Who are you to speak for your spouse? He or she probably has his or her own business to sign for or his or her own assets to protect. Pressuring your spouse to sign the guarantee is the kind of thing that destroys a relationship and causes trouble.

Make it tough for your banker to ask for your spouse's signature. Tell her, "I understand your policy is to have my wife sign. It's just that Mary doesn't really understand the necessity of this. She wants to talk to you herself. I can't really speak for her on this. I'm sorry, but I really have little choice on this one. You're going to have to talk to her yourself about having her sign, and I honestly don't see how this bank can be so chauvinistic as to require my spouse to do this. After all, she is just an innocent, uninformed third party." Let your spouse defend himself or herself. I find this is the best way to keep your spouse off the guarantee. He or she usually makes a pretty strong case for not being part of the personal guarantee. (You can always tell your spouse to say: "Did Lee Iacocca's wife have to sign personally for his loan for Chrysler?") Ask your lawyer about recent court cases concerning the liabilities of innocent spouses; they are being decided increasingly in favor of the spouse.

BUILD YOUR CASE PIECE BY PIECE

Don't forget to decide how much it is really worth to you to avoid signing personally, so you don't get carried away during the negotiations. Start by telling your banker how much it would mean to your peace of mind not to have to sign. Tell her the "Matilda" story, have her meet Matilda, and then have Matilda mention Lee Iaccoca's wife. Build your case! If you've done your homework and spent some time befriending your banker, she'll be more likely to respond to your plea.

If you do end up having to sign personally for your first loan, don't be discouraged. In the real world, you are part of the 99 percent of CEOs who do sign. At least you got the loan, and now you can put all the strategies you've learned from this book to work on your banker so that you can get off the guarantee you're already on and avoid signing personally for your next loan.

Set future milestones for getting off. Start chipping away at that guarantee from day one. Find out where and when between 0 percent and 100 percent of repayment your banker will let you off the guarantee. As soon as you take out the guarantee, write a letter to your banker letting her know that the guarantee was not given lightly, and that it bothers you.

HOMESTEADING

One final thing to look into is homesteading your primary residence. In the last century, many states enacted legislation stating that a lender who lent you money for an asset other than your primary residence could not take your principal residence toward payment on a loan. In simple language it meant that if a farmer bought a tractor and he stopped making payments on it, the lender couldn't confiscate the farm. The farmer could file a piece of paper called the Homestead Act to protect his principal residence.

The good news is that in more than half the states the Homestead Act still exists, and many lawyers recommend that you homestead your home. Depending on the state, you file one sheet of paper with the registrar of deeds in your town, and it protects a certain amount of equity in the home (in some states, homesteading is automatic, and you don't need to file anything). In Massachusetts, for example, it protects $40,000 of the equity in your home. If your home is worth $100,000 and a secondary lender (not the banker who has the mortgage on your home) tries to take your home to pay a debt on which you've defaulted, he has to leave $40,000 of equity in the home. The fact that you've filed the Homestead Act on your home is not common knowledge, either. It might not show up when you fill out the loan application or the personal financial information unless the bank decides to do a title search, which is rarely done unless you are specifically pledging the home as collateral. See your lawyer about whether your home might qualify for homesteading. It offers good protection—another step in the strategy of getting off personal loan guarantees.

The states of Florida, Texas, and Oklahoma have outstanding homestead protection. In these entrepreneurial states you can protect the entire homestead and all its equity. Always speak to your lawyer, though, to make sure you're up to date on any recent changes in state laws.

I never said it would be easy to get off personal loan guarantees, but it is certainly possible if you follow the strategy I have given step-by-step in this book. A good negotiating plan will increase your probability of getting off personal loan guarantees just as a good business plan guides the growth of your business. In each case you set goals and work toward achieving those goals.

If you go away with just one thought from this book, I hope it will be that, just like the rest of us, a banker is a human being and, like any human being, she responds to warmth and friendly interest in herself. Do all your research and have all the facts and figures she needs, but don't forget to treat her as you would any friend from whom you want a favor. Be her best customer, and you'll get off those personal loan guarantees. And remember, the best way to get off a personal loan guarantee is not to sign the damn thing in the first place!

HOW TO AVOID PERSONAL GUARANTEES IN THE FIRST PLACE

1. Decide on value.
2. Offer other collateral.
3. Ask if everyone signs personally.
4. Never let a nonworking spouse be forced to sign. Have the banker speak to the spouse one on one.
5. Home mortgage—sleeping well. "Matilda."
6. Have your board of directors sign a policy statement against personal guarantees. Put it in the minutes book. Make sure you date it.

7. Personal statements come back to haunt you. Attachable real estate. Use your own form.
8. Set specific future milestones for getting off.
9. Mention Lee Iacocca.
10. Ask if the bank ever volunteered to let anyone off?
11. Caruth Institute, SMU, bank earnings on small-business loans 2.7 percent higher, i.e., 17.7 percent versus 15.0 percent.

HOW TO GET OFF PERSONAL GUARANTEES

1. Decide what it's worth:
   A. Interest rate
   B. Amount of money
   C. Compensating balance
   D. Maturity
2. The best way to get off is not to get on in the first place.
3. Questions for you to ask:
   A. Does everybody who borrows here sign personally?
   B. What do they have that I don't have?
4. Questions for you to practice answering:
   A. Why don't you want to personally guarantee the loan?
   B. Don't you plan to pay it back? (Use the home mortgage example.)
5. Ask for the future, not for now.
6. Forms of guarantees:
   A. Joint and several
   B. Payment versus collection indemnity versus guarantee
7. Jury trial takes six years—contract statute of limitations is six years.
8. With multiple stockholders, limited guarantees.
9. Trigger when guarantees could go into effect.

A LAWYER'S VIEW

What follows is a commentary by one of Chicago's premier legal firms on the topic of avoiding personal guarantees. Because it's a legal point of view, which is different than mine, I feel it is valuable to know. The following are excerpts from a presentation given by the firm of Levin & Ginsburg Ltd. to certain of its business clients.

As a CEO for a privately held business you are often asked to personally guarantee loans for your business. This means that if the business is unable to repay the lender, you, the guarantor, must personally pay the loan. By providing a personal guarantee on any obligation incurred by your business, you not only substantially increase your potential liability, but you also put too many of your "eggs in one basket" and thereby jeopardize your family's security. Do not allow failure of the business to result in your personal bankruptcy. What can you, the CEO of a privately held business, do to avoid giving a personal guarantee on a loan needed by the business?

Lenders generally require collateral, such as accounts receivable, inventory, and equipment, as security for their loan. Lenders to privately held businesses typically seek a guarantee by the CEO because lenders want to be sure their loans will be protected. The value of your personal guarantee may be as important to the lender as collateral. By requiring your personal guarantee a lender receives both your financial and "emotional" commitment to monitor the business and repay the loan. The implications of the financial commitment are clear, while the consequences of the emotional commitment are less apparent. The knowledge that the security of your family's "nest egg" depends on your business's success can delay and actually hinder the effective decision making required from a CEO. As a result, your personal guarantee, with its emotional commitment, may weaken your business and lessen its value, both to the lender and to you. The personal guarantee can produce the opposite of its desired effect. Trying to convince your lender of this result could prove very difficult.

In demanding your personal guarantee, the lender seeks accountability from the CEO, the person who is in control of what is effectively the lender's collateral. As CEO, you are in a better position than the lender to evaluate market demand, resale value of inventories, maintenance needs of equipment, and the creditworthiness or general desirability of your customers. You do have control over various aspects of the operation of your business, and may agree to be accountable for those. However, you do not have control over market fluctuations or customer purchasing behaviors. Although you may seek to make prudent, informed business decisions, you cannot be assured that the market and your customers will remain stable and unchanged.

Attempt a favorable resolution of the personal guarantee issue by convincing the lender that it will have to make concessions on this issue in order to win your loan business. This works, particularly in a competitive lending environment, and you should attempt to create that environment. If your business is strong, more than one lender will be interested in your loan business.

A strong earnings history, financial and credit controls, net worth, and good management make your business loan more desirable to a lender. If you do not have these credentials try:

1. Asking the lender what it will take to eliminate the personal guarantee; or
2. Offering a personal guarantee, but limiting your liability, for example, to 10 percent of the loan principal or a fixed dollar amount; or
3. If the business has multiple owners, allocating the guarantee liability on a pro rata basis so each owner is individually liable only for a pro rata share of the personal guarantee; or

4. Offering a guarantee of certain issues; you can address the lender's concerns over accountability for adequate accounts receivable, inventory levels, and equipment maintenance without providing your unlimited personal financial guarantee of payment or value; or

5. Seeking out another lender; or

6. Replacing some or all of the debt with equity by taking in a venture capitalist or other partner.

Remember, when pursuing loans for your privately held business, there is or can be a competitive market for your loan business. You can negotiate giving the guarantee and its terms in the same manner you negotiate the interest rate and other economic terms of the loan. When negotiating with your lender, establish at the outset that the personal guarantee will be a pivotal issue. You may have to make concessions on other loan issues to avoid or reduce your guarantee, but these concessions may be worthwhile in order to protect your family's security and your personal assets. Before negotiating loan terms or signing loan documents, seek the advice of an experienced attorney. The lender's form documents and "boilerplate" language are written to protect the lender and are not designed to favor the borrower.

(The law firm of Levin & Ginsburg consists of twelve attorneys and twenty-two support staff. We provide a broad range of legal services to entrepreneurs and other businesses including the negotiating and documentation of commercial loan transactions. Our practice stresses client communications, timely service, planning and risk analysis, and general counsel services. Please call us if we can be of service.)

Levin & Ginsburg Ltd.
Attorneys at Law
180 N. LaSalle St.
Chicago, IL 60601-2702
(312) 368-0100

7. Small Business Administration Loans

WHY YOU SHOULD KNOW ABOUT THE SBA

I can already hear the question in your mind: "Why is there a chapter on SBA loans in this book? Isn't this book about how to get off personal loan guarantees? SBA loans require personal guarantees, don't they?"

Well, the bad news is yes, most Small Business Administration (SBA) loans do require a personal guarantee, but the good news is that the SBA loan program is probably the best thing the federal government has ever done for entrepreneurs, and you should know about it. You probably wouldn't even pick up a book about the SBA, but now that you've read the first six chapters of this book I hope you're thinking, "Well, I guess Mancuso wouldn't waste my time with a textbook study of the SBA. He must have a few tricks to show me."

Some academics say that the SBA loan program hasn't *created* one major company in this country, and they're probably right, but it has financed a lot of mom-and-pop stores, a lot of restaurants, and a lot of service companies that really had no place else to go for financing. Several large companies like Federal Express have used SBA financing, but the critics claim this financing wasn't instrumental in the start of these growth businesses.

The SBA is a small, independent federal agency that was created by Congress in 1953 to assist, counsel, and champion small businesses. The agency has about five thousand employees in more than one hundred offices nationwide. Local offices have decision-making authority in most instances.

The best way to obtain the SBA loan application package is to visit your local SBA office. If you call to order one, the office may insist that you get two loan rejections first—simply because the office is probably understaffed. In cities with populations of more than 200,000, you must be rejected by two lenders before you can seek a loan from the SBA.

This is a downright silly requirement, isn't it? In all my travels—and I claim to know probably more entrepreneurs than just about anyone—I've never met an entrepreneur who couldn't get turned down for a loan by a bank. I've always wondered if this requirement should be toughened up a little to something like "must be turned down by two banks within sixty days."

Going down to the local SBA office in person is a much better idea than calling. That way you can also pick up any free literature. The SBA offers a host of valuable free literature on management, support services, etc. If you ever need a quick answer about something, the SBA hotline number is 1-800-368-5855.

In fiscal 1986, the SBA approved 16,768 business loans, for a total of $2.5 billion. The SBA has been making special efforts to increase the involvement of private lenders. SBA Development Company Programs, for example, offer state and local development companies special financing that enables them to extend long-term, fixed-asset financing to small businesses in their area.

THE SBA PERSONAL GUARANTEE

Keep in mind that you have to go on the personal guarantee for the SBA loan because the government is also on the guarantee. You can negotiate to keep your spouse off the guarantee, however, in the way I outlined in chapter 6. The bank lends you the money and then the SBA takes a percentage of the guarantee. Usually the SBA takes 70 percent of the loan (they can take up to 90 percent), so if the loan goes bad, the SBA would step up and pay 70 percent of the loan to the bank right away. The SBA, in turn, wants your guarantee.

The interesting thing about SBA administrators, though, is that they get your personal guarantee, but they're not vicious about executing against your home. I have a very close friend who had his home up for collateral on an SBA loan for $150,000 for a solar energy company. The loan went bad, and he was able to settle with the SBA for a very reasonable payout about four years afterward. The SBA is usually pretty reasonable. They aren't quite as concerned as banks are with being paid back. Banks are dogged about getting all their money back from whatever collateral is available.

Some people think it's useful to tell the bank that you'll guarantee only the 30 percent that the bank is guaranteeing. In other words, if you borrow $100,000, the SBA will guarantee $70,000. Let's say the bank doesn't want to go along with the deal because it has to be exposed for $30,000. You can't offer to guarantee the $30,000 because it's against the law. The SBA guarantee is not $70,000 first and the bank's $30,000 second. It's pro rata, meaning out of every dollar collected, seventy cents goes to SBA and thirty cents goes to the bank.

There are some SBA direct loans that don't go through a bank, but they represent less than 1 percent of all SBA-guaranteed loans. SBA direct loans have an administrative maximum of $150,000 and are available only to applicants unable to secure an SBA-guaranteed loan. Before applying for an SBA direct loan, an applicant must first seek financing from his bank and, in cities with populations of more than 200,000, from at least one other lender. Direct loans usually are available only when there is a direct allocation from Congress to encourage small business or a specific industry (businesses located in high-unemployment areas, or those owned by low-income individuals, handicapped individuals, Vietnam veterans, or disabled veterans, for example). Those windows last for only about 30 days, so check the newspaper or with your local SBA office for information about these allocations to see if one comes up that might fit your business.

Most SBA loans are guaranteed loans made by private lenders (although the Money Store is the country's largest SBA lender), usually banks, and guaranteed up to 90 percent by the SBA. The maximum guarantee percentage on loans exceeding $155,000 is 85 percent. The SBA can guarantee up to $500,000 of a private sector loan.

There are three principal parties to an SBA guarantee loan: the SBA, the small-business owner, and the private lender. The small-business owner submits the loan application to the lender, who makes the initial review. If the lender approves it for submission to the SBA, the application is forwarded for analysis to the local SBA office. If the SBA approves the loan, the lender closes the loan and disburses the funds.

I'll tell you a secret. Banks actually like SBA loans because the bank can take that guarantee for 70 percent of the loan and turn around and sell it in the open market for cash. For example, if you borrow $100,000 from the bank, the bank gets an SBA guarantee for $70,000. You might be paying 13 percent interest on the loan, but the bank might be able to sell the $70,000 for 9 percent because it has a government guarantee on it. The bank can make 4 percent of $70,000, but it will also get the $70,000 back to lend out again. The bank might get another SBA loan on that money and turn it around to make 4 percent of $49,000 (70 percent of $70,000 is $49,000), and so on. It's the same principle banks use to turn around home mortgages.

HOW TO APPLY FOR AN SBA LOAN

By law, an applicant must first seek financing from a bank or other lending institution before seeking SBA loan assistance. You have to be turned down twice for a loan by a private source before you can go SBA. I think you'll agree with me that this isn't an obstacle for the average entrepreneur. I'm sure if you put your mind to it, you can be turned down for a loan by at least two banks. Actually, you don't need to be turned down by two banks to get a bank-generated SBA loan; only to get a direct (no bank) SBA loan.

To be eligible for SBA loan assistance your business must be operated for profit and qualify as small under SBA criteria (except for sheltered workshops under the Handicapped Assistance loan program). Loans cannot be made to businesses involved in the creation or distribution of ideas or opinions. This provision includes newspapers, magazines, and academic schools. Other ineligible borrowers are businesses engaged in speculation or investment in (rental) real estate.

SBA General Size Standards

Size eligibility is based on the average number of employees for the preceding twelve months or on sales volume averaged over three years.

> *Manufacturing*. The maximum number of employees may range from 500 to 1,500, depending on the type of product manufactured.
>
> *Wholesaling*. The maximum number of employees may not exceed 500.
>
> *Services*. Annual receipts may not exceed $3.5 to $14.5 million, depending on the industry.
>
> *Retailing*. Annual receipts may not exceed $3.5 to $13.5 million, depending on the industry.
>
> *Construction*. General construction annual receipts may not exceed $9.5 to $17 million, depending on the industry.
>
> *Special trade construction*. Annual receipts may not exceed $7 million.
>
> *Agriculture*. Annual receipts may not exceed $500,000 to $3.5 million, depending on the industry.

Here are some tips on applying for an SBA loan. First, don't let the paperwork scare you. It's really not that bad, no matter what you've heard. There are a few forms to fill out, but they are fairly straightforward. You'll find examples in this chapter. The SBA responds quickly—usually within two or three weeks.

The SBA wants to see the following:

1. A current business balance sheet listing all assets, liabilities, and net worth. New business applicants should prepare an estimated balance sheet as of

SBA Loan Number	SMALL BUSINESS ADMINISTRATION		Loan Submitted As:
	LENDER'S APPLICATION FOR GUARANTY OR PARTICIPATION		☐ Reg. 7(a)
Name of Applicant			☐ CLP
			☐ PLP

Name of Lender		Telephone (Inc A/C)	R. L. Polk's Lender No.
Street Address		City	State	Zip

WE PROPOSE TO MAKE A (Check One)

		Lenders Share	SBA Share	Term of Loan	Amount of Loan $
	Guaranteed Loan	%	%	Years	
	Immediate Participation Loan (Lender to make and service)	Lender's Share %	SBA Share %	Payment Beginning _____ Months from Date of Note	Monthly Payment $ _____

Lenders Interest Rate		If Interest Rate is to be Variable	Adjustment Period	Base Rate Source
% Per Annum		Base Rate	Spread	

CONDITIONS OF LENDER (e.g., Insurance requirements, standbys other conditions. Use additional sheets)

I approve this application to SBA subject to the terms and conditions outlined above. Without the participation of SBA to the extent applied for we would not be willing to make this loan, and in our opinion the financial assistance applied for is not otherwise available on reasonable terms. I certify that none of the Lender's employees, officers, directors or substantial stockholders (more than 10%) have a financial interest in the applicant.

Lender Official:	Title	Date

ON PLP SUBMISSION ONLY: I approve and certify that the applicant is a small business according to the standards in 13 CFR 121, the loans proceeds will be used for an eligible purpose and the owners and managers of the applicant business are of good character.

Approving/Certifying Lender Official	Title	Date

FOR SBA USE ONLY

Loan Officers Recommendation	☐ Approve	☐ Decline State Reason(s)
Signature	Title	Date

Other Recommendation, if Required	☐ Approve	☐ Decline State Reason(s)
Signature	Title	Date

THIS BLOCK TO BE COMPLETED BY SBA OFFICIAL TAKING FINAL ACTION

☐ Approve ☐ Decline State Reason(s)		
Signature	Title	Date

Sample Small Business Administration Lender's Application for Guarantee or Participation

Sample Small Business Administration Lender's Application for Guarantee or Participation (*cont.*)

INSTRUCTIONS: Lender will complete and enclose as part of this application package, all working papers, support material and agreements requested herein, specifically including:

1. Balance sheet and ratio analysis - comment on trends, debt to worth and current ratio.
2. Lenders analysis of repayment ability.
3. Management skill of the applicant.
4. Collateral offered and lien position, and analysis of collateral adequacy.
5. Lenders credit experience with the applicant. Identify weaknesses.

FINANCIAL SPREAD

BALANCE SHEET	As of	Fiscal Year Ends	AUDITED ☐	UNAUDITED ☐
		DEBIT	CREDIT	PRO FORMA
Assets				
Cash	$	$	$	$
Accounts Rec.				
Inventory				
Other				
Total Current Assets				
Fixed Assets				
Other Assets				
Total Assets	$	$	$	$
Liabilities & Net Worth				
Accounts Payable	$	$	$	$
Notes Payable				
Taxes				
Other:				
SBA				
Total Current Liabilities	$	$	$	$
Notes Payable	$	$	$	$
SBA				
Other				
Total Liabilities	$	$	$	$
Net Worth	$	$	$	$
Total Liab. & Net Worh	$	$	$	$

Profit & Loss	PRIOR THREE YEARS			INTERIM		PROJECTIONS	
Sales	$	$	$	$	$	$	
Depreciation							
Income Taxes							
W/D Officer Comp.							
Net Profit After Tax/Deprec.	$	$	$	$	$	$	

PRO FORMA SCHEDULE OF FIXED OBLIGATIONS

	YEAR 1	YEAR 2	YEAR 3	YEAR 4
	$	$	$	$

Lenders Analysis:

SBA Form 4-1

GPO 928-864

the day the business starts. The amount that you and/or others have to invest in the business must be stated. The SBA requires you to show that you have an economic stake in the business.

2. Income (profit and loss) statements should be submitted for the current period and for the most recent three fiscal years, if available. New business applicants should prepare a detailed projection of earnings and expenses at least for the first year of operation. (A monthly cash flow is recommended.)

3. A current personal financial statement of the proprietor, or each partner or stockholder owning 20 percent or more of the corporate stock. Personal guarantees are required from all the principal owners and from the chief executive officer, regardless of his ownership interest.

4. A list of collateral to be offered as security for the loan, along with an estimate of the present market value of each item, as well as the balance of any existing liens. SBA literature says the SBA requires that sufficient assets be pledged to adequately secure the loan to the extent that they are available. Liens on personal assets of the principals also may be required where business assets are considered insufficient to secure the loan.

5. A statement as to the amount of the loan request and the purposes for which the loan will be used.

The SBA expects you to take this information to a bank and be turned down—then you can ask the banker to apply to the SBA for you. Don't think for a minute, however, that your presentation to the lender can be sloppy or inadequate. You may just be seeing him to be turned down, but he will be filling out a "lender's application" when he sends your package into the SBA. On the back of this form is a section called "lender's analysis." Your banker will give a detailed evaluation here of your debt and capital ratios, your management, your repayment of past loans, and the present state of your financials. Now you should understand why it is crucial for you to be thoroughly prepared before you see that banker.

Every community has some bank that is involved with the SBA's preferred lender program (PLP). In Chicago, for example, there are banks that have been identified as SBA banks. They have already advanced in Washington, D.C., at SBA headquarters, a certain amount of money to be held in escrow should they make any bad SBA debts. This allows these banks to approve SBA loans right from the bank, because they're now qualified as members of PLP. If you're going to apply for an SBA loan, it obviously makes sense to apply at a PLP bank because the PLP bank can approve your loan simultaneously as the bank and as a representative of the SBA. It's quicker than going through the bank and then through the SBA. To find out what bank in your community is a PLP bank, call the SBA hotline number (1-800-368-5855), ask your banker, or ask your accountant or lawyer.

DON'T BELIEVE ALL THOSE MYTHS ABOUT SBA LOANS

Probably the most common myth is that SBA loans take forever to be approved. Don't be fooled by the entrepreneur's traditional mistrust of bureaucracy into thinking this is true. An entrepreneur I know—Joe Maroni, owner of the Northworks restaurant in Worcester, Massachusetts—got an SBA loan processed in about five weeks. He submitted his business plan (see his full business plan in my book *How to Prepare and Present a Business Plan*), filled out the forms, and got a four-to-one debt ratio—in other words, he put up $50,000 and got $200,000—within five weeks. The average time from your presentation of a well-prepared loan package to your banker to the moment you receive your SBA check ranges from three to six months in the real world.

People tell me an SBA loan can't be done quickly, but it can if you know how to prepare your application so that it doesn't get stuck in any files on its way through the SBA office. The chief factor in the expedition of your loan request is the completeness of your loan application. If your application is inadequate, the SBA will keep rejecting it until it meets the agency's minimum standards.

The SBA examines not only all aspects of the business venture but also the applicant's personal qualifications. Three qualifications are considered essential:

1. You must have an economic stake in the venture. A stake is not collateral, nor is it time invested in the business. You must show that you have made an economic contribution to the business. You are expected to have contributed 20 percent to 30 percent when purchasing an existing business and 30 percent to 50 percent when you are starting a business from scratch.

2. You must be able to present a lease agreement. Your lease agreement should be for at least the period of the loan you are requesting.

3. You must show some collateral.

The SBA looks at several other factors when it runs its evaluation analysis, but those three are the most important personal qualifications.

The SBA divides its loans into three categories: loans for the start-up of a business, loans for the purchase of a business, and loans for the expansion of an existing business. Here is a list of the documents required from applicants in all loan categories.

1. Two loan rejections from two acceptable lenders
2. SBA loan application
3. Statement of personal history
4. Personal financial statement
5. Summary of collateral
6. Operating plan forecast

7. Cash flow projections
8. Résumé and work experience
9. Copy of lease agreement
10. Business plan

Look at the checklists I've provided for each category to determine your needs. I've included in this chapter some SBA forms for your perusal and convenience, but be sure to obtain updated copies, as the rules and forms change frequently.

EVALUATION ANALYSIS FOR SBA LOAN APPLICATIONS

1. Your own stake in the business venture (*essential*)	(Purchase of business) if less than 20%	= 0 pts.	_____ pts.
	(Start-up business) if less than 30%	= 0 pts.	
	(Purchase of business) if 20% to 30%	= 15 pts.	
	(Start-up business) if 30% to 50%	= 15 pts.	
	(Purchase over 30% or (Start-up) 50%	= 20 pts.	_____ pts.
2. Special consideration loans	Veteran/minority/women	= 5 pts.	
	Handicapped	= 10 pts.	
	None of the above	= 0 pts.	_____ pts.
3. Combined conditions on your lease agreement (*essential*)	Less than 7 years remaining	= 0 pts.	
	8 to 10 years remaining	= 3 pts.	
	11 or more years remaining	= 4 pts.	_____ pts.
A. Condition of lease	Straight percentage lease	= 2 pts.	
	Minimum + percentage lease	= 3 pts.	
	Reasonable fixed rate lease	= 4 pts.	_____ pts.
B. Type of lease	Triple net lease (tax + insurance + maintenance)	= 2 pts.	
	Net-net lease (you pay tax + insurance)	= 3 pts.	
	Net lease (you pay taxes only)	= 4 pts.	_____ pts.
4. Your credit history	Derogatory (bankruptcy/write-off, etc.)	= 0 pts.	
	Acceptable (some slow payments)	= 5 pts.	
	Good to excellent	= 10 pts.	_____ pts.
5. Collateralizable assets (*essential*)	If less than 50% of amount applied for	= 0 pts.	
	If 60% to 100% of amount applied for	= 10 pts.	
	If more than 100% of amount applied for	= 15 pts.	_____ pts.
6. Type of loan	Start-up loan	= 2 pts.	
	Purchase of business loan	= 5 pts.	
	Business expansion loan	= 10 pts.	_____ pts.
7. How long have you operated your business?	Less than 1 year	= 2 pts.	
	At least 2 to 5 years	= 6 pts.	
	6 or more years	= 10 pts.	_____ pts.
8. How many years of experience in this business?	Less than 3 years	= 1 pt.	
	At least 4 to 8 years	= 4 pts.	
	9 or more years	= 6 pts.	_____ pts.

9. Profit potential of your proposed business	Average	= 1 pt.	
	Good	= 2 pts.	
	Exceptional	= 4 pts.	_____ pts.
10. Category of business	Sunset (declining potential)	= 1 pt.	
	Stable (most businesses)	= 2 pts.	
	Sunrise (upswing potential)	= 3 pts.	_____ pts.
	Total		_____ pts.

Maximum obtainable score = 100

START-UP

Documentation requirements to apply for an SBA Direct/Guaranteed/Participation loan for a new business to be established or created with SBA start-up capital:

☐ 1. Statements of rejection from two lenders where you have previously applied for a commercial bank loan, stating the reasons for loan disapproval

☐ 2. Lender's application for guarantee or participation (SBA form 4–1)

☐ 3. SBA application for business loan (SBA form 4)

☐ 4. Recommendations from lenders, civic leaders, professionals, businesspeople if possible

☐ 5. Statement of personal history (SBA form 912)

☐ 6. Résumé and work experience

☐ 7. Personal financial statement (SBA form 413)

☐ 8. Summary of collateral (SBA form 4, schedule A)

☐ 9. Statements required by law and executive orders (SBA form 1261)

☐ 10. Compensation agreement (this form is now part of SBA application, form 4)

☐ 11. Comprehensive business plan

☐ 12. Operating plan forecast/profit and loss projection (SBA form 1099)

☐ 13. Monthly cash flow projection (SBA form 1100)

☐ 14. Copy of lease agreement

☐ 15. Other

Note: SBA may require additional information and documentation since every loan application is processed and evaluated on its individual merit.

PURCHASE OF EXISTING BUSINESS

Documentation requirements to apply for an SBA Direct/Guaranteed/ Participation loan to purchase an existing business:

☐ 1. Loan disapproval statements from two previous lenders

☐ 2. Lender's application for guarantee or participation (SBA form 4–1)

☐ 3. SBA application for business loan (SBA form 4)

☐ 4. Recommendations from lenders, civic leaders, professionals, businesspeople, etc.

☐ 5. Statement of personal history (SBA form 912)

☐ 6. Résumé and work experience

☐ 7. Personal financial statement (SBA form 413)

☐ 8. Statements required by law and executive orders (SBA form 1261)

☐ 9. Summary of collateral (SBA form 4, schedule A)

☐ 10. Compensation agreement (this form is now part of SBA application form 4)

☐ 11. Jurat (SBA generally supplies this form) = certification of balance sheet by seller

☐ 12. Agreement of compliance (SBA forms 601 and 601-B)

☐ 13. Operating plan forecast/profit and loss projection (SBA form 1099)

☐ 14. Monthly cash flow projection (SBA form 1100)

☐ 15. Comprehensive business plan and lease agreement

Documentation and information to be furnished by *seller* of business:

☐ A. The reason the present owner is selling the business

☐ B. A copy of the proposed buy-sell agreement

☐ C. Income tax returns for the past three years for the seller

☐ D. A balance sheet for the business being sold, dated within the last ninety days. (If the income tax returns are more than ninety days old, a current interim operating statement for the seller dated within ninety days of the application is needed.

☐ E. Independent appraisal(s) of assets changing hands, if value cannot be readily determined from the other material submitted.

Note: SBA may require additional information and documentation since every loan application is processed and evaluated on its individual merit.

EXISTING BUSINESS EXPANSION LOAN

Documentation requirements to apply for an SBA Direct/Guaranteed/Participation loan to expand an existing business:

- [ ] 1. Loan disapproval statements from two previous lenders
- [ ] 2. Lender's application for guarantee or participation (SBA form 4–1)
- [ ] 3. SBA application for business loan (SBA form 4)
- [ ] 4. Statement of personal history (SBA form 912)
- [ ] 5. Personal financial statement (SBA form 413)
- [ ] 6. Statements required by law and executive orders (SBA form 1261)
- [ ] 7. Summary of collateral (SBA form 4, schedule A)
- [ ] 8. Compensation agreement (this form is now part of SBA application, form 4)
- [ ] 9. Agreement of compliance (SBA form 601) nonsegregation facilities (601–B)
- [ ] 10. Jurat (SBA generally supplies this form) = certification of balance sheet by seller
- [ ] 11. Resolution of board of directors (if corporation) (SBA form 160)
- [ ] 12. Operating plan forecast/profit and loss projection (SBA form 1099)
- [ ] 13. Monthly cash flow projection (SBA form 1100)
- [ ] 14. Résumé and work experience
- [ ] 15. Recommendations from lenders, civic leaders, professionals, businesspeople, etc.
- [ ] 16. Comprehensive business plan and lease agreement
- [ ] 17. Exhibit A: Description of existing machinery and equipment, plus furniture, etc., offered as collateral
- [ ] 18. Exhibit C: Balance sheets, net worth reconciliation, aging of accounts receivable and accounts payable
- [ ] 19. Exhibit D: Brief history of company, benefits to company from the proposed loan
- [ ] 20. Exhibit F: My/our wife(s) _____ are willing to sign any necessary loan documents
- [ ] 21. Exhibit G: List of all equipment and/or fixtures to be purchased with this loan

Note: SBA may require additional information and documentation since every loan application is processed and evaluated on its individual merit.

Another SBA myth that dies hard is "Only minorities get SBA loans." The fact is, the amount of SBA-guaranteed loans to minorities is approximately proportionate to minorities' representation in the U.S. population.

The myth that SBA loans require too much paperwork and struggles with red tape has, I hope, been debunked by what you've read so far. The documentation requirements for SBA loans don't differ much from those for a regular commercial bank loan. The SBA makes it easier, in fact, by providing a complete loan application that makes your obligations quite clear (in other words, the SBA doesn't delight in playing go fetch the way your banker does). You may think, for that matter, that both banks and the SBA are too demanding but, take my word for it, you ain't seen nothing until you deal with a venture capital firm. Its requirements will be far more demanding.

AVOID "LITTLE" THINGS THAT WILL SLOW DOWN YOUR LOAN

Here are some tips on how to prepare your application for the speediest possible SBA processing:

1. Don't check the box on your application that says you pay a consultant because if you do, your application is flagged and it might be slowed down. Your accountant is not a consultant; your lawyer is not a consultant. A consultant is not a consultant as far as that application is concerned. You may be getting advice from people—just don't call them consultants. The SBA uses this information to uncover illegal operations that charge large unwarranted fees to "help" small-business owners seeking SBA financing.

2. The SBA will lend you money for more than one year, unlike your friendly banker. Banks, as I'm sure you know by now, are not keen on long-term lending. At most, they like to let you borrow money on an annual basis. Banks aren't in the business of long-term lending, they are in the business of covering short-term needs. An SBA loan is one way to handle a long-term need. The typical SBA loan is for seven years. So how many years should you ask for on your application? Obviously you should ask for the maximum, seven years. A word here about interest rates on SBA loans: Interest rates in the guarantee program are negotiated between the borrower and the lender, but are subject to SBA maximums. For a seven-year SBA loan, the interest cannot exceed $2^{3}/_{4}$ percent over the New York prime, and an SBA loan with a maturity of less than seven years cannot charge interest more than $2^{1}/_{4}$ percent over the New York prime. Interest rates on direct loans are based on the cost of money to the federal government and are calculated quarterly.

3. If you ask the SBA for a seven-year loan, the SBA wants to see financial projections for seven years. In some regions of the country, the SBA office will reject your loan application if you apply for a seven-year loan but don't include a seven-year financial projection. Imagine that! You're sitting at home, desperate for the cash, and you get a call from the SBA official, who says, "We can't process your application because you didn't forecast years six and seven, and you're asking for a seven-year loan." You think to yourself, "Those guys are crazy. How am I supposed to forecast what I'm gonna do in 1997 and 1998 when I don't know what I'm gonna do tomorrow?" Then you say to the caller: "I'll tell you what you do. Take the year five projection, multiply it by 10 percent, take the year six and multiply it by 10 percent, and voilà! Year seven's financial projection." Projecting for years six and seven when you submit your financials can make a difference.

4. The most money that the SBA wants you to borrow is three times what you put up. If you put up $50,000, the SBA will lend you $150,000. I have seen one case of a five-to-one debt/equity ratio, and a few cases of four-to-one arrangements with the SBA. More common is two-to-one, but you can target three-to-one. This debt/equity ratio is a good balance between what's enough and what's reasonable.

5. Don't try to use the SBA to bail you out of a bad conventional loan. SBA has set a policy that it doesn't do that. So if you get a conventional loan and it goes bad, the likelihood that you can then get a SBA loan is very small. It might actually be best to start with an SBA loan because, as I said earlier, the SBA is much nicer to deal with on a bad loan than a bank is. The SBA even has a fancy word for a bad loan—a moratorium. A fantastically high proportion of SBA loans go through a moratorium period; there's even a form to fill out called the moratorium form. When you fill it out and submit it, you have a moratorium on your loan, i.e., you only have to make interest payments, not principal payments, for the length of the moratorium. Commercial banks have nasty lawyers who don't like moratoriums—that's why it's much nicer to deal with the SBA.

6. A lot of entrepreneurs mistakenly believe that politicians can help you get an SBA loan. A lot of politicians like to claim this is the case, but it's not true. Stay away from politicians or from big-name lawyers or accountants who say they can get your loan pushed through the SBA. The SBA has a system, and you have to wait your turn. If you try to speed up your loan approval by having a letter from a politician "friend" tacked on, the red flag will go up and your application will be slowed down.

7. If you are a manufacturer, be careful about how you classify your product. You must prove to the SBA that your product will compete successfully in the existing market, especially in its specific category. Determine the general field in which your product will best compete, then state this in your application

OMB Approval No. 3245-0016
Expiration Date: 10-31-87

U.S. Small Business Administration

Application for Business Loan

Applicant	Full Address

Name of Business	Tax I.D. No.

Full Street Address	Tel. No. (Inc. A/C)

City	County	State	Zip	Number of Employees (Including subsidiaries and affiliates)

Type of Business	Date Business Established	At Time of Application _____

Bank of Business Account and Address	If Loan is Approved _____
	Subsidiaries or Affiliates _____ (Separate from above)

Use of Proceeds: (Enter Gross Dollar Amounts Rounded to Nearest Hundreds)	Loan Requested	SBA USE ONLY
Land Acquisition		
New Construction/ Expansion/Repair		
Acquisition and/or Repair of Machinery and Equipment		
Inventory Purchase		
Working Capital (Including Accounts Payable)		
Acquisition of Existing Business		
Payoff SBA Loan		
Payoff Bank Loan (Non SBA Associated)		
Other Debt Payment (Non SBA Associated)		
All Other		
Total Loan Requested		
Term of Loan		

Collateral

If your collateral consists of (A) Land and Building, (D) Accounts Receivable and/or (E) Inventory, fill in the appropriate blanks. If you are pledging (B) Machinery and Equipment, (C) Furniture and Fixtures, and/or (F) Other, please provide an itemized list (labeled Exhibit A) that contains serial and identification numbers for all articles that had an original value greater than $500. Include a legal description of Real Estate offered as collateral.

	Present Market Value	Present Loan Balance	SBA Use Only Collateral Valuation
A. Land and Building	$	$	$
B. Machinery & Equipment			
C. Furniture & Fixtures			
D. Accounts Receivable			
E. Inventory			
F. Other			
Totals	$	$	$

PREVIOUS SBA OR OTHER GOVERNMENT FINANCING: If you or any principals or affiliates have ever requested Government Financing, complete the following:

Name of Agency	Original Amount of Loan	Date of Request	Approved or Declined	Balance	Current or Past Due
	$			$	
	$			$	

SBA Form 4 (2-85) Previous Editions Obsolete

Sample Small Business Administration Application for Business Loan

Sample Small Business Administration Application for Business Loan (*cont.*)

INDEBTEDNESS: Furnish the following information on all installment debts, contracts, notes, and mortgages payable. Indicate by an asterisk (*) items to be paid by loan proceeds and reason for paying same (present balance should agree with latest balance sheet submitted).

To Whom Payable	Original Amount	Original Date	Present Balance	Rate of Interest	Maturity Date	Monthly Payment	Security	Current or Past Due
	$		$			$		
	$		$			$		
	$		$			$		
	$		$			$		

MANAGEMENT (Proprietor, partners, officers, directors and all holders of outstanding stock — 100% of ownership must be shown). Use separate sheet if necessary.

Name and Social Security Number	Complete Address	% Owned	*Military Service From	To	*Race	*Sex

*This data is collected for statistical purposes only. It has no bearing on the credit decision to approve or decline this application.

ASSISTANCE   List the name(s) and occupation(s) of any who assisted in preparation of this form, other than applicant.

Name and Occupation	Address	Total Fees Paid	Fees Due

Signature of Preparers if Other Than Applicant

THE FOLLOWING EXHIBITS MUST BE COMPLETED WHERE APPLICABLE. ALL QUESTIONS ANSWERED ARE MADE A PART OF THE APPLICATION.

For Guaranty Loans please provide an original and one copy (Photocopy is Acceptable) of the Application Form, and all Exhibits to the participating lender. For Direct Loans submit one original copy of application and Exhibits to SBA.

Submit SBA Form 1261 (Statements Required by Laws and Executive Orders). This form must be signed and dated by each Proprietor, Partner, Principal or Guarantor.

1. Submit SBA Form 912 (Personal History Statement) for each person e.g. owners, partners, officers, directors, major stockholders, etc.; the instructions are on SBA Form 912.

2. Furnish a signed current personal balance sheet (SBA Form 413 may be used for this purpose) for each stockholder (with 20% or greater ownership), partner, officer, and owner. Social Security number should be included on personal financial statement. Label this Exhibit B.

3. Include the statements listed below: 1, 2, 3 for the last three years; also 1, 2, 3, 4 dated within 90 days of filing the application; and statement 5, if applicable. This is Exhibit C (SBA has Management Aids that help in the preparation of financial statements). All information must be signed and dated.

1. Balance Sheet   2. Profit and Loss Statement
3. Reconciliation of Net Worth
4. Aging of Accounts Receivable and Payable
5. Earnings projections for at least one year where financial statements for the last three years are unavailable or where requested by District Office.
    (If Profit and Loss Statement is not available, explain why and substitute Federal Income Tax Forms.)

4. Provide a brief history of your company and a paragraph describing the expected benefits it will receive from the loan. Label it Exhibit D.

ALL EXHIBITS MUST BE SIGNED AND DATED BY PERSON SIGNING THIS FORM.

SBA Form 4 (2-85) Previous Editions Obsolete

Sample Small Business Administration Application for Business Loan (*cont.*)

5. Provide a brief description of the educational, technical and business background for all the people listed under Management. Please mark it Exhibit E.

6. Do you have any co-signers and/or guarantors for this loan? If so, please submit their names, addresses and personal balance sheet(s) as Exhibit F.

7. Are you buying machinery or equipment with your loan money? If so, you must include a list of the equipment and cost as quoted by the seller and his name and address. This is Exhibit G.

8. Have you or any officers of your company ever been involved in bankruptcy or insolvency proceedings? If so, please provide the details as Exhibit H. If none, check here: ☐ Yes ☐ No

9. Are you or your business involved in any pending lawsuits? If yes, provide the details as Exhibit I. If none, check here: ☐ Yes ☐ No

10. Do you or your spouse or any member of your household, or anyone who owns, manages, or directs your business or their spouses or members of their households work for the Small Business Administration, Small Business Advisory Council, SCORE or ACE, any Federal Agency, or the participating lender? If so, please provide the name and address of the person and the office where employed. label this Exhibit J. If none, check here: ☐ Yes ☐ No

11. Does your business, its owners or majority stockholders own or have a controlling interest in other businesses? If yes, please provide their names and the relationship with your company along with a current balance sheet and operating statement for each. This should be Exhibit K.

12. Do you buy from, sell to, or use the services of any concern in which someone in your company has a significant financial interest? If yes, provide details on a separate sheet of paper labeled Exhibit L.

13. If your business is a franchise, include a copy of the franchise agreement and a copy of the FTC disclosure statement supplied to you by the Franchisor. Please include it as Exhibit M.

CONSTRUCTION LOANS ONLY

---

14. Include a separate exhibit (Exhibit N) the estimated cost of the project and a statement of the source of any additional funds.

15. File the necessary compliance document (SBA Form 601).

16. Provide copies of preliminary construction plans and specifications. Include them as Exhibit O. Final plans will be required prior to disbursement.

DIRECT LOANS ONLY

---

17. Include two bank declination letters with your application. These letters should include the name and telephone number of the persons contacted at the banks, the amount and terms of the loan, the reason for decline and whether or not the bank will participate with SBA. In cities with 200,000 people or less, one letter will be sufficient.

EXPORT LOANS

18. Does your business presently engage in Export Trade?
Check here ☐ Yes ☐ No

19. Do you plan to begin exporting as a result of this loan?
Check here ☐ Yes ☐ No

20. Would you like information on Exporting?
Check here ☐ Yes ☐ No

AGREEMENTS AND CERTIFICATIONS

Agreements of Nonemployment of SBA Personnel: I/We agree that if SBA approves this loan application I/We will not, for at least two years, hire as an employee or consultant anyone that was employed by the SBA during the one year period prior to the disbursement of the loan.

Certification: I/We certify: (a) I/We have not paid anyone connected with the Federal Government for help in getting this loan. I/We also agree to report to the SBA office of the Inspector General, 1441 L Street N.W., Washington, D.C. 20416 any Federal Government employee who offers, in return for any type of compensation, to help get this loan approved.

(b) All information in this application and the Exhibits are true and complete to the best of my/our knowledge and are submitted to SBA so SBA can decide whether to grant a loan or participate with a lending institution in a loan to me/us. I/We agree to pay for or reimburse SBA for the cost of any surveys, title or mortgage examinations, appraisals etc., performed by non-SBA personnel provided I/We have given my/our consent.

I/We understand that I/We need not pay anybody to deal with SBA. I/We have read and understand Form 394 which explains SBA policy on representatives and their fees.

If you make a statement that you know to be false or if you over value a security in order to help obtain a loan under the provisions of the Small Business Act, you can be fined up to $5,000 or be put in jail for up to two years, or both.

If Applicant is a proprietor or general partner, sign below:

By: _____
                                                                    Date

If Applicant is a Corporation, sign below:

_____
Corporate Name and Seal   Date

_____

By: _____
                    Signature of President

Attested by: _____
                    Signature of Corporate Secretary

ALL EXHIBITS MUST BE SIGNED AND DATED BY PERSON SIGNING THIS FORM.

SBA Form 4 (2-85) Previous Editions Obsolete   ✭U.S.GPO:1986-0-623-058/281

United States of America

SMALL BUSINESS ADMINISTRATION

STATEMENT OF PERSONAL HISTORY

Please Read Carefully - Print or Type

Each member of the small business concern requesting assistance or the development company must submit this form in TRIPLICATE for filing with the SBA application This form must be filled out and submitted by

1. If a sole proprietorship by the proprietor.
2. If a partnership by each partner.
3. If a corporation or a development company, by each officer, director, and additionally by each holder of 20% or more of the voting stock.
4. Any other person including a hired manager, who has authority to speak for and commit the borrower in the management of the business

Name and Address of Applicant (Firm Name) (Street, City, State and ZIP Code)	SBA District Office and City
	Amount Applied for:

1. Personal Statement of: (State name in full, if no middle name, state (NMN), or if initial only, indicate initial). List all former names used, and dates each name was used. Use separate sheet if necessary.	2. Date of Birth: (Month, day and year)
First . Middle Last	3. Place of Birth: (City & State or Foreign Country):
	U.S. Citizen? ☐ YES ☐ NO If no, give alien registration number: #

4. Give the percentage of ownership or stock owned or to be owned in the small business concern or the Development Company.	Social Security No.

5. Present residence address:	City	State
From: To: Address:		
Home Telephone No. (Include A/C):	Business Telephone No. (Include A/C):	
Immediate past residence address:		
From: To: Address:		

BE SURE TO ANSWER THE NEXT 3 QUESTIONS CORRECTLY BECAUSE THEY ARE IMPORTANT.

THE FACT THAT YOU HAVE AN ARREST OR CONVICTION RECORD WILL NOT NECESSARILY DISQUALIFY YOU. BUT AN INCORRECT ANSWER WILL PROBABLY CAUSE YOUR APPLICATION TO BE TURNED DOWN.

6. Are you presently under indictment, on parole or probation?

☐ Yes ☐ No   If yes, furnish details in a separate exhibit. List name(s) under which held, if applicable.

7. Have you ever been charged with or arrested for any criminal offense other than a minor motor vehicle violation?

☐ Yes ☐ No   If yes, furnish details in a separate exhibit. List name(s) under which charged, if applicable.

8. Have you ever been convicted of any criminal offense other than a minor motor vehicle violation?

☐ Yes ☐ No   If yes, furnish details in a separate exhibit. List name(s) under which convicted, if applicable.

9. Name and address of participating bank

The information on this form will be used in connection with an investigation of your character. Any information you wish to submit, that you feel will expedite this investigation should be set forth.

Whoever makes any statement knowing it to be false, for the purpose of obtaining for himself or for any applicant, any loan, or loan extension by renewal, deferment or otherwise, or for the purpose of obtaining, or influencing SBA toward, anything of value under the Small Business Act, as amended, shall be punished under Section 16(a) of that Act, by a fine of not more than $5000, or by imprisonment for not more than 2 years, or both.

Signature	Title	Date

It is against SBA's policy to provide assistance to persons not of good character and therefore consideration is given to the qualities and personality traits of a person, favorable and unfavorable, relating thereto, including behavior, integrity, candor and disposition toward criminal actions. It is also against SBA's policy to provide assistance not in the best interests of the United States, for example, if there is reason to believe that the effect of such assistance will be to encourage or support, directly or indirectly, activities inimical to the Security of the United States. Anyone concerned with the collection of this information, as to its voluntariness, disclosure or routine uses may contact the FOIA Office, 1441 "L" Street, N.W., and a copy of §9 "Agency Collection of Information" from SOP 40 04 will be provided

SBA FORM 912 (5-87) SOP 9020 USE 6-85 EDITION UNTIL EXHAUSTED   **1. SBA FILE COPY**

Sample Small Business Administration Statement of Personal History

Statement of Personal History (SBA Form 912)

It is necessary to submit this form for *each* of the business principals, the owners, the partners, the major stockholders, and corporate officers. The same statement of personal history must also be filed by the spouse of the owner and by the employee(s) hired specifically to manage the business.

Name and address of applicant. Enter company name and address of proposed business. If no permanent location has been chosen, fill in your home address.

SBA district office and city. Give location of SBA office where application will initially be submitted to. Use the list of SBA Field Offices in the back of this book.

Amount applied for. Enter the full amount of the loan you are applying for.

1. Enter your full legal name, and the full legal name of your spouse.
2. Fill in only applicant's date of birth.
3. Only applicant's place of birth is needed.
4. If yours is a sole proprietorship, enter 100 percent; if a partnership, give your actual percentage as defined by your agreement; if a corporation, state percentage of your stock ownership.
5. Enter your present home address, and also give previous addresses.

     You must answer the following questions truthfully and correctly. It is required by law. If you fail to do so you are violating the law!

6. If your answer is *yes,* a separate letter of explanation is required.
7. Speeding or drunk driving convictions are considered *major* violations.
8. If your answer is *yes,* furnish a separate letter explaining in detail what the circumstances were. Do not hesitate to present your case in the best possible light. SBA is not out to "get you"; it will not disqualify applicants who have made a mistake and paid their debt.
9. Here, you will enter the name and address of the lending institution that has shown the most positive interest to participate in your loan request. It is helpful to furnish the name of the loan officer who has discussed the application with you, and also give the loan officer's telephone number.

     If you wish to furnish special information pertaining to such matters as U.S. citizenship, name changes, etc., use the space provided directly beneath question no. 9.

     Sign your full name, and state your title (in relation to your business position), and, lastly, enter the date.

Small Business Administration Statement of Personal History Instructions

Form Approved
OMB No. 100-R-0081

PERSONAL FINANCIAL STATEMENT

As of _March 31_ , 19___.

Return to: Small Business Administration

For SBA Use Only

SBA Loan No.

Complete this form if 1) a sole proprietorship by the proprietor, 2) a partnership by each partner, 3) a corporation by each officer and each stockholder with 20% or more ownership; 4) any other person or entity providing a guaranty on the loan.

Name and Address, Including ZIP Code (of person and spouse submitting Statement)

Timothy and Marilyn Wilson
2000 Knoll Road
Anytown, Anystate 00000

SOCIAL SECURITY NO. _473-32-1700_
Business (of person submitting Statement)

This statement is submitted in connection with S.B.A. loan requested or granted to the individual or firm, whose name appears below:

Name and Address of Applicant or Borrower, Including ZIP Code

ACME Sheetmetal
123 Main Street
Anytown, Anystate 00000

Please answer all questions using "No" or "None" where necessary

ASSETS		LIABILITIES	
Cash on Hand & in Banks	$ 620	Accounts Payable	$ 350
Savings Account in Banks	4,500	Notes Payable to Banks	1,200
U. S. Government Bonds	800	(Describe below - Section 2)	
Accounts & Notes Receivable	None	Notes Payable to Others	-0-
Life Insurance-Cash Surrender Value Only	2,100	(Describe below - Section 2)	
Other Stocks and Bonds	10,200	Installment Account (Auto)	2,100
(Describe - reverse side - Section 3)		Monthly Payments $ 180.00	
Real Estate	65,000	Installment Accounts (Other)	-0-
(Describe - reverse side - Section 4)		Monthly Payments $	
Automobile - Present Value	6,200	Loans on Life Insurance	-0-
Other Personal Property	12,000	Mortgages on Real Estate	42,170
(Describe - reverse side - Section 5)		(Describe - reverse side - Section 4)	
Other Assets	40,120	Unpaid Taxes	Current
(Describe - reverse side - Section 6)		(Describe - reverse side - Section 7)	
		Other Liabilities	-0-
		(Describe - reverse side - Section 8)	
		Total Liabilities	45,820
		Net Worth	95,720
Total	$ 141,540	Total	$ 141,540

SAMPLE

Section 1. Source of Income
(Describe below all items listed in this Section)

		CONTINGENT LIABILITIES	
Salary	$ 17,000	As Endorser or Co-Maker	$ -0-
Net Investment Income	735	Legal Claims and Judgments	-0-
Real Estate Income	-0-	Provision for Federal Income Tax	Current
Other Income (Describe) *	9,400	Other Special Debt	-0-

Description of items listed in Section 1
All items are stated on an annual basis.

*Military disability of $200/mo.
Wife's salary of $7,000/yr.

Note: Banks own form of Personal Financial Statement may be used instead.

Not necessary to disclose alimony or child support payments in "Other Income" unless it is desired to have such payments counted toward total income.

Life Insurance Held (Give face amount of policies - name of company and beneficiaries)

$50,000 - American Life - Marilyn Wilson is beneficiary.
$50,000 - National Life - Marilyn Wilson is beneficiary.

SUPPLEMENTARY SCHEDULES

Section 2. Notes Payable to Banks and Others

Name and Address of Holder of Note	Amount of Loan		Terms of Repayments	Maturity of Loan	How Endorsed, Guaranteed, or Secured
	Original Bal	Present Bal			
Bank of 1st Nat'l State	$ 2,000	$ 1,200	$ 100/mo.	1-1-19xx	Unsecured
Crack Finance Co.	3,600	2,100	180/mo.	4-10-19xx	1973 Pontiac

SBA FORM 413 (12-78) REF: SOP 50 50   Edition of 8-67 May Be Used Until Stock Is Exhausted

Sample Small Business Administration Personal Financial Statement

Sample Small Business Administration Personal Financial Statement (*cont.*)

Section 3. Other Stocks and Bonds: Give listed and unlisted Stocks and Bonds *(Use separate sheet if necessary)*

No. of Shares	Names of Securities	Cost	Market Value Statement Date Quotation	Amount
80	ABM Ltd.	3,400	65	5,200
100	NNN Corp.	6,000	50	5,000

Section 4. Real Estate Owned. *(List each parcel separately. Use supplemental sheets if necessary. Each sheet must be identified as a supplement to this statement and signed). (Also advises whether property is covered by title insurance, abstract of title, or both).*

Title is in name of
Timothy and Marilyn Wilson

Type of property
Personal Home

Address of property (City and State)
2000 Knoll Road
Anytown, Anystate 00000

Original Cost to (me) (us) $	50,000	
Date Purchased	Aug 1971	
Present Market Value $	65,000	
Tax Assessment Value $	55,000	

Name and Address of Holder of Mortgage (City and State)
Bruce Savings & Loan
220 Elton Ave.
Anytown, Anystate 00000

Date of Mortgage	Aug 1971
Original Amount $	45,000
Balance $	42,170
Maturity	2001
Terms of Payment	$321/month

Status of Mortgage, i.e., current or delinquent. If delinquent describe delinquencies

Current

Section 5. Other Personal Property. *(Describe and if any is mortgaged, state name and address of mortgage holder and amount of mortgage, terms of payment and if delinquent, describe delinquency.)*

Household Furnishings
Personal Property
Jewelry

SAMPLE

Section 6. Other Assets. *(Describe)*

$40,120 - Value of partnership interest in Acme Sheetmetal

Section 7. Unpaid Taxes. *(Describe in detail, as to type, to whom payable, when due, amount, and what, if any, property a tax lien, if any, attaches)*

All taxes are current.

Section 8. Other Liabilities. *(Describe in detail)*

No other liabilities.

(I) or (We) certify the above and the statements contained in the schedules herein is a true and accurate statement of (my) or (our) financial condition as of the date stated herein. This statement is given for the purpose of: *(Check one of the following)*

☒ Inducing S.B.A. to grant a loan as requested in application, of the individual or firm whose name appears herein, in connection with which this statement is submitted.

☐ Furnishing a statement of (my) or (our) financial condition, pursuant to the terms of the guaranty executed by (me) or (us) at the time S.B.A. granted a loan to the individual or firm, whose name appears herein.

Timothy G. Wilson	*Marilyn Wilson*	April 15, 19xx
Timothy G. Signature Wilson	Marilyn Signature Wilson	Date

SBA FORM 413 (12-78) REF: SOP 50 50

GPO : 1979 O - 296-994

and be prepared to substantiate your claim. The SBA uses the classification guidelines of the *Standard Industrial Classification* (SIC) *Manual* published by the Bureau of the Budget in Washington, D.C. If your product is classified incorrectly, your loan application might be rejected. For example, let's say that

---

INSTRUCTIONS

Personal Financial Statement (SBA Form 413)

A copy of this form is required to be completed by *each* owner, partner, or corporate officer, and each stockholder with 20 percent or more ownership.

The example shown is self-explanatory, so we don't have to go into extensive instructions. However, do your best to fill out the form; SBA may reject your application if incorrect statements are detected.

Assets. Leave no blanks! If answer is 0, so enter. Check with your insurance agent to calculate your life insurance cash value.

Liabilities. Fill out completely. Your net worth is your assets minus your liabilities. The totals of the assets and the liabilities should balance.

Section 1. Enter all your sources of income from the previous year; this should reflect your income tax statement. Omission of any unpaid claim, a lawsuit, or judgment, is fraud. Your life insurance policy should be available for inspection by the SBA.

Section 2. Your notes payable should be made available for SBA inspection. Make sure all payments are current.

Section 3. Enter the names, number of shares, their cost, and present value of any corporate stock you own.

Section 4. Describe all real estate interests you may have; SBA may require independent appraisals. Have your payments up to date.

Section 5. List all your household goods, jewelry, artworks, etc.

Section 6. List all nonpersonal property of value, such as commissions due you, patents you hold, partnership interests, coin collections, and other such valuables.

Section 7. Do *not* file your application until all of the tax obligations are completely satisfied.

Section 8. List any other liabilities which exist, but are not covered on this form.

Your final step is to review your own statements carefully, then sign this form and date it.

Small Business Administration Personal Financial Statement Instructions

you manufacture an educational game, but the way you describe it in your application (by using the SIC code) leads the SBA to classify it as a toy. The price for your game is too high to be competitive in the toy market, however, so the SBA might reject your loan application. The moral of the story is be careful, and if in doubt about the classification of your product, talk to someone at the SBA office who can help you.

The best thing to remember about dealing with the SBA is that it was created to help the entrepreneur. The SBA has been loaning money to small-business owners for more than thirty years, and in all that time I doubt that it's ever taken someone's first-born child. Can your bank make the same claim? Both have foreclosed on homes, but the SBA takes longer to do it and is a bit more gentle—of course, it hurts just the same. I put all this information on the SBA into this book because I really think it's a worthwhile source of financing. At the very least, visit your local SBA office and pick up some of that free literature. You might learn something, and six weeks from now you might have a new loan!

SBA FIELD OFFICES

Alabama
908 S. 20th St.
Birmingham, AL 35205
(205) 254-1344

Alaska
Federal Bldg.
701 C St., Box 67
Anchorage, AK 99513
(907) 217-4022

Box 14
101 12th Ave.
Fairbanks, AK 99701
(907) 452-0211

Arizona
3030 N. Central Ave.
Ste. 1201
Phoenix, AZ 85012
(602) 241-2200

301 W. Congress St.
Federal Bldg., Rm. 3V
Tucson, AZ 85701
(602) 792-6715

*Regional Office.

Arkansas
P.O. Box 1401
Little Rock, AR 72203
(501) 378-5871

California
1229 "N" St.
Fresno, CA 93712
(209) 487-5189

350 S. Figueroa St.
6th Fl.
Los Angeles, CA 90071
(213) 688-2956

1515 Clay St.
Oakland, CA 94612
(415) 273-7790

2800 Cottage Way
Rm. W2535
Sacramento, CA 95825
(916) 484-4726

880 Front St.
Rm. 4-S-33
San Diego, CA 92188
(714) 293-5440

*450 Golden Gate Ave.
P.O. Box 36044
San Francisco, CA 94102
(415) 556-7487

211 Main St., 4th Fl.
San Francisco, CA 94105
(415) 556-2820

Fidelity Federal Bldg.
2700 N. Main St.
Santa Ana, CA 92701
(714) 547-5089

Colorado
*Executive Tower Bldg.
1405 Curtis St.
22d Fl.
Denver, CO 80202
(303) 837-5763

721 19th St.
Rm. 407
Denver, CO 80202
(303) 837-2607

Connecticut
One Hartford Square W.
Hartford, CT 08106
(603) 224-4041

Delaware
844 King St.
Rm. 5207
Lockbox 16
Wilmington, DE 19801
(302) 573-6294

District of Columbia
1111 18th St., N.W.
Sixth Fl.
Washington, DC 20417
(202) 634-1818

Florida
2222 Ponce De Leon Blvd.
5th Fl.
Coral Gables, FL 33134
(305) 350-5521

400 W. Bay St.
Rm. 261
P.O. Box 35067
Jacksonville, FL 32202
(904) 791-3782

700 Twiggs St.
Ste. 607
Tampa, FL 33602
(813) 228-2594

701 Clematis St.
Rm. 229
West Palm Beach, FL 33402
(305) 659-7533

Georgia
*1375 Peachtreet St., N.W.
5th Fl.
Atlanta, GA 30309
(404) 881-4943

*Regional Office.

1720 Peachtree Road, N.W.
6th Fl.
Atlanta, GA 30309
(404) 881-4325

Federal Bldg.
52 N. Main St.
Statesboro, GA 30458
(912) 489-8719

Guam
Pacific Daily News Bldg.
Rm. 508
Martyr and Chara Sts.
Agana, GU 96910
(671) 477-8420

Hawaii
300 Ala Moana
Rm. 2213
P.O. Box 50207
Honolulu, HI 96850
(808) 546-8950

Idaho
1005 Main St.
2d Fl.
Boise, ID 83702
(208) 334-1096

Illinois
*219 S. Dearborn St.
Rms. 438 and 838
Chicago, IL 60604
(312) 353-4528

Illinois National Bank Bldg.
1 N. Old State
Capital Plaza
Springfield, IL 62701
(217) 492-4416

Indiana
New Federal Bldg.
5th Fl.
575 N. Pennsylvania St.
Indianapolis, IN 46204
(317) 269-7272

501 E. Monroe St.
Ste. 120
South Bend, IN 46601
(219) 232-8163

Iowa
373 Collins Road, N.E.
Cedar Rapids, IA 52402
(319) 399-2571

210 Walnut St.
Des Moines, IA 50309
(515) 284-4422

Kansas
Main Place Bldg.
110 E. Waterman St.
Wichita, KS 67202
(316) 267-6311

Kentucky
Federal Office Bldg.
P.O. Box 3517
Rm. 188
Louisville, KY 40201
(502) 582-5971

Louisiana
Ford-Fish Bldg.
1661 Canal St.
2d Fl.
New Orleans, LA 70112
(504) 589-6685

500 Fannin St.
Federal Bldg. & Courthouse
Rm. 5 B04
Shreveport, LA 71101
(318) 226-5196

Maine
40 Western Ave.
Rm. 512
Augusta, ME 04330
(207) 622-6171

Maryland
8800 LaSalle Rd.
Rm. 630
Towson, MD 21204
(301) 962-4392

Massachusetts
*60 Batterymarch St.
10th Fl.
Boston, MA 02110
(617) 223-2100

150 Causeway St.
10th Fl.
Boston, MA 02114
(617) 223-2100

302 High St.
4th Fl.
Holyoke, MA 01040
(413) 536-8770

Michigan
Michigan Ave.
Samara Bldg.
Rm. 515
Detroit, MI 48226
(313) 226-6000

Don H. Bottum University Ctr.
540 W. Kaye Ave.
Marquette, MI 49885
(906) 225-1108

Minnesota
610-C Butler Square
100 N. 6th St.
Minneapolis, MN 55403
(612) 725-2928

Mississippi
Gulf National Life Insurance
   Bldg.
111 Fred Haise Blvd.
2d Fl.
Biloxi, MS 39530
(601) 435-3676

*Regional Office.

100 W. Capitol St.
New Federal Bldg.
Ste. 322
Jackson, MS 30201
(601) 969-4371

Missouri
*911 Walnut St.
23d Fl.
Kansas City, MO 64106
(816) 374-3316

1150 Grand Ave.
5th Fl.
Kansas City, MO 64106
(816) 374-5557

815 Olive St.
Rm. 242
St. Louis, MO 63101
(314) 425-6600

731 N. Main
Sikeston, MO 63801
(314) 471-0223

309 N. Jefferson
Springfield, MO 65806
(417) 864-7670

Montana
301 S. Park Ave.
Rm. 528, Drawer 10054
Helena, MT 59601
(406) 449-5381

Nebraska
Empire State Bldg.
19th & Farnum St.
Omaha, NE 68102
(402) 221-4691

New Jersey
1800 E. Davis St.
Camden, NJ 08104
(609) 757-5183

970 Broad St.
Rm. 1635
Newark, NJ 07102
(201) 645-3683

New Mexico
Patio Plaza Bldg.
5000 Marble Ave., N.E.
Albuquerque, NM 87110
(505) 766-3430

New York
99 Washington Ave.
Rm. 921
Albany, NY 12210
(518) 472-6300

111 W. Huron St.
Rm. 1311
Buffalo, NY 14202
(716) 846-4301

180 Clemens Center Pkwy.
Rm. 412
Elmira, NY 14901
(607) 733-4686

35 Pinelaw Rd.
Rm. 102 E.
Melville, NY 11747
(516) 454-0764

*26 Federal Plaza
Rm. 29-118
New York, NY 10007
(212) 264-7772

26 Federal Plaza
Room 3100
New York, NY 10278
(212) 264-1766

100 State St.
Rm. 601
Rochester, NY 14614
(716) 263-6700

100 S. Clinton St.
Rm. 1073
Federal Bldg.
Syracuse, NY 13260
(315) 423-5382

North Carolina
230 S. Tryon St.
Ste. 700
Charlotte, NC 28202
(704) 371-6111

215 South Evans St.
Rm. 206
Greenville, NC 27834
(919) 752-3798

North Dakota
P.O. Box 3086
Fargo, ND 58102
(701) 237-5131

Ohio
550 Main St.
Rm. 5028
Cincinnati, OH 45202
(513) 684-2814

1240 E. 9th St.
Rm. 317
AJA Federal Bldg.
Cleveland, OH 44199
(216) 522-4194

85 Marconi Blvd.
Columbus, OH 43215
(614) 469-6860

Oklahoma
200 N.W. 5th St.
Ste. 670
Oklahoma City, OK 73102
(405) 231-4301

333 W. Fourth St.
Rm. 3104
Tulsa, OK 74103
(918) 581-7495

Oregon
1220 S.W. Third Ave.
Rm. 676
Federal Bldg.
Portland, OR 97204
(503) 221-5209

Pennsylvania
*One Bala Cynwyd Plaza
231 St. Asaphs Rd.
Ste. 640
West Lobby
Bala Cynwyd, PA 19004
(215) 596-5889

*Regional Office.

One Bala Cynwyd Plaza
231 St. Asaphs Rd.
Ste. 400
East Lobby
Bala Cynwyd, PA 19004
(215) 596-5889

100 Chestnut St.
Rm. 309
Harrisburg, PA 17101
(717) 782-3840

1000 Liberty Ave.
Rm. 1401
Pittsburgh, PA 15222
(412) 644-2780

Penn Place
20 N. Pennsylvania Ave.
Wilkes-Barre, PA 18702
(717) 826-6497

Puerto Rico
Federal Bldg.
Rm. 6991
Carlos Chardon Ave.
Hato Rey, PR 00919
(809) 753-4572

Rhode Island
40 Fountain St.
Providence, RI 02903
(401) 528-4586

South Carolina
1835 Assembly St.
3rd Fl.
P.O. Box 2786
Columbia, SC 29201
(803) 765-5376

South Dakota
101 S. Main Ave.
Ste. 101
Sioux Falls, SD 57102
(605) 336-2980

Tennessee
Fidelity Bankers Bldg.
502 S. Gay St.
Rm. 307
Knoxville, TN 37902
(615) 251-5881

211 Federal Office Bldg.
167 N. Main St.
Memphis, TN 38103
(901) 521-3588

404 James Robertson Pkwy.
Ste. 1012
Nashville, TN 37219
(615) 251-5881

Texas
Federal Bldg.
Rm. 780
300 E. 8th St.
Austin, TX 78701
(512) 397-5288

3105 Leopard St.
P.O. Box 9253
Corpus Christi, TX 78408
(512) 888-3331

*720 Regal Row
Rm. 230
Dallas, TX 75235
(214) 767-7643

1100 Commerce St.
Room 3C36
Dallas, TX 75242
(214) 767-0605

4100 Rio Bravo St.
Ste. 300
Pershing W. Bldg.
El Paso, TX 79902
(915) 543-7586

222 E. Van Buren St.
Ste. 500
Harlingen, TX 78550
(512) 423-4533

2525 Murthworth #705
Houston, TX 77054
(713) 660-2409

1205 Texas Ave.
Rm. 712
Lubbock, TX 79401
(806) 762-7466

100 S. Washington St.
Rm. G-12
Marshall, TX 75670
(214) 935-5257

727 E. Durango St.
Rm. A-513
Federal Bldg.
San Antonio, TX 78206
(512) 229-6260

Utah
125 S. State St.
Rm. 2237
Salt Lake City, UT 84138
(801) 524-5800

Vermont
87 State St.
Rm. 204
Montpelier, VT 05602
(802) 229-0538
* Regional Office.

Virginia
400 N. 8th St.
Rm. 3015
P.O. Box 10126
Richmond, VA 23240
(804) 771-2617

Virgin Islands
Veterans Dr.
Rm. 283
St. Thomas, VI 00801
(809) 774-8530

Washington
*710 2d Ave.
5th Fl.
Seattle, WA 98104
(206) 442-5676

915 Second Ave.
Rm. 1744
Seattle, WA 98174
(206) 442-5534

651 U.S. Courthouse
P.O. Box 2167
Spokane, WA 99210
(509) 456-5310

West Virginia
Charleston National Plaza
Ste. 628
Charleston, WV 25301
(304) 343-6181

109 N. 3d St.
Rm. 301
Clarksburg, WV 26301
(304) 623-5631

Wisconsin
500 S. Barstow St.
Rm. 89AA
Eau Claire, WI 54701
(715) 834-9012

212 E. Washington Ave.
Rm. 213
Madison, WI 53703
(608) 264-5205

517 E. Wisconsin Ave.
Rm. 246
Milwaukee, WI 53202
(414) 291-3941

Wyoming
P.O. Box 2839
Casper, WY 82602
(307) 265-5550

OTHER WAYS TO USE THE SMALL BUSINESS ADMINISTRATION

When most people think of SBA, they think of small-business loans and loan guarantees. But loans and loan guarantees make up only a portion of the services the SBA provides. As they describe it, "The mission of the SBA is to help get people into business and to stay in business." And when you consider, as venture capitalist and chairman of *Venture* magazine Arthur Lipper III recently remarked, that "In our lifetime the Fortune 500 companies are not likely to create a single net new job," this mission becomes all the more important.

Management Assistance

Statistics show that most small-business failures can be directly attributed to management weaknesses. So perhaps the most valuable services provided by the SBA are its one-on-one consulting and management training programs. These programs include the Active Corps of Executives (ACE), the Service Corps of

Retired Executives (SCORE), the Small Business Institute (SBI), and Small Business Development Centers (SBDC).

Through the ACE program, small-business owners can get free hands-on management assistance from active executives in all major industries, professions, and trades. SCORE offers a similar program, the chief difference being that the counselors, who are retired executives, are able to devote more time to visiting business owners on-site to help analyze problems and develop solutions. In both cases, counselors with expertise in one or more business disciplines (such as marketing, personnel, and production) offer seasoned advice, both to start-up operations hoping to solve specific problems, and to well-established businesses in the process of reviewing objectives and making long-range plans.

The Small Business Institute is a more extensive program. An alliance of nearly 500 colleges and universities, it provides an opportunity for business owners to get extended on-site management advice from senior and graduate business students and their faculty advisers. Students are guided by faculty advisers as well as SBA management assistance experts. The SBI can be instrumental in helping entrepreneurs channel their energies into long-range strategies.

Finally, the university-based Small Business Development Centers are a cooperative effort between federal, state, and local governments and the private sector to provide management training and technical assistance to the small-business community. SBDCs, which were begun with a pilot program in 1976, have been so successful (there are some 35 "lead" centers around the country and an additional 175 subcenters) that Congress has extended their funding through 1990.

Recently SBDCs have also increased their efforts at helping small companies that are interested in exporting their goods as well as making special efforts to reach women, minorities, and veterans.

Procurement Assistance

The SBA also offers procurement assistance to small businesses in the form of counseling on how to prepare bids and obtain prime government contracts and subcontracts. And perhaps more important, the computerized Procurement Automated Source System (PASS) makes the names and capabilities of small companies available to federal procurement officers as well as to purchasing officials working with large private contractors. For example, a small manufacturing company could list its products in the PASS data base. Then government agencies, which are required by law to purchase a portion of their goods from small vendors, can quickly review manufacturers who suit their needs. This program is especially valuable when you consider that in 1983, $49.3 billion in government contracts went to small businesses.

Research and Development

The Small Business Innovation Research Grant Program (SBIR) is, in my opinion, the most exciting thing the government has done for small business since it put the SBA in place. Begun in 1982, the SBIR program, which is a cooperative effort between the SBA and eleven separate government agencies, can provide a small business with up to $550,000 in government grants for research and development. Up to $50,000 can be awarded in phase I of the program for six months of feasibility-related research on a wide range of topics of interest to the federal government. Following the results of this research, promising projects become eligible for up to $500,000 in follow-up money for twenty-four months of related research and development. The positive effect of a large chunk of government R&D money ($1.3 billion over five years) going into small entrepreneurial companies cannot be overestimated. And more significantly, this money is available to start-ups as well as established small companies.

SBA Publications

Each year the SBA's Office of Management Assistance distributes 10 million books and pamphlets on subjects ranging from "The ABCs of Borrowing" to "Managing the Small Service Firm for Growth and Profit." These publications (more than 200 different titles) are geared primarily toward people just going into business or in their first two years of business and are available free or at a nominal cost (never more than seven dollars). Of particular interest to new businesses is the "Starting Out Series," which has almost thirty pamphlets on specific types of businesses, including "Roofing Contractors," "Interior Design Services," "Marine Retailers," and "Selling by Mail Order." I also recommend the two substantial booklets in the "Starting and Managing Series," "Starting and Managing a Business of Your Own" and "Starting and Managing a Small Service Firm," which are written to help the small entrepreneur "look before leaping."

Finding Assistance

Services provided by the SBA are available to all types of small businesses (and about 98 percent of the nonfarm business in the United States meet the SBA's definition of "small business"), so no matter what your situation, the SBA is well worth looking into. There are 10 regional offices and 100 district offices throughout the country. To find out more about the programs listed above, and many more, call your local SBA office (listed in your local telephone book under Federal Government), or contact the U.S. Small Business Administration at 1441 L St., N.W., Washington, DC 20416; (800) 368-5855.

8. The Ethics of Banking

In this chapter I only plan to sketch other alternatives to avoid losing your home and life savings to an overzealous bank. In practice, I don't believe any of what I am about to discuss is completely ethical, and I much prefer the direct confrontation method I have outlined in the seven previous chapters. Though I have seen a number of banks and lenders who would surely not win any ethics prizes for their behavior in pursuing bad debts, two wrongs don't make a right, and so I judged it best to briefly acquaint the reader with these additional alternatives: increasing lender liability, protecting assets, and avoiding lawsuits.

INCREASING LENDER LIABILITY

In many cases, entrepreneurs sign the personal guarantee and then rely on inherent inequities in the U.S. legal system to avoid totally living up to the commitment. One reason for this is their claim that the lender performed in bad faith. So when the bank seeks to foreclose, the entrepreneur countersues, claiming the problems were due to the bank's behavior. These lawsuits are increasing and entrepreneurs are winning a number of claims. This success has to do in part with the ineptness of the U.S. court system and the ability of lawyers to argue both sides of an issue.

An excellent synopsis of current events in the area of Lenders' Lawsuits can be found in an article by Jay Finegan entitled "Bankers' Suits" in the November 1989 issue of *Inc.* magazine. It begins on page 109 and is subtitled "How small companies victimized by their lenders are fighting back." It ends on page 114 and has a good deal of current legal data. To get a copy, contact:

> Reprint Dept.
> *Inc.* Magazine
> 38 Commercial Wharf
> Boston, MA 02110

Or call (617) 227-4700.

Lender Liability Newsletter

It had to happen. As the banking crisis deepens, more and more entrepreneurs are passing along their financial problems and are suing their lenders (banks). A whole category of law is emerging called lender liability.

Financial institutions are under attack for their lending practices. In suits around the country, debtors unable to repay their loans have turned the tables and sued their lenders. They are creatively crafting common law theories of fraud, duress, negligence, and interference with contractual relations to win multi-million-dollar verdicts against their creditors.

- *Washington, D.C.* The U.S. Supreme Court is scheduled to hear an oral argument in a case where a Texas company contends that it should be able to take a claim against an insolvent thrift into federal court instead of to the Federal Savings and Loan Insurance Corporation.
- *California.* The state supreme court refused to review a ruling by a state appellate court that overturned a $26 million judgment in a lender liability suit against the Bank of America in which an apple grower and an apple processor claim the bank fraudulently induced them to borrow funds for a processing plant.
- *Texas.* The First National Bank of Beeville has filed an application for a writ of error with the state supreme court in a case in which plaintiffs claim the bank acted out of self-interest. And the Hunt brothers effectively utilized their bank lawsuit to settle their bankruptcy.

Other debtors have struck back with suits brought under the Federal Racketeer Influenced and Corrupt Organizations Act (RICO):

- *Chicago.* The U.S. District Court for Northern Illinois ruled that more than one borrower can act as representative for a group of other borrowers and that the lending institution is not entitled to summary judgment on claims that it overcharged borrowers in creating loan interest rates.

In addition to suits by borrowers, lenders are also confronting efforts by the Environmental Protection Agency (EPA) to impose liability on them for the costs of cleaning up hazardous waste sites:

- *Philadelphia.* A federal judge is scheduled to hear arguments in a case in which the EPA is trying to recover from Turner & Newall PLC the cost of cleaning up asbestos waste piles near Ambler, Pennsylvania. T&N is a mortgagee of the operator of the site, T&N subsidiary Keasbey & Mattison.
- *Georgia.* Justice Department attorneys are contending that a lender with a

security interest in a printing company's assets is liable for costs incurred under CERCLA to clean the company's property.

The *Lender Liability Litigation Reporter* is a new twice-monthly national journal of record from Andrews Publications Inc., P.O. Box 200, Edgemont, PA 19028. It can keep you abreast of the most recent developments in this new field of litigation. Based on reports from a nationwide network of correspondents, each issue includes summaries of new filings, settlements, pretrial maneuverings, trials, and appellate court activity. The bad news is that the service is expensive and aimed primarily at attorneys. The subscriber price is $450 per year. Call 1-800-345-1101 or (215) 253-2565.

PROTECTING ASSETS AND AVOIDING LAWSUITS

Another alternative is to shield your assets from any creditor. Many entrepreneurs choose to do this, but the exact execution of it is a tricky legal matter. Two options that seem to be growing in popularity are using offshore banking to protect assets and avoid lawsuits and using limited partnerships to avoid lawsuits and protect assets.

The stability of offshore banking is always a question. I recommend that you contact:

> J. F. (Jim) Staw
> 301 Plymouth Drive, N.E.
> Dalton, GA 30721-9983
>
> Jerome Schneider
> WFI Corporation
> 357 S. Robertson Blvd.
> Beverly Hills, CA 90211

Attorney Jay Mitton believes in creating limited partnerships as a preferred method of avoiding lawsuits. This is the logic of his reasoning:

1. Limited partnerships can allow you to control an asset as the general partner without owing it as the limited partner.

2. A judgment against a limited partnership can only be collected from any distribution to the partners. If there is no distribution, the judgment becomes academic. Assets within a limited partnership cannot be attacked, only the income they produce to partners.

3. In Mitton's opinion, U.S. courts haven't overturned the limited partnership structure as they have the corporate structure. This structure has stood the test of time.

4. In most cases, a judgment creditor against a limited partnership must declare income upon receipt of the judgment, not upon receipt of the cash. So, the enthusiasm for a creditor to attack a limited partnership given that the cash flow from a judgment could well mean a significant up-front cash payment for taxes before (and if) any payments are made makes this a desirable structure to protect assets.

While we are on the subject of banking ethics, I believe the following story, which appeared as a cover story of *Inc.* magazine in April 1988, will broaden your banking perspective. I have also included a rebuttal in a letter to the *Inc.* editors in the October 1988 issue. Bill Rodgers is a real person—a relatively well known person. And this is a real story.

HEARTBREAK HILL

BY JOSEPH P. KAHN

"I'm basically a compromiser," Bill Rodgers was saying, sitting on the patio outside his Phoenix condominium. "If a bad situation came up, I always preferred going around it to colliding with it. And the last thing I ever wanted to do was collide with a $30-billion bank."

It was a balmy day in January, and Rodgers was enjoying his annual mid-winter desert sabbatical, far from the snows of New England and the aftershocks of a corporate disaster. In eight weeks' time he would be back home in Boston, tuning up for this month's 92d running of the Boston Marathon, the oldest and most hallowed of American road races, one that the man dubbed "Boston Billy" had won four times in his prime. This year, having turned forty, Rodgers would be competing for the first time in the marathon's masters division, and he was clearly relishing the challenge: enough to be putting in 115-mile training weeks, despite an aggravating case of tendinitis and some dark storm clouds hanging over his financial future.

While returning to Boston was not in doubt, he could not be so sure it would feel like home this time around. In many ways, "home" had become a tenuous concept for him, thanks largely to the collision he alluded to, a collision that was both fierce and final. Indeed, when the clothing company that bore his name staggered across the finish line a year ago, drained of cash and oxygen and wobbling on its last legs, it looked less like a veteran marathoner than the victim of a street mugging. On April 7, two weeks before the 1987 Boston Marathon, the Bank of Boston had laid a billy club to the head of Bill Rodgers & Co. (BRC) by calling its loan, padlocking its doors, and selling off its inventory at fire-sale prices.

After shutting down the ailing business, the bank subsequently opened even deeper wounds for Rodgers and company president Rob Yahn. To guarantee the company's loans, both had pledged personal assets as collateral, including second mortgages on their houses. Now, the two were being held accountable for an estimated $700,000 shortfall, and Rodgers's seventeen-room house in Dover, Massachusetts, was under imminent threat of foreclosure. For Rodgers, who had neither a business background nor, he admitted, a meaningful role in the management of the company, the sense of helplessness was acute. There was pain in his eyes and strain in his voice as he recounted the sequence of events leading up to and through the liquidation of his company. Doubts about Yahn's judgment mingled with an air of disbelief that the bank could have pushed them so hard to the wall—and then just kept right on pushing.

"If I come off sounding overly emotional," Rodgers said, "you have to understand what we've been through. First there were the tough times with the business. Then there were tough times with Rob. Finally there were *very* tough times with the bank. I'm tired of the struggle. Tired of meetings with bankers and lawyers, hassles with creditors, the whole deal. That isn't me. I'm an athlete, not a businessman. My total goal was to be the best marathon runner on the planet."

As he spoke, Elise Rodgers, two, sprinted through the doorway and crawled into her father's lap. "I've been to Japan several times," he continued, "and over there, you know, company managers make it a point of honor to take full responsibility for their failures. Maybe that's part of this story—how nobody wanted to take responsibility. It's sad, really. I wish I knew where to place the blame, but I don't. See, it was never a black-and-white thing. It was always . . . shades of gray."

He shook his head. "The bank must realize that," he sighed. "Or am I still being an optimist?"

What he was, a decade or so ago, was one of the stardust twins of American distance running: a fair-haired schoolteacher from Everett, Massachusetts, who burst to the forefront of his sport with dramatic victories in the Boston (1975) and New York City (1976) marathons. Three times in five years Rodgers held the world's number-one ranking in the marathon. Together with Frank Shorter, winner of the 1972 Olympic Marathon in Munich, he helped spark the distance-running craze that swept America in the late 1970s.

The Shorter-Rodgers rivalry was a spirited one, both on and off the roadways. The two men did not particularly like each other and were not bashful about saying so in print. If a common purpose united them, however, it was their effort to lead road racing out of its economic Dark Ages and into the realm of free enterprise. This was not always easy to do. At the time, there were severe restrictions on appearance money, personal endorsements, and other for-profit arrangements that might "compromise" the standing of amateur athletes. To a runner like Rodgers, trying to make the 1976 Olympic team on a schoolteacher's $10,000 salary—and schedule—compromise was not the overriding issue. Survival was.

"I knew how the best runners in the world trained," he explains, "and I knew what it would take to compete with them. There came a point when I couldn't do that and keep my teaching job. At the same time, you had to be real careful how you set up any [business deals] or risk losing your amateur status."

Rodgers's first business venture was Bill Rodgers Running Center, a retail clothing-and-shoe store on Chestnut Hill Avenue, facing the Boston Marathon course near the twenty-three-mile mark. Opened in 1977, the store was capitalized with $40,000 put up by Bill and his then-wife, Ellen, and managed by his brother, Charlie. In addition to becoming Bill's training headquarters and a hangout for serious runners, the store was a modest commercial success, spawning a second venue at Boston's Quincy Market and eventually grossing as much as $1 million yearly. As the financial strictures on amateur athletes were relaxed, Rodgers also retained a personal agent—Drew Mearns of the International Management Group—to represent him in licensing arrangements.

But it was Shorter's decision to jump into the wide-open marketplace for running apparel that inspired his old rival to consider doing the same. In 1976, Shorter launched Frank Shorter Running Gear. To manage it, Shorter turned to Yale classmate and former miler Rob Yahn, a Harvard M.B.A. who'd worked in the small-business division of a large public accounting firm.

"We *were* the market when we opened," says Yahn. "I'd projected first-year sales of $250,000 or something, and in our first three months we booked $3.5 *million* in orders. It was crazy." And short-lived. Within months, there was a falling out. Yahn left and "started looking around for something else to do."

Rodgers had met Yahn at a trade show, where he was ordering Shorter's shorts for his Boston store. When Yahn later heard of Rodgers's interest in doing his own clothing line, he offered his services. Rodgers accepted. He valued Yahn's experience, and did not mind in the least that Yahn had recently defected from Frank's ranks.

And so, in 1978, Bill Rodgers & Co. was launched and began producing BR running gear. Under guidelines laid down by the amateur athletic establishment, Rodgers himself was required to hold a majority share in the enterprise. Accordingly, he and his wife kept 60 percent of the stock. The rest was spread among a handful of others, including Yahn, Charlie Rodgers, and Russell McCarter, Bill's personal accountant and business manager for the Bill Rodgers Running Center stores. With the exception of Yahn and McCarter, none of them knew a balance sheet from a balance beam, but that hardly seemed much of a handicap. They put up $60,000 in capital and retained a New York City–based factor to handle inventory and receivables financing. Suppliers were numerous, and the market primed to explode. When it did, so did Bill Rodgers & Co.

In 1981, Rodgers won more than twenty races, establishing himself as the premier distance runner on the planet. That same year, BRC did $3 million in sales and established itself as the hottest company in the running-clothes industry. Seizing the opportunity, it grew at a breakneck pace, pushing revenues to $6.5 million at the end of fiscal '83, $8.4 million a year later. That growth rate would eventually land the company at #29 on the 1984 INC. 500, the highest-ranked apparel business on the list. In the meantime, however, growth was putting a strain on BRC's finances. Though the company was profitable, it was not generating nearly enough cash to keep up with production demands. So Yahn had begun looking for outside capital, approaching several Boston-area banks, none of which was eager to back a narrow-niche clothing company with few fixed assets.

But one banker was receptive—Ann Hartman, then an assistant vice president at the Bank of Boston. Hartman, who had worked on the Running Centers' accounts, liked Yahn personally and thought highly of his business plan. Two capital needs were identified: a term loan of $350,000 to finance office improvements and new equipment; and a $200,000 line of credit to cover the more seasonal requirements of fabric ordering, finished-goods production, and marketing and selling costs.

It was not an easy sell. "The first time I pitched the loan to my department," Hartman recalls, "they turned it down." But on the second pass, in September 1980, she was able to push the package through by cementing it with a Small Business Administration guarantee. In addition, she secured a lien on inventory. "That was a concession on the company's part, true," she admits. "But when you're in a no-asset, fast-growth situation like Bill Rodgers & Co., it's hard to get credit unless the lender feels secure." For that same reason, Rodgers and Yahn also had to sign "unlimited" personal guarantees. At the time, this seemed a minor detail. Given the amount of the loan and the market value of company inventory, where was the risk?

The first suitor to approach BRC was CML Group Inc., an Acton, Massachusetts–based holding company with a variety of retail businesses catering to the aging baby-boom market. It made its offer in the fall of 1982. Looking back, the shareholders wish they had grabbed it, for it had long been their plan to grow the company to a respectable size and cash out via the acquisition route. But by then, there were a lot of oars in the water, and not all of them were pulling smartly in the same direction. For one thing, Bill and Ellen Rodgers had had a less-than-friendly divorce. Ellen controlled 30 percent of the stock, with a seat on the board. When the issue of selling the company arose, she had her own interests to assert, and assert them she did.

"CML was basically offering a five-year earn-out with some cash up front," says Yahn, "but [Ellen's] attorneys were having problems with the concept. Bill's agent, meanwhile, was warning Bill about selling an outsider the rights to his name. So we started renegotiating his licensing deal, and *that* took a year. By the time we got [the licensing contract] resolved, CML was gone."

Yahn himself was in what Rodgers now characterizes as "an embattled position," pinned in the crossfire between the agent, Mearns; Ellen Rodgers; and Russell McCarter, who worried about growth pressures and Yahn's ability to manage them. "Rob refused to be concerned with problems," says McCarter. "He was off doing his own thing, not really accountable to anyone. I could never get answers from him. I'd worked in a lot of troubled businesses, and even though we were profitable those first few years, I knew we could have been twice as profitable. Rob just wasn't keeping receivables or expenses under control, turning inventory fast enough, doing all the things the business really needed."

Indeed, through a combination of bad luck and bad management, the company was getting deeper and deeper into trouble, even as its revenues continued to grow. First there was an ill-conceived attempt to establish a British operation, which wound up costing BRC $400,000. Even more problematical was the increase in competition back home, as a number of large shoe manufacturers—Nike, Adidas, New Balance, Saucony—brought out clothing lines of their own. The timing couldn't have been worse, coming just as the market was nearing saturation. The combination of a softening market and steeper competition squeezed everybody's margins. And to make matters worse, BRC was having problems with a new subcontractor in Puerto Rico, where Yahn had begun to do some manufacturing in a cost-cutting move. Quality suffered, and flexibility disappeared.

Such troubles only intensified the shareholders' desire to sell, but internal dissension continued to be an obstacle. "I bumped into a guy from Levi Strauss," remembers Rodgers, "who knew the running world and was very interested in our business. He told me Levi was also looking at Frank Shorter's company, but that he'd rather deal with me. Unfortunately, there was a lot of disagreement [among the shareholders] over what the company was worth. Drew [Mearns] was telling me one thing, Ellen was insisting on a figure of her own, and Rob was probably worried about his own future with the company if we sold it. While all that was going on, the deal fell through. And then Levi Strauss turned around and bought Frank Shorter. I was really depressed."

This setback notwithstanding, the shareholders retained the investment banking firm of Bear, Stearns & Co. to value BRC and to help sell the company. At the time, Bill Rodgers & Co. (with '84 revenues of $8.5 million and pretax profits of $634,000) still looked like an attractive property; Bear, Stearns fixed the selling price at somewhere between $2.5 and $4 million.

Throughout 1985, Yahn concentrated his energies on finding a buyer. Several seemed interested, but none followed through. His efforts, he now agrees, were a form of managerial denial—a way to avoid admitting how fast things were going downhill. "I'm sure I could have spent my time better managing the company," Yahn offers, "but I didn't. And every time somebody looked us over, we looked worse." On that score, anyway, he finds himself in unusual agreement with McCarter, who was appalled at the company's credit-control policies and incensed that BRC kept shipping to delinquent accounts.

"Rob's standard line was, 'We're working on it,' " says McCarter. "Maybe he was in over his head, and maybe he didn't want to let go. But the Bank of Boston was still enthusiastic about the company. And the bottom line was, we were still showing a profit at that point. By the end of '85, the consensus among the [shareholders] was, let's sell this sucker and get out."

By the end of '85, some of the players already had gotten out. One was Mearns, who left Bill Rodgers's employ to open his own sports agency. More unsettling was Ann Hartman's leavetaking from the Bank of Boston. Hartman had been the company's main contact there, a sympathetic insider who, according to Yahn, knew more about the company's financial position than anyone but himself. Well she might. BRC's debt to the bank was mushrooming. In addition to the original loan, the company now had an overadvance, or seasonal loan, which allowed it to borrow above its standard credit line during periods when sales were slow and production needs high. As a result, BRC was into the bank for more than $2.5 million.

So Yahn was shocked when he stopped by Hartman's office one morning and found it empty. "My first thought," he says, "was that she'd been fired for loaning us too much money." When he finally tracked her down at home, Hartman told Yahn not to worry—that her departure was voluntary and had nothing to do with the amount of money the bank had fronted to BRC. She did say, however, that she'd been admonished for promoting management's point of view and warned Yahn that the bank might start "clamping down pretty hard."

Shortly thereafter, Yahn got a call from his new loan officer. "Hi," she said cheerily. "When are you planning to sell the company?"

Ody Cormier attended the February '86 trade show in Dallas at which Bill Rodgers & Co. was showing its new fall line. His presence was indicative of his concern, and his concern was understandable. As founder and president of Cormier Corp., a Laconia, New Hampshire–based apparel manufacturer, he was one of BRC's principal suppliers of finished goods at a time when the company was having trouble paying its creditors. It owed its advertising agency and its main fabric supplier, W. L. Gore & Associates Inc., sums in the six-figure range, and Cormier himself had advanced BRC $500,000 in unsecured trade credit, allowing the company to continue manufacturing while it searched for a solution to its problems. The solution, everyone agreed, was to sell the business. Yahn pulled Cormier aside in Dallas and assured him that the sale of BRC to CB Sports Inc. was a couple of weeks away. "Rob was giving me just the highlights," says Cormier, "but he really believed the company was still viable in the marketplace, and I had faith in him."

The bank, on the other hand, was rapidly losing faith. At its insistence, the shareholders had anted up an additional $130,000 in working capital, but that was not enough to keep the BRC file from being kicked upstairs to the twelfth floor, where "troubled loans" were handled. The bank also informed the company that it had no obligation to lend it further funds beyond July 1, 1986, and demanded that Yahn and Rodgers take out second mortgages on their houses to guarantee the overadvance, which had previously gone uncollateralized. At the time, Rodgers had just bought a new house in Dover, Massachusetts. Believing the sale of the company to CB Sports was imminent, he gave the bank the guarantee it was seeking.

Then CB Vaughan stopped returning Yahn's phone calls. Yahn says he still doesn't understand what went wrong. Vaughan, president of CB Sports, says the deal was just too complex. In any case, the sale fell through, and with it went BRC's last chance to cash out with its hands clean.

Bill Rodgers & Co. was now running on empty. A vicious cycle had set in: as creditors' bills piled up, there were increasing delays in the shipment of fabric and finished goods. The longer stores had to wait to get their goods, the less inclined they were to pay their bills promptly. This, in turn, aggravated the situation with creditors and put the company in a desperate cash bind. It responded by laying off its sales and credit managers, thereby compounding its problems.

By the summer of 1986, BRC was down to ten employees, from a high of twenty-one. It had even stopped paying Rodgers his licensing fee. Nevertheless, says Yahn, it was still receiving plenty of moral support from its four largest suppliers, with whom he managed to negotiate letters of forebearance, and from the bank, which was working hard to get its money back.

"Our third loan officer was Julie Bertinette," he remembers, "and she was very straightforward. We knew where we stood anyway—you don't get to the twelfth floor of the Bank of Boston as a 'valued customer.' Up there, you're not a customer at all—you're a problem. But Julie said that since our creditors and shareholders were obviously willing to be supportive, the bank should be too."

With few options left, Yahn approached Ody Cormier. Would he consider putting up a new round of financing in exchange for equity in the company? Cormier was interested. He already had an intimate knowledge of the company's manufacturing operations, plus a large chunk of unsecured credit sitting on BRC's books. What he did not have was any real understanding of its debt profile to the Bank of Boston. So he met several times with Bertinette, finally asking the bank to produce a letter spelling out the terms of its lending arrangement with BRC. Meanwhile, he had his own lawyers and accountants evaluate the company's viability. But, all things being equal, Cormier was inclined to do a deal. "There was no question" that a market existed for BR clothes, he says. "BRC had always been first with new products, plus Bill had tremendous name recognition."

Yahn and Bertinette soon had a written agreement designed to accomplish two major objectives. The first was to protect the bank's exposure by reducing both the loan and the overadvance; the second was to provide sufficient cash flow for the company to stay in business while Cormier reorganized it. The bank would advance BRC money (up to a limit of $1.75 million) on the basis of 80 percent of new sales and 30 percent of inventory. "When the cash payment was received," noted Yahn in a later memo to the bank, "it was applied to the loan so the loan balance and receivables were reduced by the same amount. Recalculating the formula resulted in 20 percent of the cash received being available for new borrowing. In other words, we were advanced 80 percent when the sale was made and received the remaining 20 percent when the bill was paid. Under this system, we were always being advanced 80 percent of sixty-day receivables."

For its part, the bank required BRC to pay down its overadvance in an orderly fashion, from its current level of $700,000 to zero by February 1988. To meet that requirement, BRC would either have to increase its profitability or decrease its asset base (principally inventory, since it had almost no fixed assets). BRC also had a $395,000 income-tax refund coming in November, $350,000 of which was pledged to the bank. Bertinette monitored the account closely. "Julie said that the plan looked fine," says Yahn, "and that she felt comfortable with it as long as they could check it every month."

Satisfied that a workable accommodation had been reached, Cormier and Yahn signed a purchase-and-sale agreement in late August. In exchange for approximately $300,000 in cash and another $400,000 in trade debt, plus some personal loans and promissory notes to the shareholders, Ody Cormier assumed control of the company. Most of the cash went to suppliers, as per the letters of forebearance.

During the second half of 1986, everything went pretty much as planned. Although the company ran into delivery problems with its fall line, sales picked up, and by Christmas BRC was breaking even again. And then, one fateful December day, Yahn went up to Bertinette's office to drop off some papers. Her desk was empty.

"What happened to Julie?" Yahn asked one of her coworkers.

"Oh," came the reply, "she left to get married." Yahn's heart sank. "Sit tight," he was told. "We'll let you know who your new loan officer is."

Conflicts between lending officers and "asset recovery" personnel are not uncommon at banks. Lenders, after all, are in the business of finding new customers and helping them meet their borrowing needs. Loan-review officers, on the other hand, have the often disagreeable task of resolving bad-debt situations.

"You hear a lot of gestapo stories from customers in [bad-loan] situations," says Ann Hartman, who did her own tour of duty in that department, "and some of them are true. Banks do get trigger-happy at times. Particularly when dealing with a clothing company, where the inventory is perceived to have a short shelf life. The mentality becomes, 'Let's sell this crap by the pound.' But it depends on the circumstance."

The circumstance Bill Rodgers & Co. now found itself in was awkward indeed, and the dialogue between management and the company's new loan officer, Jack Bradley, did not get off to a propitious start. At their first meeting in mid-January, Bradley brought up a $138,000 debt with the bank's London office, left over from the ill-fated British expansion; he said he wanted to fold it into the current repayment formula. Yahn replied that such a change would cripple BRC's cash flow and insisted the debts stay separate. Bradley demurred, but at their next meeting he fired a larger shot across their bow: As of February 1, a new repayment formula would take effect. The old advance rate of 80 percent of new sales would remain intact; in the future, however, the company would hand over the remaining 20 percent of all cash receipts, to be applied directly to the loan paydown. No longer would that money be available as working capital.

At first Yahn surmised that Bradley simply didn't understand the implications of what he was proposing. On February 18, he composed a memo to Bradley, spelling out those implications. "Obviously, very rapid debt reduction takes place [under the new formula]," he conceded, "but there is not enough cash to operate the business." He then essayed a compromise: cut the 20 percent of cash receipts down to 10 percent and administer the formula as before. To counter two of Bradley's concerns, he also pointed out that the bank would still be protected against declining cash receipts in that a) it was lending only on sixty-day receivables, and b) there was a cap on the total advance available. Yahn concluded with a plea that BRC be allowed to make "an orderly withdrawal from the bank."

"During this entire time," he wrote, "Bill and I have been very cooperative. Subordinated debt was put in by the stockholders when required. We have both pledged a large majority of our assets to secure the overadvance, so that the Bank would not be taking an equity risk. . . . Ody has invested a considerable amount of money under the belief that we would have a reasonable amount of time to resolve our situation. I feel that the Bank should . . . allow us enough cash flow to operate while we seek replacement financing."

Yahn's plea fell on deaf ears. The question was, why? Why was the bank suddenly pressing for a new repayment formula (one that even Hartman later termed "draconian") when the old formula had apparently been working as it was supposed to? Had the bank lost faith in the company's ability to repay? Or was Bradley gambling, as some suspected, that Ody Cormier's deep pockets would keep BRC from going under? If so, then he badly misread the new owner. Informed by Bradley that the bank wanted him personally to guarantee the overadvances, Cormier refused. "Bradley told me that I already had a sizable investment in the company," remembers Cormier, "and I'd better sign the agreement. There's no question he was putting a gun to my head. If he didn't know me then, it didn't take him long to find out."

Cormier came back with one more counterproposal, whereby the bank would handle BRC's receivables through its own in-house factoring division, in return for which the company would cease shipping to overdue accounts. In addition, the bank would let BRC take all the "good" (that is, current) inventory and flush it out through the system, at full value on the dollar.

Bradley wouldn't budge. He told Cormier and Yahn that he didn't want anyone "cherry-picking" the inventory and that the new formula was "cast in stone." Things went downhill from there.

Over the ensuing weeks, Yahn and Cormier debated a number of emergency alternatives. The most logical one was to take Bill Rodgers & Co. into bankruptcy court, liquidate its assets, set up a successor company, and buy the existing BR inventory from the bank, using the proceeds from its sale to pay off the loan. Ultimately, however, they rejected this course of action—first, because it would mean blowing off their creditors, who had stuck by them during tough times; second, because they didn't want to risk losing credibility in the marketplace by stopping production. "Besides," adds Yahn, "bankruptcy didn't seem like a good career move."

On Friday, April 3, Yahn's lawyer called to say that he'd been sent a hand-delivered letter from Bradley demanding full repayment of the $1.3-million loan balance. When Yahn finally reached Bradley, the loan officer was gruff. "Negotiations have gone on long enough," he said ominously. "If you won't take action, we will."

Yahn spent the weekend discussing the situation with Rodgers and Cormier, and they decided to hold a board meeting in Boston on Tuesday afternoon. On Monday morning, Yahn called Bradley back and informed him of the board meeting. The two agreed to meet at the bank at 10:00 A.M. on Wednesday.

At 7 o'clock Tuesday morning, Jack Bradley turned up at one of Cormier's plants. With him was a driver and a moving van. Cormier was away. They told the plant manager, Carole Wallace, that they had come to pick up the BRC inventory. She blocked the door and ran back to call Cormier. He was not amused. For one thing, he did not believe the bank had any legal right to take so much as a drawstring out of his factory. For another, the goods on his shop floor belonged to other customers besides Bill Rodgers & Co., and Jack Bradley was hardly capable of identifying which was which. Cormier had Wallace tell them to get lost.

"Then they asked to use the telephone," she recalls, "and while they were on it, Ody called back on the other line and told me under no circumstance to let them make a call. There wasn't much I could do, so I pushed the button down on them." Vowing to return with a court order, Bradley left. Meanwhile, Ody Cormier made two more phone calls—one to his attorney, and one to Rob Yahn.

The scene that morning at Bill Rodgers & Co.'s headquarters in Weymouth, Massachusetts, resembled an outtake from an episode of "The Untouchables." Ten minutes after Cormier's warning call to Yahn, the Bank of Boston asset-recovery team pulled up. Company employees were just drifting into work. The atmosphere quickly went from frosty to confrontational. Yahn asked to see a court order and, assured one was not needed (in fact, it was not), was informed that his house might be seized as well. Christine Scanlon, BRC's customer-service manager, got into a shouting match with one bank representative when she tried to remove some personal effects from her desk. Security guards were posted and padlocks installed. Bank representatives then disappeared into the warehouse to count inventory.

Even then, the principals tried hard not to panic. That they owed the Bank of Boston $1.3 million was indisputable. Still, as best they could calculate, finished-goods inventory totaled $660,000 at cost, and gross receivables came to $920,000. Furthermore, all of the current inventory (roughly 80 percent of the total) was on open order—the retailers still wanted it. Yahn and Rodgers talked things over and could see "no way" that liquidation would leave them with a deficit for which they would be personally liable. "I knew things were complicated," says Rodgers, "but I did not think, 'Uh oh, there goes my *house.*' "

How complicated things really were soon became painfully apparent. Yahn summarized the chronology of events in a letter to the Bank of Boston dated January 20, 1988.

"First Bill, myself, and [Cormier] wanted to start a successor company, which would buy the current inventory items and arrange for the disposition of [other] items. We felt a successor company would also be very helpful in receivables collection. Jack refused to sell part of the inventory. He said he did not want it 'cherry-picked.' The bank then obtained bids from local merchants, with the high bid being 50 percent, or $330,000. Jack felt this amount was totally inadequate. Bill and I then offered to sell the inventory to a few selected customers. We informed Jack that if it had to be done quickly (within two weeks), $475,000 could be realized. Jack replied that much more could be realized with a plan he had worked out with MVP Sports [a sporting-goods chain]—the inventory was to be sold to the public at the Northeast Trade Center.

"I told Jack this was not an economically viable plan because the quantities were too large. The amount was more than we had sold in all of New England in a year. It was not reasonable to sell it all in one location over four days. . . ."

Reasonable or not, the sale proceeded as Bradley had planned. Four days later, the gross profits came to $235,000, minus advertising costs and other fees totaling $110,000. The net was thus roughly $125,000—significantly below the firm outside bid for the inventory, and far off the $475,000 promised by Yahn and Cormier.

"Bill and I then asked if we could at least sell what was left over after the MVP sale," Yahn's letter continued. "When asked what I thought could be realized, [I replied] $120,000 to $200,000, depending on the condition. Only one problem—I was repeatedly told that I could not see the goods in order to make a specific determination. Besides, [Bradley told me] if my maximum was $200,000, it didn't matter, because the bank expected more. [The remaining inventory] was still [worth] $450,000 at cost, and the bank thought that something close to the original bid (50 cents on the dollar) could be obtained at auction. I said I thought Jack was dreaming and would be lucky to get $50,000 for goods that had already been through a sale. The result was $47,000, less expenses, but that included fixed assets.

"So the final tally was $155,000 for all finished goods, and Bill and I are expected to make up the $320,000 difference. . . . We expect to pay for our mistakes. It is paying for the bank's mistakes that is brutal."

Yahn's list of complaints did not end there, either. "After the auction," he continued, "I asked Jack if he wanted me to remove the records from the company offices. He replied that he was only obligated to give up the payroll records and intended to put the rest in storage. Despite several calls from the landlord, the records were never picked up and were eventually thrown out. Obviously the bank did not want the records; they just did not want us to have them. [Those records] may have been helpful for future tax filings. . . .

"I don't know the total expenses at the moment, because I have not received a loan statement in over six months. The worst example, however, was being required to pay $2,400 per week for twenty-four hour-a-day security service—this went on for about twelve weeks. For nine years we had just locked the door . . . and our insurance premiums were only about $250 a week. What was even worse, the first security company had to be fired because they stole two personal computers and who knows what else. The charges for the service were promptly made to our account, but I have never seen any credit for the computers.

"Obviously," Yahn concluded, "this course of events has left [Rodgers and me] very frustrated. . . . If we were allowed to cooperate with the bank in the liquidation of the assets, there would have been at least $400,000 less for us to pay. The whole matter would have been over by now. Instead, interest and expenses continue to pile on. It appears that the bank or Jack or both wanted more than their money. They wanted as much as possible to come from [us]."

Ody Cormier got the new business, Bill Rodgers Sportswear, up and running last June. Cormier's company and his wife own 84 percent of the new venture, Bill Rodgers 9 percent, Rob Yahn the remaining 7 percent. The first five months' sales totaled $1 million, and sales for '88 are projected at $4 million. Moreover, the company is already profitable, thanks to tight production controls, more pricing diversity, and the ability to make quick design changes.

"We did have marketing problems," concedes Christine Scanlon, who joined the new company as a vice president. "There was a lot of negative press over what happened to Bill, especially in the Boston area. People still say, 'Gee, we thought Bill Rodgers had gone out of business.' But my question is: If Bill Rodgers & Co. was so sick, why are we so healthy now?"

Seated next to her in the offices of their St. Johnsbury, Vermont, factory, Ody Cormier bangs his hand on a metal table. "I've dealt with a lot of bankers over the years," he snorts, "and I've been in problem situations before. But I've never experienced anything like this in my life. This whole thing was a bad circumstance orchestrated by the bank, and everybody lost in the end—especially the creditors. All Bradley seemed to care about was clearing the decks, and . . ." bang! again ". . . that's just what they did. If you need a doctor, you don't call in an undertaker."

For understandable reasons, the Bank of Boston remains tight-lipped about the whole matter, preferring to invoke the principle of client confidentiality. Jack Bradley himself has been unavailable for comment, but bank spokesperson Wayne Taylor does concede that the contretemps is a "no-win situation for everyone."

"I will say, though," Taylor commented recently, "that we find ourselves bridling at the characterization that the bank took precipitious action. Our business is one of nurturing entrepreneurial effort and helping small businesses grow. When we assume possession of collateral, it's the last thing we want to do—a last resort. But it's also a necessary and accepted guarantee in order to protect the interests of the very businesses that we're trying to grow, as well as the interests of our depositors and the community at large."

As for Rob Yahn, he is now working for CML Group—the very first company that wanted to buy Bill Rodgers & Co. His travails with the Bank of Boston are not over yet. Last fall, he reached an agreement on the sale of his house; the day before the closing, however, he discovered that the SBA had not come through with the necessary approval to release him from his obligations on the original loan. The deal collapsed. On Christmas Eve, Rodgers's attorney was told by the bank that foreclosure proceedings would be reinstated unless the two principals began making monthly payments of $7,000 on the outstanding interest.

"My wife kept telling me that Bradley really wanted to go after us," Yahn says today, "that the bank didn't just want its money back—it wanted it from *us*. I never really believed that before, but I guess I believe it now."

Rodgers spent the winter in Arizona, training for the Boston Marathon and seeking corporate sponsorship for the masters' road-racing circuit he and old rival Frank Shorter are trying to put together. Beyond that, he plans to keep a hand in the promotional and marketing efforts of the new clothing company. What he won't do is get into another business venture with any element of personal risk. He says he wants only "small-scale, short-term, no-risk deals."

"One thing I realize now," says Boston Billy, "is that I do a better job of communicating than a lot of the lawyers and agents and businessmen who've represented me. Once you start bringing in all those layers, things deteriorate. I know that's what happened here. To this day, I have mixed feelings about Rob. To a certain extent I feel misled by him—and it's cost me a lot of money."

For the money—and because it is what he has always done best—Rodgers will keep running. And no race brings out the warrior in him like the Boston Marathon. When the pack takes off from Hopkinton, twenty-six miles and change from the finish line, the biggest challenge facing it will be Heartbreak Hill. Rodgers should take it in stride. After all, he's a master.

Postscript

After weeks of preliminary negotiations, Rodgers returned to Massachusetts for a meeting on February 19, at which he concluded a settlement with the Bank of Boston. Under the terms of the agreement, the bank purchased his house in Dover in exchange for the extinguishing of his remaining indebtedness. Rodgers also signed a personal-service contract that provides for him to represent the bank at a number of public functions. Describing the meeting as "businesslike but friendly," Rodgers said, "I've always been a compromiser, and in the end that's what we achieved, a compromise. My financial—and athletic—future is now secure." Asked how it felt to see Jack Bradley again, he said, "There was some tension in the air, but I think we were more relieved than anything. Business is business, and sometimes it gets tough. I'm just glad I don't have his job."

In Defense of Bankers

At last, a reader has come forward with a hard-hitting, straight-talking, no-holds-barred defense of the way bankers deal with their small-business customers. What prompted his letter was our July "Focus" section, in which readers responded to our story about Bill Rodgers's run-in with the Bank of Boston ("Heartbreak Hill," April). Several of them recounted their own misfortunes at the hands of their lenders. Edward J. Healy Jr. shed no tears:

I have been involved with the banking industry for thirty years, and I am still fascinated when an article like your Bill Rodgers story generates interpretation that turns night into day and black into white. Someone should remind your readers that most of America's businesses, large and small, got where they are with the help of full-service commercial banks, and that those institutions can't just serve borrowers' needs—they must also provide a return on investment to shareholders and prudence to depositors. Your Indianapolis attorney and Clinton, Iowa, manufacturer would seem to prefer the mad-dog lending practices of Penn Square and Continental Illinois to those at the typical heartland bank. Your correspondent from Cohasset, Massachusetts, mentions that he owed his bank $35,000 *plus some $70,000 in bad checks.* This guy wants sympathy?

I have seen too many ebullient, overconfident supermen (and superladies) who are only too happy to suck up the bucks at the beginning, but who hate financial records; pay inadequate attention to their businesses; cheat Uncle Sam unmercifully; resort to all sorts of sneaky, underhanded, and often illegal behavior; and then whine and moan when the bank wants the money back. A pox on all of them! They embarrass the legions of hardworking small-business people who pay attention and play it straight.

I concede that your letter-writer Brenda Koskinen makes a very good point. I have witnessed the scenario she relates, wherein a bank's senior officers become peeved at a loan officer who quits or is fired and proceed to attack every borrower who dealt with that lender. The result is always the same. *The marketplace solves the problem.* If the business is viable, another bank will finance it.

Lending money is not a lot of fun. Many people are like Mr. Rodgers. Beset with adversity caused by themselves, their associates, their advisers, or the marketplace, they regard the mess as not of their doing and refuse to accept responsibility. They seem to feel that the money they've borrowed is all play money and need not be repaid. Wrong. The bank does indeed want its depositors' money back. Not the tools, the machinery, the buildings, the guarantor's house—the money! Perhaps if failing borrowers and their well-paid attorneys gave more attention to methods of repayment and less to debt evasion, these problems would not occur, and a lot of pain would be avoided.

Edward J. Healy, Jr.
President
Bloomsburg Bank
Columbia Trust Co.
Bloomsburg, Pennsylvania

We doubt that Mr. Healy's letter will win him a lot of friends among small-business borrowers, but we hope that it will generate an equally articulate response.

Appendix I

Acid test ratio. Cash plus those other assets that can be used *immediately* converted to cash should equal or exceed current liabilities. The formula used to determine the ratio is as follows:

$$\frac{\text{cash plus receivables (net) plus marketable securities}}{\text{current liabilities}}$$

The acid test ratio is one of the most important credit barometers used by lending institutions, as it indicates the abilities of a business enterprise to meet its current obligations.

Aging receivables. A scheduling of accounts receivable according to the length of time they have been outstanding. This shows which accounts are not being paid in a timely manner and may reveal any difficulty in collecting long overdue receivables. This may also be an important indicator of developing cash flow problems.

Amortization. To liquidate on an installment basis; the process of gradually paying off a liability over a period of time, i.e., a mortgage is amortized by periodically paying off part of the face amount of the mortgage.

Assets. The valuable resources or properties and property rights owned by an individual or business enterprise.

Balance sheet. An itemized statement that lists the total assets and the total liabilities of a given business to portray its net worth at a given moment in time.

Breakeven analysis. A method used to determine the point at which the business will neither make a profit nor incur a loss. That point is expressed in either the total dollars of revenue exactly offset by total expenses (fixed and variable) or in total units of production, the cost of which exactly equals the income derived by their sale.

Capital equipment. Equipment that you use to manufacture a product, provide a service, or use to sell, store, and deliver merchandise. Such equipment will not be sold in the normal course of business, but will be used and worn out or be consumed over time as you do business.

Cash flow. The actual movement of cash within a business: cash inflow minus cash outflow. A term used to designate the reported net income of a corporation plus amounts charged off for depreciation, depletion, amortization, and extraordinary charges to reserves, which are bookkeeping deductions and not actually paid out in cash. Used to offer a better indication of the ability of a firm to meet its own obligations and to pay dividends rather than with the conventional net income figure.

Cash position. See *Liquidity*.

Corporation. An artificial legal entity created by government grant and endowed with certain powers; a voluntary organization of persons, either actual individuals or legal entities, legally bound to form a business enterprise.

Current assets. Cash or other items that will normally be turned into cash within one year, and assets that will be used up in the operations of a firm within one year.

Current liabilities. Amounts owed that will ordinarily be paid by a firm within one year. Such items include accounts payable, wages payable, taxes payable, the current portion of a long-term debt, and interest and dividends payable.

Current ratio. A ratio of a firm's current assets to its current liabilities. The current ratio includes the value of inventories that have not yet been sold, so it is not the best evaluation of the current status of the firm. The acid test ratio, covering the most liquid of current assets, provides a better evaluation.

Deal. A proposal for financing business creation or expansion; a series of transactions and preparation of documents in order to obtain funds for business expansion or creation.

Depreciation. A reduction in the value of fixed assets. The most important causes of depreciation are wear and tear, the effect of the elements, and gradual obsolescence that make it unprofitable to continue using some assets until they have been exhausted. The purpose of the *bookkeeping charge for depreciation* is to write off the original cost of an asset (less expected salvage value) by equitably distributing charges against operations over its entire useful life.

Entrepreneur. An innovator of a business enterprise who recognizes opportunities to introduce a new product, a new production process, or an improved organization, and who raises the necessary money, assembles the factors of production, and organizes an operation to exploit the opportunity.

Equity. The monetary value of a property or business that exceeds the claims and/or liens against it by others.

Illiquid. See *Liquidity*.

Liquidity. A term used to describe the solvency of a business that has special reference to the degree of readiness in which assets can be converted into cash without a loss. Also called *cash position*. If a firm's current assets cannot be converted into cash to meet current liabilities, the firm is said to be *illiquid*.

Long-term liabilities. These are liabilities (expenses) that will not mature within the next year.

Market. The number of people and their total spending (actual or potential) for your product line within the geographic limits of your distribution ability. The *market share* is the percentage of your sales compared to the sales of your competitors in total for a particular product line.

Net worth. The owner's equity in a given business represented by the excess of the total assets over the total amounts owing to outside creditors (total liabilities) at a given moment in time. Also, the net worth of an individual as determined by deducting the amount of all his personal liabilities from the total value of his personal assets.

Partnership. A legal relationship created by the voluntary association of two or more persons to carry on as co-owners of a business for profit; a type of business organization in which two or more persons agree on the amount of their contributions (capital and effort) and on the distribution of profits, if any.

Profit. The excess of the selling price over all costs and expenses incurred in making the sale. Also, the reward to the entrepreneur for the risks assumed by him in the establishment, operation, and management of a given enterprise or undertaking.

Pro forma. A projection or estimate of what may result in the future from actions in the present. A pro forma financial statement is one that shows how the actual operations of the business will turn out if certain assumptions are realized.

Sole proprietorship or proprietorship. A type of business organization in which one individual owns the business. Legally, the owner *is* the business and personal assets are typically exposed to liabilities of the business.

Sub-Chapter S corporation or tax option corporation. A corporation that elected under Sub-Chapter S of the IRS Tax Code (by unanimous consent of its shareholders) not to pay any corporate tax on its income and, instead, to have the shareholders pay taxes on it, even though it is not distributed. Shareholders of a tax option corporation are also entitled to deduct, on their individual returns, their shares of any net operating loss sustained by the corporation, subject to limitation in the tax code. In many respects, Sub-Chapter S permits a corporation to behave for tax purposes as a proprietorship or partnership.

Take-over. The acquisition of one company by another company.

Target market. The *specific* individuals, distinguished by socioeconomic, demographic, and/or interest characteristics, who are the most likely potential customers for the goods and/or services of a business.

Working capital, net. The excess of current assets over current liabilities. These excess current assets are available for carrying on business operations.

Appendix II

As the author of eighteen books, I am commonly asked some foolish questions. My all-time favorite occurred at a seminar. An attendee was debating about spending $7.95 for my first book, *Fun and Guts.* The purchasing decision was contingent on how long it took me to write the book, and the potential customer was making a mental calculation of the ratio of his cost to my time invested. Fortunately, since this was my first book, it took me forever to write (at least twenty versions). The customer was impressed and made the economic plunge for $7.95.

From this and other experiences, I have always wondered why someone would want to know how long it took an author to write a book before making the decision to purchase it. Time to write seems like such an unrelated variable, I almost never mention it in describing any of my books. That is, until my sixteenth book, released in July 1988, entitled *Mancuso's Small Business Resource Guide.* It's 572 pages and contains thousands of annotated original resources I've uncovered for entrepreneurs since founding the Center for Entrepreneurial Management Inc. in 1978. This book is a reference guide that began as my Rolodex, and it is where I turn to answer questions from members or to suggest a place to write or call. Because it is jammed full of hard-to-find resources with names, addresses, and telephone numbers, I thought I'd list the Five Best Reference Books that are a must for an entrepreneur's library.

1. *A.T.&T's toll-free Business-to-Business Directory.* There are a half million 800 numbers in the United States and this directory lists 100,000 of them. What's nice is the yellow pages section, which lists 1,000 categories of products and services in the United States and Canada. And when you look for hard-to-find items or do some comparison purchasing, all the phone calls are free. To get a directory call 1-800-426-8686. It's $14.95.

2. *The Directory of Directories.* It always seems as if you need a directory for some purpose or another and this reference book listing all the directories published is an excellent original source of information. It is published once per year. The current edition has 2,171 pages and the price is $195. It can be purchased from the publisher, Gale Research Co., Book Tower, Detroit, MI 48226; (313) 961-2242 or 1-800-223-GALE.

3. *The Encyclopedia of Associations.* This is also a classic because there is usually an association that has answers to all your questions. There are literally thousands of associations, and they hold meetings, run conferences, publish resources and studies, and are original sources of information. Published annually, this encyclopedia has 2,666 pages and its price is $230. Order from Gale Research Co.

4. *The National Directory of Addresses and Telephone Numbers.* This is a national telephone book that lists the telephone numbers of all places frequently called. Because an information call costs fifty cents or more, this directory has become invaluable. It's wonderfully organized into sections, and it even lists zip codes and addresses, along with the most commonly used telephone numbers. Priced at $45, it is published annually by General Information Inc., 401 Park Pl., Kirkland, VA 98033; (206) 828-4777 or 1-800-722-3244.

5. *Bacon's Publicity Services.* For an entrepreneur, a disproportionate amount of questions are generated that can be answered by print and broadcast media. One of the better original sources of these directories and services (they also do clippings) is the Bacon Publicity Checker. All the 1989 editions are $155 each, and they are listed below.

A. Publicity Checker
B. Media Alerts Directory
C. Radio & TV

Purchase from R. H. Bacon & Co., 332 S. Michigan Ave., Chicago, IL 60604; (312) 922-2400 or 1-800-621-0561.

Appendix III

SAMPLE APPLICATION FOR A BUSINESS PLAN LOAN

CHEMICALBANK
New York, New York

Application for Business Plan Loan

Note: All stockholders, officers, or partners (herein referred to as "Principal(s)") must complete the Personal History Section on page 2. If additional space is necessary, use a separate sheet of paper. This application must be accompanied by full and complete financial statements, satisfactory to the Bank, as to the applicant firm and each individual principal.

The undersigned hereby make application for a loan of $ _____ Net _____ repayable in _____ Number of _____ monthly instalments beginning _____ Date _____

(Please indicate preference) ☐ ONE MONTH FROM DATE OF LOAN ☐ ON THE FOLLOWING DATE _____

Purpose of Loan

PURCHASE OF	(Describe Item and Cost)
PROPERTY IMPROVEMENT	(Describe Improvement)
	(Describe Location of Property) At
OTHER	(Describe Exact Use of Loan Proceeds)

Business Record   Please check One: ☐ Proprietorship ☐ Partnership ☐ Corporation

Name of Business	Kind of Business	Year Established
Business Address (No. & Street, City, State)	Zip Code	Telephone Number

Has this business ever applied for a loan or borrowed from this Bank? ☐ Yes ☐ No	Name of Business Bank and Address	Account Number
Name & Address of Landlord	Lease Expiration Date	Annual Rent

Name of Partners', Officers or Stockholders (Principals)	Title	No. of Shares Owned	Percentage Owned
1.			
2.			
3.			
4.			

The undersigned (applicant and each individual principal) represents, warrants, and affirms that the statements made in this application and accompanying financial statements are true and correct and have been made to induce you to grant a loan to the undersigned with knowledge that you will rely thereon. For the same purpose, the undersigned affirms, represents, and warrants that undersigned is not obligated to any bank, loan company, corporation or individual, and that no suits, judgments or legal claims of any kind whatsoever are now pending against undersigned, except as stated in the financial statements.

The undersigned (applicant and each individual principal) agrees that you may exchange credit information about the undersigned with others. You may request a credit report on the undersigned and if the undersigned asks you will tell the undersigned the name and address of the consumer reporting agency that furnished it. If you update, renew, or extend the loan, you may request a new credit report without telling the undersigned.

You are authorized to deduct from the proceeds of the loan, at your option, any monies which may be owing to you by the undersigned and to remit the balance to the undersigned by ordinary mail by your official check, the responsibility for receipt of which is assumed by the undersigned. If this application is not approved, the undersigned authorizes you to return the note by ordinary mail at the risk of the undersigned, but you may retain this application for your records.

	By _____		
(Name of Applicant)		(Title, if any)	Date
Signatures verified by _____	By _____	(Title, if any)	Date
Means of verification _____	By _____	(Title, if any)	Date
	By _____	(Title, if any)	Date

03 2061* (4-79)   Principals: Kindly complete the personal history on the reverse side of this form.   Page 1

Sample Application for a Business Plan Loan

Sample Application for a Business Plan Loan (*cont.*)

Principals   Unless this is an application for individual, unsecured credit, please indicate your marital status.

Print Full Name (List on Page 3 all other names in which you have applied for or been granted credit)			Date of Birth	Marital Status ☐ Married ☐ Unmarried ☐ Separated
Home Address	City	State	Zip Code	☐ Own this Dwelling ☐ Rent this Dwelling
Home Phone No.	Social Security No.	Your Position		Yearly Income from applicant firm $
Previous Home Address	City	State		Have you ever applied for a loan or been a borrower or co-maker or guarantor with this Bank? ☐ Yes ☐ No

IMPORTANT: Income from alimony, child support or separate maintenance payments, need not be revealed if you do not choose to disclose such income and do not wish the Bank to consider it in its credit decisions.

Describe all sources of income, other than wages, including without limitation, interest, dividends, alimony, child support or separate maintenance payments, annuities, pensions and royalties. *Attach additional sheet if necessary.*	Annual Other Income *(Describe below or Page 3.)* $

Source of Other Income — Name and Address of Firm (If from a business)							
Personal Checking Acct:	Name of Bank	Branch	A/C Number	Savings Account:	Name of Bank	Branch	A/C Number

Principals   Unless this is an application for individual, unsecured credit, please indicate your marital status.

Print Full Name (List on Page 3 all other names in which you have applied for or been granted credit)			Date of Birth	Marital Status ☐ Married ☐ Unmarried ☐ Separated
Home Address	City	State	Zip Code	☐ Own this Dwelling ☐ Rent this Dwelling
Home Phone No.	Social Security No.	Your Position		Yearly Income from applicant firm $
Previous Home Address	City	State		Have you ever applied for a loan or been a borrower or co-maker or guarantor with this Bank? ☐ Yes ☐ No

IMPORTANT: Income from alimony, child support or separate maintenance payments, need not be revealed if you do not choose to disclose such income and do not wish the Bank to consider it in its credit decisions.

Describe all sources of income, other than wages, including without limitation, interest, dividends, alimony, child support or separate maintenance payments, annuities, pensions and royalties. *Attach additional sheet if necessary.*	Annual Other Income *(Describe below or Page 3.)* $

Source of Other Income — Name and Address of Firm (If from a business)							
Personal Checking Acct:	Name of Bank	Branch	A/C Number	Savings Account:	Name of Bank	Branch	A/C Number

Principals   Unless this is an application for individual, unsecured credit, please indicate your marital status.

Print Full Name (List on Page 3 all other names in which you have applied for or been granted credit)			Date of Birth	Marital Status ☐ Married ☐ Unmarried ☐ Separated
Home Address	City	State	Zip Code	☐ Own this Dwelling ☐ Rent this Dwelling
Home Phone No.	Social Security No.	Your Position		Yearly Income from applicant firm $
Previous Home Address	City	State		Have you ever applied for a loan or been a borrower or co-maker or guarantor with this Bank? ☐ Yes ☐ No

IMPORTANT: Income from alimony, child support or separate maintenance payments, need not be revealed if you do not choose to disclose such income and do not wish the Bank to consider it in its credit decisions.

Describe all sources of income, other than wages, including without limitation, interest, dividends, alimony, child support or separate maintenance payments, annuities, pensions and royalties. *Attach additional sheet if necessary.*	Annual Other Income *(Describe below or Page 3.)* $

Source of Other Income — Name and Address of Firm (If from a business)							
Personal Checking Acct:	Name of Bank	Branch	A/C Number	Savings Account:	Name of Bank	Branch	A/C Number

Principals   Unless this is an application for individual, unsecured credit, please indicate your marital status.

Print Full Name (List on Page 3 all other names in which you have applied for or been granted credit)			Date of Birth	Marital Status ☐ Married ☐ Unmarried ☐ Separated
Home Address	City	State	Zip Code	☐ Own this Dwelling ☐ Rent this Dwelling
Home Phone No.	Social Security No.	Your Position		Yearly Income from applicant firm $
Previous Home Address	City	State		Have you ever applied for a loan or been a borrower or co-maker or guarantor with this Bank? ☐ Yes ☐ No

IMPORTANT: Income from alimony, child support or separate maintenance payments, need not be revealed if you do not choose to disclose such income and do not wish the Bank to consider it in its credit decisions.

Describe all sources of income, other than wages, including without limitation, interest, dividends, alimony, child support or separate maintenance payments, annuities, pensions and royalties. *Attach additional sheet if necessary.*	Annual Other Income *(Describe below or Page 3.)* $

Source of Other Income — Name and Address of Firm (If from a business)							
Personal Checking Acct:	Name of Bank	Branch	A/C Number	Savings Account:	Name of Bank	Branch	A/C Number

Page 2

Sample Application for a Business Plan Loan (*cont.*)

Automatic Charge Authorization

If you have a checking account at Chemical you may prefer having the monthly payments on your loan charged to your account. If so, please complete the following authorization.

Checking Account Title

Account Number

This is your authorization to charge the above checking account each month for payments becoming due on this loan until further written notice, or until paid. I understand this will be done automatically without further notice to me.

Authorized Signature _____ Date _____

Title _____

Authorized Signature _____ Date _____

Title _____

Additional Space

_____
_____
_____
_____
_____
_____
_____
_____
_____
_____
_____
_____
_____
_____
_____
_____
_____
_____

Comments: (For Bank Use Only) _____
_____
_____
_____
_____
_____

Page 3

149

Sample Application for a Business Plan Loan (*cont.*)

For Bank Use Only

Loan Amount	Term	First Payment Due	Interest Rate	Date Discounted

Collateral:

Remarks:

Source of Business

Loan Documentation

Req.	Name of Document	In File	Following	Date Expected	Req.	Name of Document	In File	Following	Date Expected
	Security Agreement					Real Estate Mortgage			
	U.C.C. Filing N.Y. State					Assignment of Mortgage			
	U.C.C. Filing County					Assignment of Lease			
	MV 900 Not of Lien					Landlords Consent			
	Schedule A					Note			
	Corporate Resolution					Ins. Coverage Loss Payee			
	Corporate G/A/L					Invoices			
	Personal G/A/L or Endorsers					Disb. Auth.			
	Sub								
	Sub.								

_____ Negotiated By _____   _____ Approved By _____   _____ Closed By _____

Face Amount	$
Life Insurance Premium	
A & H Premium	
Appraisal Fee	
Inv. & Filing Fee	
Finance Charge	
Net Proceeds	
Deduct SBL No.	
Other	
Disbursed (Auth.)	
Net Proceeds	$

Type of Loan ☐ Secured ☐ Unsecured   APR _____

Deduct Balance on _____

Loan Class: ☐

Special Instructions:

Approved By:

_____ Mos. _____ Per Mo.

Last Pmt. _____ Pmts. Starting _____

Page 4

Appendix IV

SAMPLE BUSINESS PLAN

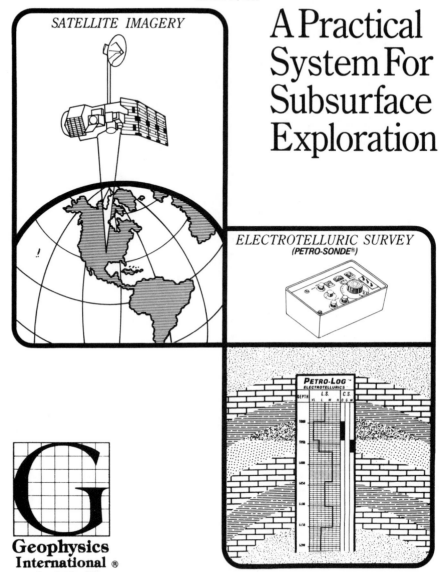

SATELLITE IMAGERY

ELECTROTELLURIC SURVEY
(PETRO-SONDE®)

A Practical System For Subsurface Exploration

Geophysics International ®

The Leader in Advanced Exploration Technologies™

Sample Business Plan

152

Satellite Imagery and
the **_PETRO-SONDE_** offer fast,
cost-effective data for use in
a variety of exploration
applications, including:
- Oil and Gas
- Coal
- Minerals
- Hydrology
- Civil Engineering
- Environmental Studies
- Archaeological Exploration

GEOPHYSICS INTERNATIONAL CORPORATION
FIVE YEAR BUSINESS PLAN
MARCH 31, 1988

"Find the best products,
hire the best people and
foster teamwork."
Jerome J. Conser - Founder

CONFIDENTIAL MEMORANDUM

Number_____

Issued to_____

EVOLUTION OF GEOPHYSICS INTERNATIONAL

"THE LEADER IN ADVANCED EXPLORATION TECHNOLOGIES"

1984 - invention of Petro-Sonde technology
- data presented in numerical format
- clientele mainly small independent operators
- initial application of Petro-Sonde is oil content identification

1985 - Petro-Log developed to format data
- first five year business plan
- Petro-Sonde for coal and minerals developed
- in-house geology staff assembled
- several mid-size companies added as clients
- Petro-Sonde modified for various weather and surface conditions
- emphasis placed on subsurface mapping with the Petro-Sonde
  (lithologic contacts, structure and stratigraphy)
- first coal contracts
- several long term contracts (50 days) in coal, oil, and gas
- selected for void detection contract, U.S. Office of Surface Mining

1986 - Satellite Imagery Analysis division formed
- first international contracts completed/China
- diversification into other industries (hydrology, engineering, archaeology,
  non-metallic minerals)
- emphasis on data quality control (data integrated with clients prospect)
- articles published in various magazines about Petro-Sonde
- contracts completed with majors (5 Oil & Gas, 6 Coal)
- seasoned and efficient staff expanded
- first offshore instrument tested

1987 - twenty-eight patents awarded and issued, U.S. Patent Office
- patents awarded and issued, Canadian Patent Office
- Australia - Oil, Gas, and Coal contracts
- Guatemala (Archaeology contract)
- additional contracts with several more major Oil & Gas and Coal companies
- U.S. government contracts (Engineering and Hydrology)
- offshore Research and Development (lakes, swamps, ocean)
- first "major" oil field discovery utilizing both Petro-Sonde and Satellite
  Imagery Analysis
- Canada - Oil and Gas Contracts
- second five year business plan

1988 - commence leasing Petro-Sonde units
- second five year business plan

TABLE OF CONTENTS

LIST OF FIGURES AND TABLES

EXECUTIVE SUMMARY

Geophysics International Corporation is revolutionizing the underground resource industries worldwide. Incorporated in February 1984, the company initially provided its services to the oil and gas industry. While the first four years' financial statements are impressive, showing gross revenues of $6,627,565, and a small profit, the next five years shall begin the real "harvest" of our efforts. Annual profits are projected to exceed the $6 million mark in 1993.

The focus of the company is a geophysical tool called the "Petro-Sonde." The tool's capabilities are tantamount to x-ray vision for the exploration of underground resources. The inventors of the tool, Dr. Carl L. Kober of Austria, and H. David Proctor-Gregg of England, combined ninety-plus years in their respective disciplines of geophysics and electronics to develop the technology of electrotellurics into a practical and multi-faceted approach. The state-of-the-art electronic hardware has been reduced to a field-portable, one-man-operated module that identifies, delineates, and quantifies subsurface elements.

Historically, underground resource industries have been forced to actually drill holes to the target depth and "hope" for discoveries of oil, gas, water, or minerals. The Petro-Sonde greatly reduces the risk, expense, danger, and impact to the environment associated with drilling programs. Savings in ratios of thousands to one can be achieved, particularly in oil, gas, and mining.

Other areas presently include: exploration for water and tracing the spread of underground contaminants affecting water supplies; and void detection. The latter has led to work contracts with the U.S. government and private industry.

Reception by underground resource industries has been gratifying and we have penetrated not only the U.S. markets but also China, Canada, and Australia.

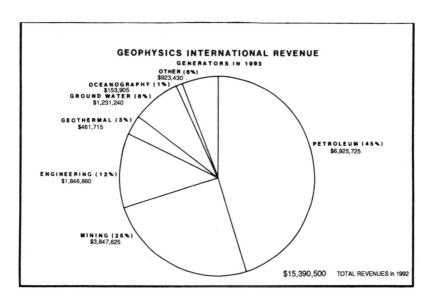

GEOPHYSICS INTERNATIONAL REVENUE
GENERATORS IN 1993

OTHER (6%)
$923,430

OCEANOGRAPHY (1%)
$153,905

GROUND WATER (8%)
$1,231,240

GEOTHERMAL (3%)
$461,715

ENGINEERING (12%)
$1,846,860

MINING (25%)
$3,847,625

PETROLEUM (45%)
$6,925,725

$15,390,500   TOTAL REVENUES in 1992

The Petro-Sonde was awarded twenty-eight patents for seventeen years by both the U.S. and Canadian patent offices in 1987. While competition can be expected, our established market presence combined with our lead time to develop both staff and applications of this technology secures our future position as the leader in this field. In addition, the purchase of patent rights, along with lifetime consulting and non-compete agreements with the inventors, enhances our strategic advantage.

Though we recognize no direct competition at this time, we acknowledge that there are alternatives to our technology. Seismic continues to be the most exploited of the geophysical exploration tools, but it has many limitations and is far more expensive. Radiometrics, geochemical, and airborne surveys run a distant second in both revenues and accuracy. And these techniques are subject to tough environmental regulations.

On the other hand, the Petro-Sonde can be carried by one man, operates with a twelve volt battery pack and generates no signal of its own. Like a radio, it is a passive device, utilizing naturally occurring signals that pass through the earth's surface to gather information.

To date, research and development programs have yielded significant advancements, however more needs to be done. Likewise, market penetration has been admirable, but much of the world is yet to be introduced to this technology. Additional staffing needs as well as investments in computers, fixtures and furnishings are required to accommodate the burgeoning growth. Our first Petro-Sonde leasing contract was executed in 1988 and we believe this to be the "wave of the future" in our marketing efforts.

In order to expedite this expansion, the company will issue stock, in combination with convertible debentures, in order to offer investors both a fixed position and the future option to enlarge this position. Projections indicate a return of investment within three to four years with a significant upside potential. The company is preparing to go public within three to five years and it is at that time that the major return on investment shall be realized.

Management is young, but presents enviable records of accomplishment. The founder and CEO has been self employed in the mining business for fifteen years and as an independent oil producer for twelve years. The president and chief geologist have combined more than twenty years of successful exploration experience. The vice-president has been with the company since its inception and is credited with achieving efficiency of operation. The controller brought five years of experience in running the accounting departments of multimillion dollar corporations. The corporate lawyer was responsible for bringing this technology to the attention of the founder.

We enjoy an excellent relationship with our bank and, from time to time, have borrowed working capital of up to $150,000 against receivables. Arthur Young is responsible for preparations to go public and has assisted in the preparation of this business plan.

This plan addresses the salient business points. An attached appendix presents the details and documentation.

THE MARKET

An estimate of market potential of the unique Petro-Sonde technology leads to an assessment of the world's needs in relationship to remaining resources. The assumption is that ultimately most resource exploration and development companies shall employ this technology.

In the 1985 business plan, Geophysics International targeted China, Australia and Canada as the next markets to penetrate. China has enormous potential which could pave the way for servicing other communist dominated markets. We have successfully completed four contracts for three ministries to date.

Canada provides a logical extension to the U.S. market and since the beginning of 1987 we have been active in the Alberta area.

Australia is a key market because of its infant stage of resource development and its pro-American environment. Most importantly, Australia's seasons are the opposite of the U.S., thus allowing us to position our field geologists in areas where the winter weather will not slow activity.

Within the U.S. our marketing has first targeted Texas, followed by Oklahoma and Louisiana. From this formidable base, we are now poised to develop the remaining U.S. and world markets. The following page is a partial listing of our major clients. We have had 106 clients employ us in the past twelve months.

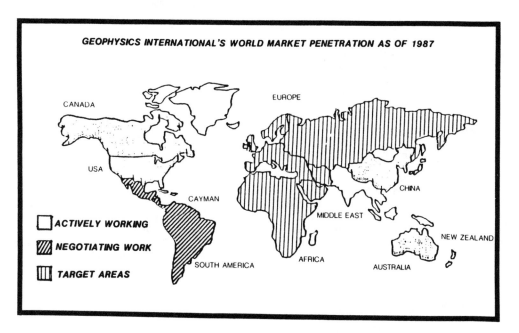

GEOPHYSICS INTERNATIONAL'S WORLD MARKET PENETRATION AS OF 1987

☐ ACTIVELY WORKING

▨ NEGOTIATING WORK

▥ TARGET AREAS

PARTIAL LISTING OF MAJOR CLIENTS

Oil & Gas Division

Chevron	Texas
Cities Service (OXY)	Texas, Louisiana, Kansas, Colorado
Phillips Petroleum Corp.	Texas
T.X.O. (USX)	Texas, Oklahoma
Sun Exploration & Production	Texas, Montana, Oklahoma
CNG Producing Company	Texas, Colorado, Oklahoma
Pennzoil Co.	Texas, New Mexico
Panhandle Eastern Pipeline	Illinois, Louisiana, Kansas, Oklahoma
Union Pacific (Champlin)	Kansas
Meridian Oil Co.	Texas
BHP (America)	Texas
Lasmo Energy	Texas, Oklahoma
Dyco Petroleum Corp.	Texas, Oklahoma
Nomeco	Mississippi, California Michigan, Louisiana, Oklahoma, Australia
Tesoro Petroleum	Texas, Mississippi
Sanguine Limited	Texas, Oklahoma
Medallion Petroleum	Wyoming, Louisiana, Kansas, Oklahoma, Colorado
Southport Exploration	Colorado, Kansas, Texas, Canada, California, Louisiana, Utah, N. Dakota, Montana, Wyoming
Jack Elam	Texas
Jay Boy Petroleum	Kansas
Hurley Petroleum	Louisiana, Arkansas, Texas
Northstar Exploration	Oklahoma
PRC Ministry of Petroleum	China

Coal & Void

Peabody Coal Company	Illinois, W. Virginia, Wyoming, Kentucky
Nomeco	Australia
Jim Walters Resources	Alabama
Utah Fuels (Coastal Corp.)	Utah
PRC Ministry of Coal	China
Goodson & Associates (O.S.M.)	Colorado, Illinois, Pennsylvania, New Mexico, Kentucky Utah

Hydrology

Morton Thiokol	Utah
Kerr McGee Corporation	Texas, Missouri
PRC Ministry of Hydrology	China

THE COMPETITION

Geophysics International is the only company in the world employing the Petro-Sonde technology, the most advanced underground exploration technology available to date. The Petro-Sonde method supplies more subsurface information than any other method or combination of methods, at any price. Yet it is one of the least expensive methods to use and there is no adverse impact to the environment.

The likelihood of Petro-Sonde technology being duplicated is remote. We recognize no present direct competition. In the face of future competition, however, we believe our aggressive research and development, our superior service, and our captive market - by virtue of being the first and therefore the most experienced - will maintain our position as the leader in this field.

We have penetrated established markets and are developing new ones. We are already working with small independent oil companies who never before considered geophysical methods because of the high costs. We are developing areas of exploration where other methods have failed (ground water and engineering studies, oil and gas exploration, and coal exploration) Other applications are archaeology, minerals, and geothermal. Geophysics International is constantly looking for new and innovative ways to apply its technology.

A thorough competitor analysis must address all geophysical service companies in order to fully explore our potential market. The following includes leading geophysical service companies and their gross revenues for the past four years as they compare to Geophysics International's first four revenue years. With gross revenues for all geophysical service companies in 1986 of $1.9 billion. We believe Geophysics International has ample room to grow.

MAJOR GEOPHYSICAL SERVICE COMPANIES

1) Geophysical Services, Inc. (G.S.I.)

	1984	1985	1986	1987
Gross Revenues:	$431,000,000	$407,000,000	$259,000,000	$240,000,000

2) Barringer Resources, Inc.

Gross Revenues:	$ 5,538,000	6,467,000	7,438,000	11,000,000

3) Tidelands Geophysical Company, Inc.

Gross Revenues:	$ 7,197,000	7,450,755	3,878,910	4,008,700

4) Digicon Geophysical Corporation

Gross Revenues:	$147,784,000	158,729,000	113,652,000	75,000,000

Geophysics International Corporation

Gross Revenues:	$ 1,515,067	1,868,865	$1,643,296	1,740,907

SATELLITE IMAGERY IN COMBINATION WITH THE PETRO-SONDE

Up until 1986, projects involving more than several hundred acres were declined because the Petro-Sonde is point specific, and it would not have been cost effective in such a large area. Only after the areas of interest are reduced to smaller blocks, can we begin the Petro-Sonde survey to confirm the presence of resources and pinpoint the very best potential well sites, mining targets, etc.

In early 1987, Geophysics International added a Satellite Imagery Analysis (Landsat) division to accommodate large scale reconnaissance projects. Already, the first discovery resulting from the combination of these two technologies is the Arapahoe Oil Field in Cheyenne County, Colorado. In this case, some four counties were reduced to thirty anomalies by the Satellite Imagery Analysis System. These were later reduced to three drillsites by the Petro-Sonde surveys. The first of these sites to be drilled came in at more than one thousand barrels per day. As of this writing there are over seventy more producers in this field, making this the largest oil field discovery in the United States during 1987. The second anomaly drilled marked the discovery of a gas field. Pipeline negotiations are ongoing.

"2 DISCOVERY, Medallion Petroleum Co., Tulsa. swabbed at a rate of more than 1000 bo/d at its 27-1 Arapahoe, SE NW 27-14n-42w. Cheyenne County, according to testimony for the state oil and gas commission. The well was put on pump in April at 230 bo/d. An eastern offset was also put on pump. The Pennsylvanian Morrow Sand was perforated from 5214-18 ft."

Source: Western Oil World, June 1987
Copyright © Hart Publications, Inc. Denver CO

With the combined technologies, Geophysics International has emerged as a complete geophysical service company.

162

Management

The owner, founder, and managing director, Jerome J. Conser, 43, has utilized a diverse background to properly staff the company and to provide industry contacts.

Trained as an instrument flight instructor in the Navy, NASA selected Mr. Conser for the "Man in Space" program which resulted in numerous commendations for his work, particularly as it related to the Apollo project.

Following his military career, Mr. Conser joined the research division of Motorola at its home office in Franklin Park, Illinois. He is credited with saving the automotive products division millions of dollars by designing and implementing a manufacturing procedure at less than half the budget assigned to the project. This procedure corrected a flaw in car tape players that reduced their return rate from more than fifty percent to less than five percent.

An interest in electronics sales led Mr. Conser to work at Engineering Agency in Chicago, an executive search firm concentrating on technologically oriented companies. Leading the seventy man agency in generated revenues his first three months, Mr. Conser was given his own agency within five months. Mr. Conser generated a profit during his first month in business, a first in the fifty-year history of the organization.

Subsequently, he accepted a full partnership in a furniture store in order to oversee its expansion. Over the next three years, two more stores were opened and then the chain was sold at a significant profit.

Mr. Conser also served as vice president of sales for an import house in San Francisco, California. There, he consummated a single sale that netted more profit than any previous year's gross of more than $1 million.

While in San Francisco Mr. Conser purchased a franchised employment agency in Phoenix, Arizona. Again Mr. Conser broke all of the old records and established new ones. Until he sold this agency in 1971, in order to go into the mining business, it had consistently led forty-plus franchises in both gross and net revenues.

In 1973, Mr. Conser's mining company, Jaries International, became the only company in Arizona to be granted the right to sell stock in a gold mine.

Mr. Conser moved to Dallas, Texas to incorporate Conser Petroleum Corporation whose first dry hole was followed by a string of producers. By age thirty two, Mr. Conser had built the company's proven oil reserves to more than 100,000 barrels.

In 1983, Mr. Conser entered negotiations with the inventors of the Petro Sonde. He believes Geophysics International to be his greatest accomplishment, not only financially, but also in terms of contributing to scientific advancement. His formula for success is simple, "Find the best products, hire the best people and foster teamwork."

Michael Birkos, President, joined Geophysics International in 1984 as a staff geologist. He holds a Bachelor of Science in Geology from Slippery Rock State College, Pennsylvania.

Upon graduation in 1975, Mr. Birkos accepted a position with Seismograph Service Corporation, of Tulsa, Oklahoma. He was promoted to Senior Surveyor, at age 22. In addition to field surveying and crew management, he was also responsible for running "point man" in front of the crew, clearing the way of all legal obstacles and securing necessary permits from state and local government officials, and land owners for the crew to run the seismic surveys.

In October of 1977, he moved to Dallas, where he served as a geologist in the Source Bed Evaluation department with Core Lab. One of his most significant accomplishments was to set up and run the "Rock-Eval" instrument, a new, state-of-the-art pyrolisis technique. The preliminary results were so impressive that Core Lab was able to begin generating revenues with the equipment within four weeks of purchase.

Mr. Birkos led his department's first foreign ventures in South America and North Africa. As a result of his efforts, the governments of Algeria and Ecuador discovered hydrocarbon reserves in unsuspected basins by using the new hydrocarbon recognition techniques offered by Core Lab.

He joined Southern Union Exploration Company in 1980. He headed the land department and his reputation as an "idea man" began to grow.

A year later, Mr. Birkos was offered a job as an exploration geologist at Triton Oil & Gas Corporation. Within a month of joining Triton Mr. Birkos accounted for approximately 90% of all exploration projects generated by the in-house geology staff of eight.

In the spring of 1983, Mr. Birkos went out on his own, assembling, selling, and drilling 14 projects in the next 12 months. Three were oil producers, and another eight were "geologic successes" - that is the reservoir came in according to projections, but there wasn't enough oil in them to make the well commercially productive.

At Geophysics International, Mr. Birkos works closely with the owner and the technical staff developing the interpretation techniques and the best application of the Petro-Sonde. His diversified background in subsurface exploration has contributed to the design of the marketing program.

In August, 1986 he was promoted to executive vice president and in 1987 he became president. Since then he has been responsible for:

Overall quality control of electrotelluric data, satellite imagery interpretation, and technical writing;

Marketing supervision and advertising;

Technical staff training;

Contract negotiations, both foreign and domestic;

Strategic planning and the coordination of expansion;

Structuring individual career development programs with technical staff members; and

Supervising research into new electrotelluric applications.

His accomplishments as a team member in special task forces, include the structuring of the company's marketing program, the writing of Geophysics International's client manual for electrotelluric/satellite imagery applications, the preparation of several papers on electrotelluric applications published in various technical journals, and the development of in-house case histories of electrotelluric applications for promotional purposes. In August 1986, he assisted in providing documentation to the U.S. Patent Office that all claims regarding the Petro-Sonde's capabilities as stated in the patent application were true.

Steven W. Dickson, Vice President, received a Bachelor of Science degree in professional geology from Stephen F. Austin State University. Mr. Dickson joined the company in March, 1984 as a Field Geologist. After becoming proficient at operating the Petro-Sonde, he spent the next six months as Training Director. Promotion to Manager of Field Operations in January 1985 and Vice-President in February 1986 reflect his abilities in organization, problem solving and people skills.

He is currently responsible for the interfacing among the in-house staff geologists (sales), field geologists (logistics and scheduling), and clients. Charged with the allocation of resources and personnel, he also oversees the day-to-day operation of the company, contract negotiations, accounting, data processing, administration, operational performance, revenue projection, and security.

Among Mr. Dickson's significant contributions to the company were assisting the inventors in development of the initial production model, the expansion into the Coal Division, and the negotiation of the largest U.S. oil and gas contract to date. He also established an Operations Department and produced an annual report regarding company wide performance and projections.

J. Davis Curlis, Manager of the Satellite Imagery Analysis Lab, has a Master's Degree in Geology with an emphasis in Remote Sensing. His background in this field includes research positions with the Kansas Geological Survey and the Center for Research, Remote Sensing Lab where he worked with a NASA sponsored team investigating the results of his first experimental mission of the Space Shuttle Imaging Radar. During his time there, he also developed and implemented a series of computer programs for digitizing and plotting coal thickness data, and implemented programs for estimating state-wide coal reserves.

More specifically, in the area of Satellite exploration, Mr. Curlis was a principal or associate investigator in more than 40 proprietary studies utilizing remotely sensed data for oil and gas exploration. He evaluated existing image processing software and assisted in implementing a variety of significant improvements. He also developed new processing techniques for image enhancement and presented his results at an international conference on Remote Sensing.

He joined Geophysics International in November 1986 as manager of the Remote Sensing division. His initial responsibilities were to become proficient in the processing techniques and operation of the analog equipment acquired first and to investigate the availability and cost of obtaining a digital image processing system. A digital system was acquired in early 1987 and is presently functional.

His duties include acquiring and processing Landsat and other types of satellite data, image analysis and interpretations, demonstrations of Geophysics International's Satellite Imagery Analysis capabilities to prospective clients, continual development and debugging of a prototype image processing computer, and technical support for all other Geophysics International staff.

His accomplishments are the set-up and operation of a new division within the company which included acquisition, development, and integration of a state of the art digital image processing system to complement the existing analog system. The digital system can provide all of the routine image enhancement operations plus some very unique image display processes, much more efficiently and cost effectively than systems commonly used only a few years ago. In addition, he has made numerous presentations on the applications of remote sensing and Geophysics International's capabilities to prospective clients, and continues to perform the analysis and interpretation of imagery for existing clients' project areas.

Gary Jackson, Controller, served for twelve years in the U.S. Army Security Agency as a Chinese Mandarin Linguist. After getting out of the army in August of 1979, he attended the University of Texas at Austin where he received a BBA degree in accounting in May, 1982. After graduation he went to work for a general contractor/developer/property management company in Brownsville, Texas where he served as Assistant Controller in charge of all construction accounting activities, payroll, and data processing until December, 1986. During his employment that company grew from $3 million volume level to more than $70 million.

Since joining the firm, he has implemented systems and procedures to maintain all records in accordance with generally accepted accounting procedures. He has also set up budgets and reporting systems enabling the company to make long range financial plans.

His responsibilities include cash planning and management, providing all financial reports, supervising accounts payable and receivable, payroll and supervision of a data processing assistant.

Guiding all of these employees is our Advisory Committee. We are fortunate to have such a diverse and experienced group of individuals.

John Spinuzzi, 58, has been a practicing attorney in Dallas, Texas for 23 years. He graduated from the University of Texas in 1960, and spent four years practicing securities law before obtaining his own practice.

Associated with the founder for more than ten years, Mr. Spinuzzi initiated the contact between him and the inventors of the Petro-Sonde, which resulted in the purchase of the exclusive worldwide marketing rights and patents. For this, and for continuing legal advice, Mr. Spinuzzi and his secretary, received five percent and one percent, respectively, of Geophysics International stock.

Richard L. Black, 62, holds a BBA degree from the University of Texas at Austin. He is a CPA and has been in public practice for ten years. Prior to that time he was a financial officer for several independent oil and gas producers for approximately 25 years. He has been Mr. Conser's CPA for more than five years and has functioned as the CPA for Geophysics International since its formation.

Dr. Jack G. Elam, 66, holds a PHD in geology from Rensselaer Polytechnic Institute and assisted in founding the University of Texas - Permian Basin Graduate School. Mr. Elam, an oil producer and geologist, was one of the company's first clients and supporters. Mr. Elam has contributed immensely in the form of feedback from the field regarding both the operation of the Petro-Sonde as well as the interpretation of its data. His reputation and contacts in the industry are major assets.

In February 1985, Mr. Elam purchased a $100,000 stock option in Geophysics International which he continues to hold.

Art Thompson, 64, holds a Chemical Engineering degree from V.T.I. and an Associate in Arts degree from William and Mary University in Virginia. Mr. Thompson has been involved in various mining projects with the founder for the past fifteen years. He offers the company an extensive executive background in addition to his experience in mining and oil and gas.

Bank

Geophysics International banks at Premier Bank, Dallas, Texas. Loan balances are presently at zero and we enjoy an excellent relationship. William (Bill) Davis, Vice President, Commercial Loans, is our officer and has helped guide the founder in properly funding and managing the company.

FINANCIAL HISTORY AND PROJECTIONS

"When there's hay in the hayloft, everyone
will get his share. Meanwhile . . . . "
Conrad Schlumberger in company memo-circa 1930

GEOPHYSICS INTERNATIONAL CORPORATION
COMPARATIVE BALANCE SHEETS
AS OF MARCH 31, 1985, 1986, 1987, 1988

	MAR 31 88	MAR 31 87	MAR 31 86	MAR 31 85
ASSETS				
Current assets				
Cash in banks	$ 16,367 $	26,757 $	28,511 $	11,499
Accounts receivable-trade	79,888	203,941	88,817	60,376
Accounts receivable-stockholder	(39,794)	58,307	3,631	54,765
Accounts receivable-other	126,147	42,820	6,010	7,785
Total current assets	182,608	331,825	126,969	134,425
Fixed assets-at cost				
Patents	913,330	744,096	521,080	274,615
Furniture & fixtures	75,445	161,146	160,824	72,484
Computerized equipment	78,435	42,744	42,744	14,437
Telephone equipment	13,088	13,088	13,088	12,000
Leasehold improvements	37,196	37,196	34,752	16,907
Automobiles & trucks	18,907	18,907	18,907	42,291
	1,136,401	1,017,177	791,395	432,734
Less accumulated depreciation	77,999	62,459	29,963	11,592
Total net assets	1,058,401	954,718	761,432	421,142
Other assets				
Deposits	6,663	14,284	3,000	3,000
Organization expense	110	110	110	110
Total other assets	6,773	14,394	3,110	3,110
TOTAL ASSETS	$ 1,247,782 $	1,300,937 $	891,511 $	558,677
LIABILITIES AND NET WORTH				
Current liabilities				
Notes payable	$ 35,530 $	160,360 $	113,074 $	43,000
Accounts payable	183,500	273,346	33,683	67,578
Payroll taxes payable	207,384	321,730	355,634	110,160
Total current liabilities	426,414	755,436	502,391	220,738
Net worth				
Common stock issued 100,000 sh.	1,000	1,000	1,000	1,000
Common stock options	100,550	103,250	103,100	100,000
Retained earnings	719,818	441,251	285,020	236,939
Total net worth	821,368	545,501	389,120	337,939
TOTAL LIABILITIES & NET WORTH	$ 1,247,782 $	1,300,937 $	891,511 $	558,677

GEOPHYSICS INTERNATIONAL CORPORATION
COMPARATIVE INCOME STATEMENTS
FOR THE FISCAL YEARS ENDED MARCH 31, 1985, 1986, 1987, & 1988

	FYE MAR 31 88	FYE MAR 31 87	FYE MAR 31 86	FYE MAR 31 85
REVENUE				
Geophysical services	$ 1,600,337	1,643,296 $	1,868,865 $	1,515,067
	----------	----------	----------	----------
COST OF SERVICES				
Sales commissions	147,264	136,168	200,883	121,480
Marketing salaries	1,750	47,720	144,875	35,159
Field operators' salaries	250,624	210,967	359,427	254,609
Sales direct expenses	89,214	36,447	48,063	81,441
Marketing direct expenses	16,855	19,795	23,750	43,890
Field operators' direct expenses	31,690	68,808	167,237	197,456
Royalties expense	4,582	6,749	6,497	474
	----------	----------	----------	----------
	541,979	526,654	950,732	734,509
	----------	----------	----------	----------
GROSS PROFITS FROM OPERATIONS	1,058,358	1,116,642	918,133	780,558
	----------	----------	----------	----------
ADMINISTRATIVE EXPENSES				
#Salaries	177,174	321,724	176,761	177,796
Advertising & promotion	9,395	6,195	42,571	49,992
*Amortization of leasehold improv	7,032	7,032	5,345	0
Auto expenses	37,946	67,538	83,979	5,938
*Depreciation	20,023	25,464	13,026	11,592
Dues & subscriptions	14,682	31,984	27,406	21,080
Employee benefits	44,225	46,226	45,508	12,606
Insurance	29,513	33,403	30,937	16,575
Interest	38,100	85,203	30,709	10,393
Legal & professional	105,050	69,768	60,449	34,574
Office supplies & expenses	51,634	65,203	67,152	46,837
Rentals	88,345	60,693	91,905	27,067
Taxes	49,717	44,418	66,448	61,165
Telephone	10,054	52,302	82,598	34,164
Travel	6,511	752	5,738	22,664
Miscellaneous	90,391	42,506	39,520	11,176
	----------	----------	----------	----------
	779,791	960,411	870,052	543,619
	----------	----------	----------	----------
NET INCOME BEFORE INCOME TAXES	$ 278,567	156,231 $	48,081 $	236,939
	==========	==========	==========	==========
*Non-cash deductions	27,055	32,496	18,371	11,592
	----------	----------	----------	----------
CASH INCOME	$ 305,623	188,727 $	66,452 $	248,531
	==========	==========	==========	==========

GEOPHYSICS INTERNATIONAL CORPORATION
COMPARATIVE CHANGES IN CAPITAL
FOR THE FISCAL YEARS ENDED MARCH 31, 1985, 1986, 1987, & 1988

	FYE MAR 31 88	FYE MAR 31 87	FYE MAR 31 86	FYE MAR 31 85
FUNDS MADE AVAILABLE				
Increase from net income	$ 278,567 $	156,231 $	48,081 $	236,939
Plus non-cash deductions	15,540	32,496	18,371	11,592
	294,108	188,727	66,452	248,531
Sale of capital stock	0	0	0	1,000
Sale of stock options	0	150	3,100	100,000
Sale of furniture and fixtures	85,701	0	0	0
Sale of automobiles & trucks	0	0	23,384	0
TOTAL FUNDS MADE AVAILABLE	$ 379,809 $	188,877 $	92,936 $	349,531
FUNDS EXPENDED				
Purchase of fixed assets:				
Patents	$ 169,234	223,016	246,465 $	274,615
Furniture & fixtures	0	322	88,340	72,484
Computerized equipment	35,691	0	28,307	14,437
Telephone equipment	0	0	1,088	12,000
Leasehold improvements	0	2,444	17,845	16,907
Automobiles & trucks	0	0	0	42,291
	204,925	225,782	382,045	432,734
Other expenditures				
Deposits	(7,621)	11,284	0	3,000
Organization expense	0	0	0	110
Repurchase of stock options	2,700	0	0	0
	(4,921)	11,284	0	3,110
Increase (decrease) in working capital	179,805	(48,189)	(289,109)	(86,313)
TOTAL FUNDS EXPENDED	$ 379,809 $	188,877 $	92,936 $	349,531

1. Petro Sonde Patent

    Denver Mineral Exploration Incorporated holds 28 patents issued in August 1987 for the
    Petro-sonde instruments used and the technology marketed by Geophysics International.
    Geophysics International pays Demex 10% of gross income per month for the purhcase
    of the patent rights. To date Geophysics International has paid $913,330
    of the $10.8 million purchase price. Geophysics may at any time cease to make
    payments and thus forfeit its ownership of the patents to the former owner
    without further liabilities.

2. Operators' Direct Expenses

    Standard contracts for services now require the customer to reimburse
    Geophysics for expenses incurred by field geologists as a result of performing
    the contract;ie. travel,lodging,meals. In the first three years
    these costs were often paid by Geophysics as a method to gain credibility
    and create a client base. Geophysics expects these expenses to continue
    their downward trend until they become a minor cost item.

3. Depreciation

    Depreciation and amortization are computed on the straight-line method
    over the estimated useful lives of the assets as shown below.

Autos & Trucks	5 yrs
Furniture & Fixtures	10 yrs
Leasehold Improvements	5 yrs
Office Equipment	10 yrs

4. Accounts Receivable

    Accounts Receivable balance of $167,479 at March 31, 1988 consists
    of the following:

		Trade Receivables *	
Trade Receivables *	79,888	Southport Exploration	590
Employee advances	1,700	Seagull Operating	400
Stockholder	(39,794)	Kulka & Schmidt	538
Conser Petroleum Corp.	120,158	Medallion Petroleum	800
Expense Advance	1,606	Dyco Petroleum	900
Commission Advance	3,921	Sanguine Ltd.	200
		Goodson & Associates	15,749
	167,479	Callon Petroleum	25,550
		Lotus-Stierwalt	400
		Mid-States General	2,050
		Arthur Hobbs	6,400
		Estoril Producing	14,000
		Peregrine Petroleum	3,463
		Gulf Tide Oil	3,200
		GHK Gas	5,350
		Coleman Morton	99
		Lasmo Energy	200
			79,888

GEOPHYSICS INTERNATIONAL
NOTES TO CONSOLIDATED FINANCIAL STATEMENTS
MARCH 31, 1985, 1986, 1987, AND 1988

5. Deposits
    Geophysics has on deposit with Vantage Management a sum equal
    to one month's rent as a security deposit for the lease of office spaces.

6. Accounts Payable
    Accounts Payable balance of $197,201 at March 31, 1988 consists of:

    | A/P Vendors | 180,533 |
    | Phil Goldstone | 2,967 |
    | | ------- |
    | | 183,500 |

7. Taxes Payable
    Payroll Taxes Payable at March 31, 1988 is composed of taxes, penalty,
    and interest for 1985, 1986, and 1987. A pay-out agreement has
    been made with the IRS concerning this obligation. Monthly payments
    of $6,350 are being made.

8. Notes Payable
    Notes Payable balance of $35,530 at March 31, 1988 consists of
    $35.530 in temporary loans from Psychical Research Foundation

9. Convertible Debentures/Stock Options
    100% of Geophysics stock is owned by Jerome J. Conser which is
    subject to stock options totalling 10% of the company.

173

```
EQUITY CAPITAL REQUIRED        $0              GEOPHYSICS INTERNATIONAL - EXECUTIVE SUMMARY
CREDIT LINE REQUIREMENTS  $244,654                         AT MARCH 31, 1988
NEW LONG TERM DEBT        $125,000                   FISCAL YEAR - APRIL 1 TO MARCH 31
                          -----------
   TOTAL FUNDS REQUIRED   $369,654
```

INCOME STATEMENT	F.Y. 1989		F.Y. 1990		F.Y. 1991		F.Y. 1992		F.Y. 1993	
GROSS SALES										
PETRO-SONDE	2,006,250	86.8%	3,150,000	81.4%	4,320,000	81.1%	5,850,000	78.7%	7,560,000	77.2%
SATELLITE IMAGERY	35,700	1.5%	70,200	1.8%	144,000	2.7%	288,000	3.9%	288,000	2.9%
OTHER SALES-PETRO SONDE LEASE	270,000	11.7%	648,000	16.8%	864,000	16.2%	1,296,000	17.4%	1,944,000	19.9%
TOTAL GROSS SALES	2,311,950	100.0%	3,868,200	100.0%	5,328,000	100.0%	7,434,000	100.0%	9,792,000	100.0%
COST OF GOODS SOLD										
PETRO-SONDE	402,495	17.4%	597,120	15.4%	751,108	14.1%	1,018,877	13.7%	1,308,096	13.4%
SATELLITE IMAGERY	70,694	3.1%	125,864	3.3%	171,212	3.2%	304,340	4.1%	340,923	3.5%
OTHER SALES-PETRO SONDE LEASE	8,100	0.4%	19,440	0.5%	25,920	0.5%	38,880	0.5%	58,320	0.6%
TOTAL C.O.G.S.	481,289	20.8%	742,424	19.2%	948,240	17.8%	1,362,097	18.3%	1,707,339	17.4%
GROSS PROFIT	1,830,661	79.2%	3,125,776	80.8%	4,379,760	82.2%	6,071,903	81.7%	8,084,661	82.6%
OPERATING EXPENSES										
TECHNICAL SUPPORT	37,484	1.6%	80,305	2.1%	274,079	5.1%	369,752	5.0%	453,617	4.6%
GENERAL AND ADMIN.	1,023,165	44.3%	1,353,349	35.0%	1,739,242	32.6%	2,201,297	29.6%	2,912,062	29.7%
MARKETING AND SELLING	308,298	13.3%	475,604	12.3%	652,540	12.2%	835,841	11.2%	1,136,165	11.6%
TOTAL OPERATING EXPENSES	1,368,947	59.2%	1,909,258	49.4%	2,665,861	50.0%	3,406,890	45.8%	4,501,844	46.0%
OPERATING PROFIT	461,714	20.0%	1,216,518	31.4%	1,713,899	32.2%	2,665,013	35.8%	3,582,817	36.6%
OTHER EXPENSES/(INCOME)										
DEPRECIATION - NEW FIXED ASSETS	0	0.0%	16,250	0.4%	55,000	1.0%	85,000	1.1%	125,000	1.3%
DEPRECIATION - EXISTING ASSETS	31,162	1.3%	31,800	0.8%	31,800	0.6%	31,800	0.4%	18,510	0.2%
INTEREST INCOME	0	0.0%	0	0.0%	0	0.0%	(5,376)	-0.1%	(27,948)	-0.3%
INTEREST EXPENSE - SHORT TERM	7,534	0.3%	14,751	0.4%	8,107	0.2%	0	0.0%	0	0.0%
INTEREST EXPENSE - LONG TERM	34,127	1.5%	27,285	0.7%	15,497	0.3%	4,934	0.1%	0	0.0%
NET PROFIT/(LOSS) BEFORE TAXES	388,891	16.8%	1,126,432	29.1%	1,603,495	30.1%	2,548,655	34.3%	3,467,255	35.4%
INCOME TAXES PAYABLE	26,243	1.1%	371,085	9.6%	545,188	10.2%	866,543	11.7%	1,178,867	12.0%
NET PROFIT/(LOSS) AFTER TAXES	362,648	15.7%	755,347	19.5%	1,058,306	19.9%	1,682,112	22.6%	2,288,388	23.4%

```
EQUITY CAPITAL REQUIRED        $0           GEOPHYSICS INTERNATIONAL - EXECUTIVE SUMMARY
CREDIT LINE REQUIREMENTS  $244,654                     AT MARCH 31, 1988
NEW LONG TERM DEBT        $125,000              FISCAL YEAR - APRIL 1 TO MARCH 31
                          -----------
   TOTAL FUNDS REQUIRED   $369,654
```

	F.Y. 1988		F.Y. 1989		F.Y. 1990		F.Y. 1991		F.Y. 1992	
PROJECTED BALANCE SHEET										
CURRENT ASSETS										
CASH-OPERATING ACCOUNT	25,000	1.6%	50,000	2.3%	50,000	1.6%	50,000	1.0%	50,000	0.7%
MARKETABLE SECURITIES	0	0.0%	0	0.0%	107,518	3.4%	558,966	11.4%	1,545,714	21.2%
ACCOUNTS RECEIVABLES	287,600	18.3%	335,000	15.6%	666,000	21.4%	1,239,000	25.3%	1,632,000	22.4%
OTHER C/A	6,773	0.4%	0	0.0%	0	0.0%	0	0.0%	0	0.0%
TOTAL CURRENT ASSETS	319,373	20.3%	385,000	17.9%	823,518	26.4%	1,847,966	37.8%	3,227,714	44.4%
FIXED ASSETS										
NEW P.P.+E.	0	0.0%	175,000	8.2%	275,000	8.8%	425,000	8.7%	625,000	8.6%
LESS ACCUM. DEPREC.	0	0.0%	(16,250)	-0.8%	(71,250)	-2.3%	(156,250)	-3.2%	(281,250)	-3.9%
EXISTING P.P.+E.	223,071	14.2%	223,071	10.4%	223,071	7.2%	223,071	4.6%	223,071	3.1%
LESS ACCUM. DEPREC.	(109,161)	-6.9%	(140,961)	-6.6%	(172,761)	-5.5%	(204,561)	-4.2%	(223,071)	-3.1%
TOTAL FIXED ASSETS	113,910	7.2%	240,860	11.2%	254,060	8.2%	287,260	5.9%	343,750	4.7%
PATENTS	1,140,955	72.5%	1,520,755	70.8%	2,039,155	65.4%	2,753,755	56.3%	3,704,155	50.9%
TOTAL ASSETS	1,574,238	100.0%	2,146,615	100.0%	3,116,733	100.0%	4,888,981	100.0%	7,275,619	100.0%
CURRENT LIABILITIES										
ACCOUNTS PAYABLE	57,520	3.7%	83,750	3.9%	146,520	4.7%	309,750	6.3%	408,000	5.6%
CREDIT LINE	167,641	10.6%	67,559	3.1%	0	0.0%	0	0.0%	0	0.0%
OTHER LIABILITIES	7,267	0.5%	0	0.0%	0	0.0%	0	0.0%	0	0.0%
TOTAL CURR. LIAB.	232,428	14.8%	151,309	7.0%	146,520	4.7%	309,750	6.3%	408,000	5.6%
LONG TERM DEBT										
NOTES PAYABLE	258,344	16.4%	156,494	7.3%	73,094	2.3%	0	0.0%	0	0.0%
TOTAL LONG TERM DEBT	258,344	16.4%	156,494	7.3%	73,094	2.3%	0	0.0%	0	0.0%
TOTAL LIABILITIES	490,772	31.2%	307,803	14.3%	219,614	7.0%	309,750	6.3%	408,000	5.6%
STOCKHOLDER'S EQUITY										
CAPITAL STOCK	1,000	0.1%	1,000	.0%	1,000	.0%	1,000	.0%	1,000	.0%
ADD. PAID IN CAPITAL	0	0.0%	0	0.0%	0	0.0%	0	0.0%	0	0.0%
RETAINED EARNINGS	1,082,466	68.8%	1,837,812	85.6%	2,896,119	92.9%	4,578,231	93.6%	6,866,619	94.4%
LESS TREASURY	0	0.0%	0	0.0%	0	0.0%	0	0.0%	0	0.0%
TOTAL EQUITY	1,083,466	68.8%	1,838,812	85.7%	2,897,119	93.0%	4,579,231	93.7%	6,867,619	94.4%
TOTAL EQUITY AND LIAB.	1,574,238	100.0%	2,146,615	100.0%	3,116,733	100.0%	4,888,981	100.0%	7,275,619	100.0%

```
EQUITY CAPITAL REQUIRED        $0            GEOPHYSICS INTERNATIONAL - EXECUTIVE SUMMARY
CREDIT LINE REQUIREMENTS    $244,654                    AT MARCH 31, 1988
NEW LONG TERM DEBT          $125,000              FISCAL YEAR - APRIL 1 TO MARCH 31
                            -----------
    TOTAL FUNDS REQUIRED    $369,654
```

	F.Y.	F.Y.	F.Y.	F.Y.	F.Y.
KEY FINANCIAL RATIOS	1988	1989	1990	1991	1992
CURRENT RATIO	1.37	2.54	5.62	5.97	7.91
PROFITABILITY					
RETURN ON GROSS SALES	16.8%	29.1%	30.1%	34.3%	35.4%
RETURN ON EQUITY	35.9%	61.3%	55.3%	55.7%	50.5%
TIMES INTEREST EARNED AFTER TAX	12.5	23.4	18.5	21.8	24.2
(NET INCOME/INTEREST EXPENSE)					
DEBT SERVICE COVERAGE AFTER TAX	2.1	9.5	11.6	16.1	27.7
(NET INCOME/(INTEREST EXP. + PRINCIPAL PAY.)					
DEBT/EQUITY RATIO (TO ONE)	0.45	0.17	0.08	0.07	0.06
DEBT	31%	14%	7%	6%	6%
EQUITY	69%	86%	93%	94%	94%
COMPANY VALUE					
PRICE EARNINGS MULTIPLY	10	10	10	10	10
MARKET VALUE	3,888,907	11,264,317	16,034,946	25,486,551	34,672,551
FUNDING REQUIREMENTS					
EQUITY	0	0	0	0	0
LONG TERM DEBT	125,000	0	0	0	0
CREDIT LINE					
BEGINNING BALANCE	0	167,641	67,559	0	0
DRAWS	343,646	37,313	0	0	0
REPAYMENTS	176,005	137,395	67,559	0	0
ENDING BALANCE	167,641	67,559	0	0	0

```
EQUITY CAPITAL REQUIRED        $0         GEOPHYSICS INTERNATIONAL - EXECUTIVE SUMMARY
CREDIT LINE REQUIREMENTS  $244,654                   AT MARCH 31, 1988
NEW LONG TERM DEBT        $125,000         FISCAL YEAR - APRIL 1 TO MARCH 31
                         -----------
    TOTAL FUNDS REQUIRED  $369,654
```

	F.Y.	F.Y.	F.Y.	F.Y.	F.Y.
PROJECTED SOURCES/(USES) OF CASH	1988	1989	1990	1991	1992
BEGINNING MARKETABLE SECURITIES BAL.	0	0	0	107,518	558,966
NET PROFIT OR LOSS	362,648	755,347	1,058,306	1,682,112	2,288,388
ADD BACK DEPRECIATION	31,162	48,050	86,800	116,800	143,510
CHANGES IN WORKING CAPITAL ACCOUNTS					
CURRENT ASSETS					
CASH - OPERATING ACCOUNT	(8,633)	(25,000)	0	0	0
ACCOUNTS RECEIVABLES	(121,360)	(47,400)	(331,000)	(573,000)	(393,000)
OTHER ASSETS	(227,625)	(373,027)	(518,400)	(714,600)	(950,400)
CURRENT LIABILITIES					
ACCOUNT PAYABLE	(125,983)	26,230	62,770	163,230	98,250
OTHER LIABILITIES	(16,500)	(7,267)	0	0	0
TOTAL WORKING CAPITAL CHANGES	(500,101)	(426,464)	(786,630)	(1,124,370)	(1,245,150)
FIXED ASSETS					
NEW P.P.+E.	0	(175,000)	(100,000)	(150,000)	(200,000)
MULT. STORE P.P.+E.	0	0	0	0	0
CHANGES IN LONG TERM DEBT POSITION					
NOTES PAYABLE	(61,350)	(101,850)	(83,400)	(73,094)	0
CHANGES IN STOCKHOLDER'S EQUITY					
CAPITAL STOCK	0	0	0	0	0
ADD. PAID IN CAPITAL	0	0	0	0	0
LESS TREASURY	0	0	0	0	0
CASH BALANCE BEFORE CREDIT LINE	(167,641)	100,083	175,076	558,966	1,545,714
CREDIT LINE					
BEGINNING BALANCE	0	167,641	67,559	0	0
DRAWS	343,646	37,313	0	0	0
REPAYMENTS	176,005	137,395	67,559	0	0
ENDING C/L BALANCE	167,641	67,559	0	0	0
ENDING MARKETABLE SECURITIES BALANCE	0	0	107,518	558,966	1,545,714

GEOPHYSICS INTERNATIONAL CORPORATION
FIVE YEAR BUSINESS PLAN
March 31, 1988

APPENDIX

CONFIDENTIAL MEMORANDUM

Number _____
Issued To
_____

TABLE OF CONTENTS

LIST OF FIGURES AND TABLES

PRODUCTS

"You can spend your time trying to sell something
no one wants, or you can spend your time trying
to find a product that everyone wants. I chose
the latter."

Jerome J. Conser, Founder

Products

While the final products of the company consist of professional reports
with accompanying exhibits, i.e., cross-sections, subsurface maps, satellite
images, and so forth, the story lies in the process of creating these
products.

Geophysics International Corporation is an international service firm
engaged in subsurface mapping and exploration. The methods employed include a
passive electrotelluric instrument known as the Petro-Sonde and Satellite
Imagery Analysis. The Petro-Sonde delineates depth, thickness and fluid
content of specific lithologic units from the surface and without a drill
hole. Data is presented in a format similar to conventional downhole logs.
The depth range of investigation is from the surface to 40,000 feet.

In 1986, Geophysics acquired the personnel, hardware, and software
necessary to process and interpret satellite imagery. This was done in
response to the growing trend in the subsurface resource industries
(particularly oil & gas exploration) to emphasize the discovery of "new"
reserves. Satellite imagery makes it possible to quickly and cost effectively
locate prospective areas of potential resource accumulation.

The combination of the two techniques allows detailed subsurface
analysis of potential resource distribution in areas identified with a high
potential to contain resources.

The sole use of the Petro-Sonde allows size and distribution evaluation
of known resource accumulations.

Applications exist in any field requiring subsurface information, as
shown on the table of applications in our manual of services.

Research and Development

Previous product development, i.e., coal instrument and void detection
techniques, was funded by two research and development programs, as was the
development of the first prototype offshore unit. The investors in these
research and development programs are receiving, as a royalty, a percentage
of gross revenues from the appropriate division of the company. We have been
making coal distributions since 1985, and void detection payments since 1986.
None of these royalties exceed two percent of gross revenues from their
respective divisions.

Future research and development projects, such as generating a field
hardcopy, would be greatly enhanced by an "in-house" research and development
group. While this represents a major investment for the company, the rewards
would be substantial.

Meanwhile, we continue to receive support from industry leaders. For instance, several major oil companies have offered to provide us access to their offshore drilling platforms for development of the offshore instrument. Peabody Coal has committed its "mainframe" computers to assist us in the development of the field hardcopy.

A significant portion of the investor funds now sought would be dedicated to research and development in order to maintain our position and market share as "The Leader in Advanced Exploration Technologies."

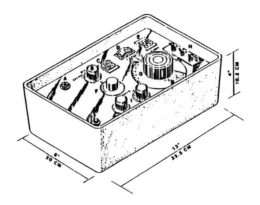

Diagram of Petro–Sonde unit. A) Charging jack,
B) On/Off/Charge switch, C) Battery on/off, D) Battery status
E) Depth x 1000 scale, F) Calibration, G) Depth vernier,
H) Weather mode control panel, I) Volume.

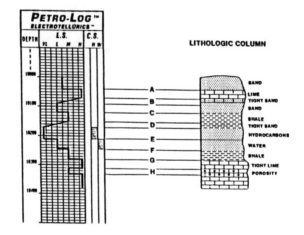

Interpretation of typical electrotelluric responses.
A,C,F,G are sharp lithologic contacts.
B, and D are gradational contacts.
E is a hydrocarbon/water contact.
H is a porosity zone.

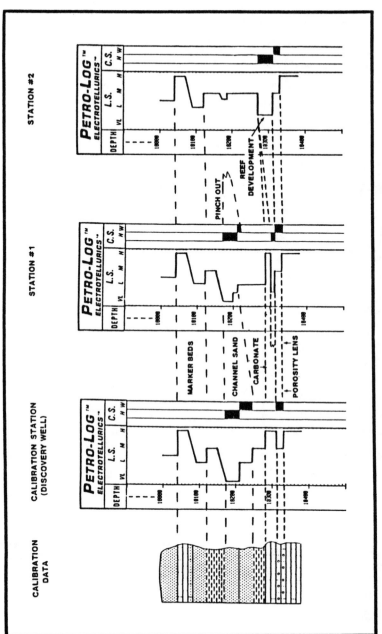

Oil and Gas division. In this idealized example, the Petro-Sonde is used to delineate lenticular reservoir distribution around a discovery well. After interpretation and correlation with available subsurface data, the lateral continuity and structural position of key formations can be inferred. In Station #1, the channel sand is thinner, and the carbonate porosity lens is thicker with an apparent hydrocarbon/water contact. In Station #2, the channel sand is gone. However, there appears to be considerable reef development. A grid survey can establish lateral limits of potential reservoirs and optimize drill site selection. Local case histories with the electrotelluric response of specific formations with subsequent drilling results are available on request.

185

A

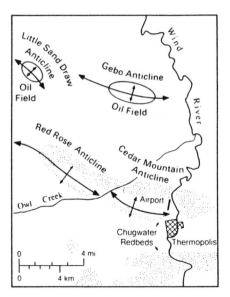

B

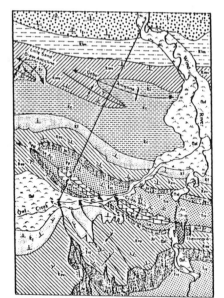

C

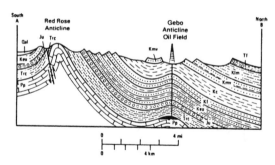

D

Thermopolis Area, Wyoming
A. Landsat Image (Band 7) showing surface structure features. B. General geologic interpretation. C. Detailed geologic interpretation after field work. D. Cross section showing subsurface configuration of two anticlines visible on Landsat image, and the structure of the Gebo Oil Field.

186

Future Product Development

As stated earlier, there seems to be virtually no limitations on applications, making this a most exciting and dynamic product. While "outer-space" appears to be the final frontier, several refinements should be accomplished prior to venturing beyond earth.

Among these enhancements would be, the improvement of the Petro-Sonde's ability to read permeability, which is necessary to oil and gas production. A secondary refinement would involve the degree to which the tool differentiates "live" oil from "dead" oil. The differences are often between a gusher and a dry hole.

Perhaps of greatest importance is the achievement of electronically produced hardcopy logs in the field. Only research and development capital can make this goal a reality. As this program affects all of our markets, we give it our highest priority. We would then be able to also perform airborn and mobile ground surveys.

Following this progression would be the final development of the offshore unit. Ideally, these projects would reach fruition by late 1989.

SUPPORTING DATA FOR
MARKETING AND SALES

Major Market Analysis

1986 was an excellent time to diversify beyond hydrocarbons. Applications were found for the Petro-Sonde in many areas. The first was civil engineering, performing bedrock detection and building foundation analysis to prevent and/or repair sinkhole related damages to buildings and structures in Florida. Our first contract involved Allstate Insurance Company.

Another project evaluated the extent of petrochemical contamination around buried fuel tanks, dump sites, and burn pits while mapping the extent and structural configuration of aquifers and indications of contamination within them. The Environmental Protection Agency is aware of our capabilities. A feasibility study conducted in August 1987 on a creosote contamination site in Missouri was attended by E.P.A. officials. That project's success led to additional contracts.

As the learning curve of the Petro-Sonde operators degreed geologists progressed, it also became possible to identify lithology, i.e. sand, limestone, etc. This breakthrough led to an interest in utilizing the tool for locating and delineating ore deposits. A very large coal company inspired the initial research and development in redesigning the tool for establishing coal reserves. In lieu of core drilling, the tool was utilized to determine thickness of coal seams across known coal deposits. Since this initial application, the tool was found to be useful for mine development due to its ability to trace fault systems. Utah Fuels, a subsidiary of Coastal States Oil and Gas, contracted Geophysics International to trace a fault system on a coal project in Utah. The company continues to be steady customers, as we are able to make their Longwall mining operations more economical.

The mining division has investigated several major mining properties in the Southwest to identify elements that could be detected by the existing hardware. At the same time, the goal has been to provide feedback to the inventors regarding necessary modifications in order to achieve accurate analysis. This research is ongoing.

The Geophysics International bid was selected from 104 proposals to perform void detection and evaluation for the United States Government through the Office of Surface Mining. This contract represents not only millions of dollars in revenues in the years to come, but establishes our technology as "state of the art" for this application. Actual work commenced in June 1987.

Recognizing that water is the easiest element to detect, the company has also initiated dialogue with both the water conservation and geothermal industries. Again, the reception has been encouraging. A monitoring of waterflood programs for the oil industry and a groundwater study to locate water well sites for the Julian Vinyards in California, showcases the versatility of both the Petro-Sonde and the company's service.

Geophysics International representatives were invited to the Peoples Republic of China to demonstrate the various applications of the technology. The demonstrations could only be overwhelming successes, resulting in immediate contracts with the Ministries of Coal, Petroleum, and Hydrology. We are in negotiations with the Hydrology Ministry of China for a major contract. Already they have agreed to our recent price increase to five thousand dollars per day.

A more "exotic" application of the Petro-Sonde is archaeology. It is a natural follow-up to the "void" detection work. Geophysics International conducted an impressive demonstration for the Academy of Science in Beijing in April 1986 and was later hired to conduct a survey for Mayan Tombs in the Yucatan Peninsula in March 1987.

In January 1987, the Petro-Sonde was applied for the first time in Australia and New Zealand. Three hydrocarbon projects and one coal project were evaluated. Geophysics International has been working in Australia ever since under agreement with NOMECO acting as our marketing agents. NOMECO is a U.S. client with major holdings in Australia. They are a wholly owned subsidiary of a Michigan utility company.

In March 1987, Albercan Corporation of Alberta Canada, began marketing our services throughout Canada. We are presently active in the Alberta area and are being very well received throughout the country.

In combination with other geophysical exploration technologies, the Petro-Sonde becomes a complimentary tool behind seismic, geo-chemical, Satellite Imagery, magnetotellurics, radiometrics, and other methods. We believe the consensus approach to finding underground resources is the most prudent.

Although competition will emerge eventually, we see this as a positive influence. Historically, competition has expedited market growth. We believe Geophysics International will be in the forefront of this expansion.

Oil and Gas

The major portion of Geophysics International's income is derived from the energy industry. Any significant change affecting the energy industry affects the company. But Geophysics International finds itself with the strategical advantage of being virtually unaffected by an industry downturn because of its unique service. When exploration industry profit margins are reduced because of lower prices for natural resources, it will actively seek alternative and less costly exploration methods. When exploration budgets are slashed, exploration managers quickly find alternatives to reducing the total areas they plan to explore. Geophysics International in the case of the petroleum industry greatly reduces the number of dry holes being drilled. And we do it more cost effectively than any other exploration method.

Energy Outlook – Energy stocks will show the smallest decline since 1977 – at 1.3 percent. Real GNP growth during 1986–87 will total 10.3 percent. The decline in energy use per dollar of GNP will amount to 2.8 percent and energy use will be up 7.2 percent.

Oil and Gas – Oil and gas will continue to be the swing fuels for heavy industry and utilities.

The Department of Energy's Energy Information Administration has maintained the stance: "Large oil discoveries will be required to replace declining production from old fields if current U.S. oil production is to be maintained." The agency's analysis showed that a little more than 1,600 large fields covered by its study accounted for 75 percent of 3.16 billion barrels produced in 1986. It took 15,000 new fields to make up the other 25 percent. Old fields had production decline at a rate of 3.1 percent per year during 1985–86.

According to Salomon Brothers, the nation's largest energy companies replaced only 41 percent of their oil reserves, and 48 percent of their gas reserves in 1986. This was the worst one year replacement rate in the last decade. It is certainly related to the 47 percent drop in exploration expenditures in 1986 down to $15.5 billion. However, prior to 1986, new reserves were being replaced not by discovery, but by secondary recovery techniques in existing fields. These techniques represent an expensive and only a short term solution.

If production from old fields continues to decline on an average of 3 percent per year, replacement oil required to maintain the 1986 level will amount to 210 million barrels in 1987, 518 million bbl in 1990, and 783 million bbl in 1995. It has been estimated that if the decline rate reverts back to its normal 6 percent figure then the numbers would be 389 million, 900 million and 1.278 billion respectively. The number of marginal producers plugged during 1986 will further exacerbate this problem. The long term exploration market looks extremely promising.

The "Oil & Gas Journal" forecasts the following for the U.S. in 1987:

- Demand for petroleum products at 16.37 million barrels per day, up .5 percent from 16.281 million barrels per day in 1986.
- 37,508 wells completed down 4.9 percent from 39,423 in 1986.
- Active rigs averaging 920, down 4.6 percent from 964 in 1986.
- Production of crude oil and condensate - 8.36 million barrels per day down 3.7 percent from 1986 and down 6.8 percent from 1985.
- Imports up 3.3 percent from 1986 averaging 6.38 million barrels per day.
- Imports represented 31.5 percent of demand in 1985, in 1987 the share will be 39 percent.

Increasing imports forces out marginal producers. This fact, combined with constant waste, finally translates to an "acknowledged" scarcity of supply. Prices of oil and gas will enter a never ending upward spiral, triggering the greatest exploration effort in the history of the world. We see this scenario beginning now and culminating into widespread panic within five years.

Electric Utilities of North America are large consumers of energy resources and therefore good indicators for future energy consumption trends.

U.S. Electric Utility Fuels Consumption, 1980-1990
(Quadrillion BTU per year)

FUELS	1980	HISTORY 1983	1985	PROJECTIONS 1990
Coal	12.1	13.2	14.4	16.5
Oil	2.6	1.5	1.4	1.6
Natural Gas	3.8	3.0	3.2	3.3
Nuclear	2.7	3.2	4.2	6.3
Other	3.2	4.0	3.3	3.3
TOTAL	24.4	24.9	26.5	31.0

Consensus opinion is that the price of gas will rebound even sooner than oil. The once ballyhooed "gas bubble" is about to burst. In either case, the race is on.

"The narrowing of price differentials has changed the economics of fuel switching and slowed the rate of decline in petroleum demand. Environmental advantages may increase demand for natural gas in the future." March '87, Oil and Gas Journal.

Projected Market Value
U.S. Dollars in Thousands

Method/Market	1987	1988	1989	1990	1991	1992	Estimated % change
Seismic	2,018,776	1,889,412	1,768,337	1,655,022	1,548,967	1,449,708	-6.41%
All Electric & Magnetic	22,881	30,616	40,966	54,815	73,346	98,141	33.81%
Gravity	14,550	16,487	18,683	21,170	23,989	27,183	13.31%
	2,056,207	1,936,515	1,827,986	1,731,007	1,646,301	1,575,032	

The decline in whole market value over a five year period is projected because of an anticipated decline in seismic exploration. It is expected that a portion of the decline in spending will be picked up by other geophysical exploration methods as oil companies seek cost-effective techniques. An overall decline in exploration expenditure is anticipated until the price of oil has again risen to a level where new field exploration gives a satisfactory return in a reasonable pay back period. It is interesting to note that 97 percent of all geophysical dollars worldwide are spent on petroleum exploration and the seismic method accounts for 94 percent of all expenditures in geophysical activity. Any change in either category has a profound change on the aggregate numbers.

The projected decline in seismic dollars and relative increases in "other methods" over the next five years is because seismic alone is inadequate for ascertaining the location and distribution of potential reservoirs. Seismic structural profiles only show the probable location of a reservoir. The Petro-Sonde can determine the depth, thickness, and content of potential reservoirs directly, thus making it a very complementary tool for seismic as well as other methods.

World Oil Production
By Region 1986

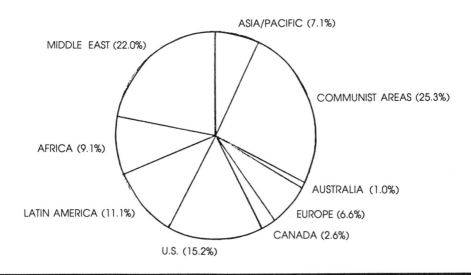

MIDDLE EAST (22.0%)

ASIA/PACIFIC (7.1%)

COMMUNIST AREAS (25.3%)

AFRICA (9.1%)

AUSTRALIA (1.0%)

LATIN AMERICA (11.1%)

EUROPE (6.6%)

CANADA (2.6%)

U.S. (15.2%)

WORLD OIL PRODUCTION BY REGION

AREAS	MILLIONS OF BBL/DAY 1986	% CHANGE	*MILLIONS OF BBL/DAY 1987	% CHANGE
Europe	3.759	+ 1.9%	3.920	+ 3.8%
Canada	1.472	− 6.1%	1.481	+ 3.1%
United States	8.668	− 3.4%	8.346	− 6.5%
Latin America	6.348	− 2.6%	5.943	− .1%
Africa	5.181	− 4.0%	4.596	− 4.3%
Middle East	12.543	+ 22.8%	11.400	− 6.7%
Asia-Pacific	4.089	+ 4.8%	3.039	− 4.9%
Communist Areas	14.464	+ 3.3%	15.531	+ 2.5%
Australia	0.542	+ 4.5%	NOT LISTED	
TOTAL	57.075		54.256	− 2.2%

* FIRST HALF OF 1987

195

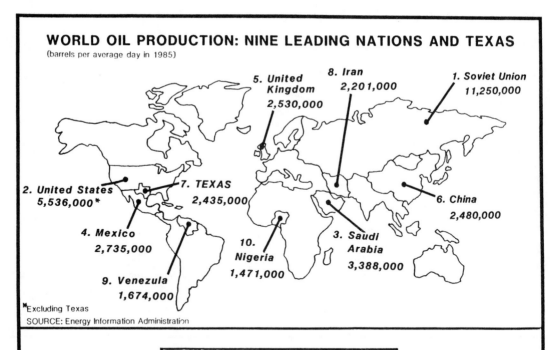

WORLD OIL PRODUCTION: NINE LEADING NATIONS AND TEXAS
(barrels per average day in 1985)

5. United Kingdom 2,530,000

8. Iran 2,201,000

1. Soviet Union 11,250,000

2. United States 5,536,000*

7. TEXAS 2,435,000

6. China 2,480,000

4. Mexico 2,735,000

10. Nigeria 1,471,000

3. Saudi Arabia 3,388,000

9. Venezuela 1,674,000

*Excluding Texas
SOURCE: Energy Information Administration

ESTIMATED WORLD PROVEN CRUDE OIL RESERVES: 19 LEADING NATIONS AND TEXAS

1.	Saudi Arabia	168.8
2.	Kuwait	89.8
3.	Soviet Union	61.0
4.	Mexico	49.3
5.	Iran	47.9
6.	Iraq	44.1
7.	Abu Dhabi	31.0
8.	Venezuela	25.6
9.	Libya	21.3
10.	United States*	20.1
11.	China	18.4
12.	Nigeria	16.6
13.	United Kingdom	13.0
14.	Norway	10.9
15.	Algeria	8.8
16.	Indonesia	8.5
17.	TEXAS	7.9
18.	Canada	6.5
19.	Oman	4.0
20.	Egypt	3.9

(as of January 1, 1986, billions of barrels)
*Excluding Texas
SOURCE: American Petroleum Institute

OFFSHORE DRILLING
===================

AREA	ACTIVE RIGS 1984	1985	PROJECTED 1986	1987
Africa	33	29	20	23
Europe	80	101	95	73
Far East	78	69	47	49
Latin America	75	81	64	45
Middle East	59	53	51	43
South Pacific	12	9	8	7
North America	210	228	107	89

Geophysics International foresees a successful entry into the offshore oil exploration market. This conclusion is based on successful research and development field tests with the Petro-Sonde offshore instrument. Offshore drilling is on the upswing worldwide as major oil companies and countries go after the remaining major oil fields. If the projection is correct that by the year 2000 about 50 percent of the oil and gas produced will come from offshore frontier areas, then the majority of the investment in exploration will go to the offshore segment of the industry. Geophysics International is well positioned to take advantage of such circumstances. The United States, the Gulf Coast, offshore California, Alaska, and the American Arctic are prime areas for exploration. The Canadian eastern coast and areas above the Arctic Circle in the Atlantic are also promising. Other high potential areas include offshore South and Central America and southwest Asia.

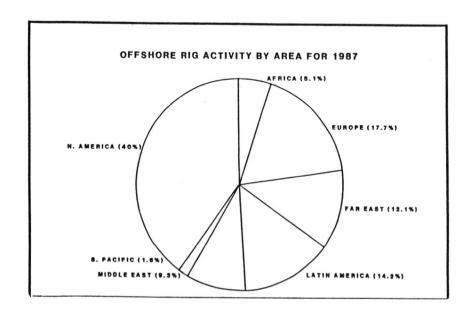

OFFSHORE RIG ACTIVITY BY AREA FOR 1987

AFRICA (5.1%)
EUROPE (17.7%)
N. AMERICA (40%)
FAR EAST (12.1%)
S. PACIFIC (1.6%)
MIDDLE EAST (9.3%)
LATIN AMERICA (14.2%)

Mining

In mining, both coal and nonmetallics, our technology reduces the need for drilling and coring to ascertain the extent and location of deposits. The same outlook appears to be true for metallic deposits, however, further research and development is necessary.

The company views coal exploration as a major source of revenue. This can be attributed to the large number of drill holes that coal companies need for ascertaining the extent of a coal field and the location of old mine workings. The Petro-Sonde will give the coal operator the same information for a fraction of the cost of cored drilling. Geophysics International is working in coal in Utah, Wyoming, Kentucky, Virginia, Texas, Ohio, Illinois, West Virginia, China, and Australia. Peabody, the largest coal company in the world, is negotiating a major worldwide contract with our coal division.

Alternative fuels, such as coal, nuclear, hydro and geothermal power, remain more economical, despite the recent closing of the gap between prices of refined coal and natural gas.

Coal demand will increase 3.2 percent this year, following a 7.8 percent increase last year. The strongest influences on coal demand are electricity demand, which is inelastic, and the prices of competing fuels such as natural gas and refined petroleum.

In summary – We see a slow but steady growth in energy demand, most likely 2-3 percent a year for the rest of the decade. This means that there will be no substantial change, in either direction, in the amount of energy being utilized on an annual basis. We anticipate a steady move away from the more expensive exploration methods as energy companies must reduce expenses.

WHOLE MARKET FORECAST
WORLD WIDE EXPENDITURE PROJECTIONS FOR GEOPHYSICAL
EXPLORATION IN MINING, U.S. $ (IN THOUSANDS).

Method/Market	1987	1988	1989	1990	1991	1992	ESTIMATED CHANGE
Seismic	6,618	6,783	6,432	6,105	5,723	5,349	-23.72%
All Electric & Magnetic	22,151	20,473	22,738	24,375	26,145	28,166	21.36%
Gravity	849	881	937	1,132	1,325	1,337	36.50%
Totals	27,618	28,137	30,107	31,612	33,193	34,852	15.02%

U.S. Coal Consumption 1986

902 Million Tons

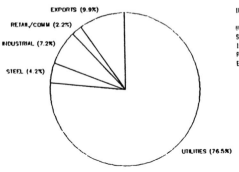

EXPORTS (9.9%)

RETAIL/COMM (2.2%)

INDUSTRIAL (7.2%)

STEEL (4.2%)

UTILITIES (76.5%)

U.S. COAL CONSUMPTION, 1986, 902 MILLION TONS

INDUSTRY	TONS (MILLIONS)	% USED
UTILITIES	690	76.5%
STEEL	38	4.21%
INDUSTRIAL	65	7.21%
RETAIL/COMM	20	2.22%
EXPORTS	89	9.87%
TOTAL	902	

THE "COAL AGE MAGAZINE" PREDICTS THE FOLLOWING FOR THE U.S. COAL INDUSTRY IN 1987

* PRODUCTION- 916.7 MILLION TONS, 3% HIGHER THAN 1986
* TOTAL U.S. CONSUMPTION- 908.3 MILLION TONS, 0.7% HIGHER THAN 1986
* EXPORTS- 84 MILLION TONS, A 5.6% DROP FROM 1986
* COAL DEMAND SHOULD BE UP BY APPROXIMATELY 40 MILLION TONS OVER 1986

1986 U.S. Coal Production

Lignite & Bituminous Combined

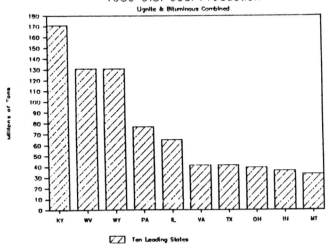

Millions of Tons

KY WV WY PA IL VA TX OH IN MT

Ten Leading States

WATER

Ground water has become a scarce resource. Geophysics International foresees a rapidly expanding effort to locate ground water resources. The company plans to be at the forefront of this effort, dominating the ground water exploration market.

==

The U.S. Water Resource Council reports the following utilization of water resources in the U.S.

- Precipitation: 4,200 billion gallons/day
- Evaporation: 2,787 billion gallons/day
- Runoff (Canada, Mexico, Ocean): 1,328 billion gallons/day.
- Input into ground water aquifer as storage: 61 billion gallons/day
- Withdrawn from aquifers for consumption: 82 billion gallons/day
- Deficit input vs. withdrawal: 21 billion gallons/day
- In 1950 the nation withdrew 12 trillion gallons of water out of the aquifers; by 1980 the figure had more than doubled
- Water table levels nationwide are dropping 6 inches to 3 feet/year
- Ground water in aquifers represents 25 percent of the nations useable water, the other 75 percent comes from rivers and lakes. The surface waters, however, are exceedingly being polluted by acid rain. This useable supply will diminish greatly over the coming years.

==

It is the combination of the ever present waste of our planetary water system, acid rain, and aquifer contamination by industry that leads us to believe our hydrology division shall ultimately become our highest revenue generator. Already, the EPA is recommending our company to industry as the most effective at assessing damage to aquifers by underground contaminants. And the scope of the activity is worldwide.

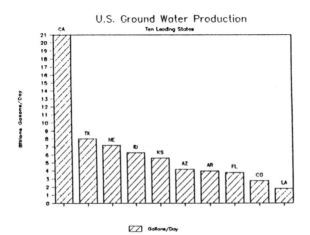

U.S. Ground Water Production

GROUND WATER PRODUCTION Ten Leading States (billions of blls. per day)	
California	21
Texas	8
Nebraska	7.2
Idaho	6.3
Kansas	5.6
Arizona	4.2
Arkansas	4
Florida	3.8
Colorado	2.8
Louisiana	1.8
TOTAL	64.7

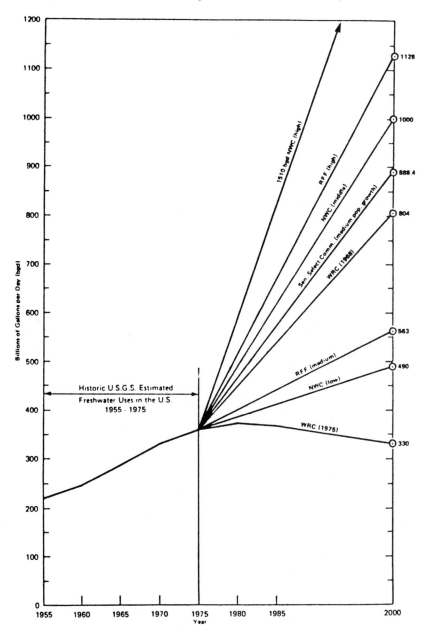

U.S. Water Resource Usage

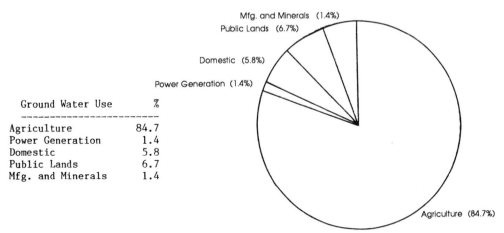

Mfg. and Minerals (1.4%)
Public Lands (6.7%)

Domestic (5.8%)

Power Generation (1.4%)

Ground Water Use	%
Agriculture	84.7
Power Generation	1.4
Domestic	5.8
Public Lands	6.7
Mfg. and Minerals	1.4

Agriculture (84.7%)

Proposed city budget would increase water rates sharply

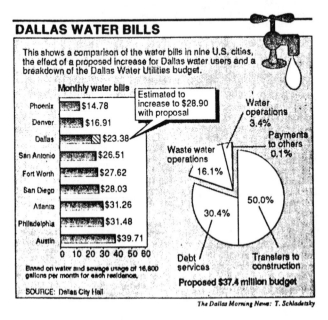

DALLAS WATER BILLS

This shows a comparison of the water bills in nine U.S. cities, the effect of a proposed increase for Dallas water users and a breakdown of the Dallas Water Utilities budget.

Monthly water bills

Phoenix	$14.78
Denver	$16.91
Dallas	$23.38
San Antonio	$26.51
Fort Worth	$27.62
San Diego	$28.03
Atlanta	$31.26
Philadelphia	$31.48
Austin	$39.71

Estimated to increase to $28.90 with proposal

0 10 20 30 40 50 60

Based on water and sewage usage of 16,800 gallons per month for each residence.

SOURCE: Dallas City Hall

Water operations 3.4%

Payments to others 0.1%

Waste water operations 16.1%

50.0%

30.4%

Debt services

Transfers to construction

Proposed $37.4 million budget

The Dallas Morning News: T. Schladetsky

202

Other Markets and Services

There are a number of other markets, all of which shall ultimately be developed. However, in our first three years we have performed work in the field of archaeology, locating buried tombs. We have served the engineering field with Dam Site and Sink Hole evaluation. One of the more exotic applications of our service to date was a search for chambers in tombs in China. Monitoring water flood programs for the oil and gas industry, detecting "bed rock" for the construction industry, and tracing contaminants in underground aquifers are also viable markets. Quantifying the size of these markets would be virtually impossible, however, they do represent a significant component of future revenues not addressed in our revenue forecast.

Our publication of geologic studies based on our technologies represents significant potential income. Beginning with our first release of Southeast Colorado in 1988, a minimum of one such study per year is set as an initial goal.

An exhaustive market analysis might suggest that the space industry could equip space probes with Petro-Sondes to ascertain the geology and resources of the other planets. In short, we have a very large market potential which is growing daily in size and needs.

Satellite Imagery

Recognizing the need for a companion technology in order for the Petro-Sonde to perform large scale reconnaissance, we chose Satellite Imagery as the desired approach. Already accepted by resource industries as a viable exploration tool, the plan was, in keeping with our "mission," to acquire the most up-to-date and comprehensive system available.

Instead of following the typical route into a digital system, as opposed to analog, we chose both; making Geophysics International the only company in the business with a dual capability. Each system has its own strengths and not all of them overlap. Specifically, the analog system is quicker and cheaper, whereas the digital can handle more data and is more accurate. Already, our Satellite Imagery Analysis System combined with Petro-Sonde surveys have yielded a major oil field discovery in Colorado.

Through our existing Petro-Sonde clientele, which number more than five hundred, we have initiated "direct mail/follow-up call" marketing efforts. It appears our satellite imagery staff shall achieve fifty percent utilization by the end of our next fiscal year and therefore we'll anticipate adding more staff by then. Fortunately, the systems can be expanded as needed.

Ironically, we view the demise of this industry in 1986, brought on by the price collapse of oil, as a unique opportunity to get in on the ground floor of a technology which is destined to have a rebirth of interest in the near future due to both technological advancements in the field and the inevitable tightening supply of all remaining resources. By starting out with "state-of-the-art" equipment and personnel at a time when most others have closed their doors, we expect to capture a market share and keep it by virtue of our exclusive Petro-Sonde rights/and our superior Satellite Imagery service. At the same time, we lock onto our Petro-Sonde customers by making it unnecessary for them to go elsewhere for their large scale reconnaissance needs. These two technologies represent a "stand alone" subsurface mapping system capable of detecting virtually any element or structural feature regardless of the amount of area under study.

The Plan (U.S.)

Our initial marketing approach was essentially a telemarketing system, wherein the office subscribed to a service which provided them copies of all drilling permits filed for oil and gas wells. These leads represented the people who were active and solvent and they simultaneously provided contact information along with well site information.

Familiarity opens many doors. Our offer to be able to pinpoint the best place to drill on a lease just "permitted," received rapt attention. In the early days of the company, the only way to establish credibility was to offer a demonstration. Normally this demonstration amounted to the potential client escorting our field geologist to an existing well. Upon arrival, our field geologist constructed a Petro-Log that duplicated the client's log without having any prior knowledge. We have actually had the majors blindfold our staff and take them on long plane rides to keep them from cheating.

Results of this technique in Texas, Oklahoma, and Louisiana proved to be effective. Eighty-three percent of the demonstrations converted to work. More than fifty percent immediately and the remainder anywhere from several days to several years – they didn't forget the demonstration! However, there was an inverse relationship between the size of the company and the decision-making ability of the person sent to witness these demonstrations. The exploration manager from Sun described his assistant, upon returning from one such demonstration, as having "stars in his eyes." It took more than two years before that translated into actual work, and yet today, Sun is a regular customer.

Having established our credibility, we can now spend more time in our customers' offices. We find that personal visits to customers and potential customers enhance not only the relationship, but also the clients' understanding of the technology and how to apply it. Presently, we have four seasoned explorationists who are responsible for this marketing effort. We must add additional staff to accommodate our growing client base.

Ultimately, this may precipitate the need for "satellite" offices strategically located to service outlying clients. Prospective sites include Denver, Bakersfield, CA, Southern Illinois, Kentucky, Tulsa, Kansas, Louisiana, Phoenix, and perhaps Pennsylvania or Ohio. These offices would be strictly marketing and scheduling offices. All accounting and billing would continue to be handled by the Dallas office.

In addition to a staff geologist, each satellite office would require a secretary/bookkeeper and as many field geologists as needed. With these elements in place, these satellite offices would grow in staff as sales dictate and perhaps spin-off additional offices.

The major benefits of expansion would be to enhance the marketing effort, expedite customers' familiarity with both technology applications and interpretation of data as well as improve communications between outlying customers and the home base in Dallas.

Like all geophysical tools including seismic, radiometrics, and other techniques — interpretation of the data is critical. Intense follow-up with the client after a survey maximizes the results of the exploration and/or development program through a joint determination of the correct interpretation of the data. Because this is a new technology with its own inherent idiosyncrasies, this follow-up is viewed as the most important ingredient to developing a satisfied client.

In early 1988, we commenced our first outright lease of a Petro-Sonde instrument to an experienced client. With the maturing of our clients' ability to interpret the data on their own, we see our leasing division growing exponentially with a significant lowering of overhead versus revenue dollars.

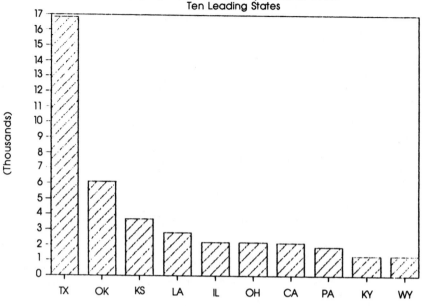

U.S. Oil & Gas Completions 1986
Ten Leading States

U.S. DRILLING –Ten Leading States Ranked by Completions

1986				1987 (estimated 7/27/87)		
Rank	State	Total		Rank	State	Total
1	Texas	16,805		1	Texas	13,868
2	Oklahoma	6,113		2	Oklahoma	4,900
3	Kansas	3,700		3	Kansas	3,150
4	Louisiana	2,805		4	Ohio	2,850
5	Illinois	2,200		5	California	2,668
6	Ohio	2,186		6	Louisiana	1,935
7	California	2,145		7	Colorado	1,200
8	Pennsylvania	1,900		8	W. Virginia	825
9	Kentucky	1,300		9	Illinois	750
10	Wyoming	1,300		10	Wyoming	700

GEOPHYSICAL EXPLORATION EXPENDITURES
BY STATE 1986

STATE	SEISMIC	OTHER	GI EARNINGS	TOTAL
TEXAS	86,757,663	2,353,996	329,230	89,440,889
OKLAHOMA	18,981,535	273,887	313,170	19,568,592
LOUISIANA	29,639,651	756,092	160,600	30,556,343

135,378,849	3,383,975	803,000	139,565,824
97.00%	2.42%	0.58%	

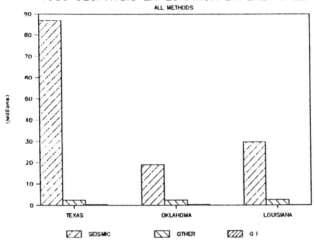

1986 GEOPHYSIC EXPLORATION EXPENDITURES
ALL METHODS

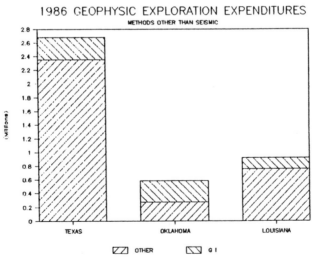

1986 GEOPHYSIC EXPLORATION EXPENDITURES
METHODS OTHER THAN SEISMIC

207

The Plan (International)

We have witnessed, and therefore are convinced of, the importance of penetrating foreign markets internally by having a physical presence with local alliances. When practicable, we shall employ local help such as the Chinese geologists in China, to further enhance this "inside out" approach.

Having had to "go it alone" in China illustrated the advantages of penetrating the international market by associating ourselves with someone with an established presence in that market. When we were approached by NOMECO regarding representation in Australia via their established contacts, we were anxious to agree. Likewise, when Albercan approached us regarding Canadian representation, we agreed.

Using these two prototype relationships as a springboard, we intend to aggressively pursue similar arrangements in as many countries as business demand dictates. Representatives pay us fifty percent of international rate plus expenses in return for all but the marketing and sales effort.

As the international markets develop, we again see the eventuality when satellite offices in those market centers will become necessary. Initially these offices would only require a single staff geologist along with a number of field geologists to service the areas.

As a minimum projection, the next five years should find us with representation in Saudi-Arabia, Kuwait, Soviet Union, Mexico, *Iran, *Iraq, Abu Dhabi, Venezuela, *Libya, Nigeria, United Kingdom, Norway, Algeria, Indonesia, Oman, and Egypt.

* Assuming war is ended and relations are neutralized.

Dollars Spent for Geophysical Exploration
Whole Market Projections
U.S. Dollars in Thousands

Method/Market	1987	1988	1989	1990	1991	1992
Petroleum	1,840,714	1,748,678	1,871,086	1,964,640	2,062,872	2,166,016
Mining	29,618	28,137	30,107	31,612	33,193	34,852
Engineering	10,716	7,556	8,689	10,079	13,103	17,034
Geothermal	1,149	660	878	1,168	1,285	1,413
Ground water	2,255	3,193	4,521	6,402	9,065	12,836
Oceanography	3,570	2,919	2,943	2,966	2,990	3,014
Other	13,863	14,004	14,146	14,290	14,435	14,581
Total	1,901,885	1,805,147	1,932,370	2,031,157	2,136,942	2,249,746

GEOPHYSICS INTERNATIONAL
PROJECTED MARKET SHARE

Whole Market Forecast
U.S. Dollars

Method/Market	1987	1988	1989	1990	1991	1992	% OF TOTAL INCOME 1992
Petroleum	816,863	1,742,004	2,863,949	3,879,817	5,621,148	6,925,725	45.00%
Mining	453,813	967,780	1,591,083	2,155,454	3,122,860	3,847,625	25.00%
Engineering	217,830	464,534	763,720	1,034,618	1,498,973	1,846,860	12.00%
Geothermal	54,458	116,134	190,930	258,654	374,743	461,715	3.00%
Ground water	145,220	309,690	509,146	689,745	999,315	1,231,240	8.00%
Oceanography	18,153	38,711	63,643	86,218	124,914	153,905	1.00%
Other	108,915	232,267	381,860	517,309	749,486	923,430	6.00%
	1,815,250	3,871,120	6,364,331	8,621,816	12,491,440	15,390,500	

GEOPHYSICS INTERNATIONAL
PROJECTED MARKET SHARE PERCENTAGE

Method/Market	1987	1988	1989	1990	1991	1992
Petroleum	0.04%	0.10%	0.15%	0.20%	0.27%	0.32%
Mining	1.53%	3.44%	5.28%	6.82%	9.41%	11.04%
Engineering	2.03%	6.15%	8.79%	10.26%	11.44%	10.84%
Geothermal	4.74%	17.59%	21.74%	22.15%	29.17%	32.67%
Ground water	6.44%	9.70%	11.26%	10.77%	11.02%	9.59%
Oceanography	0.51%	1.33%	2.16%	2.91%	4.18%	5.11%
Other	0.79%	1.66%	2.70%	3.62%	5.19%	6.33%

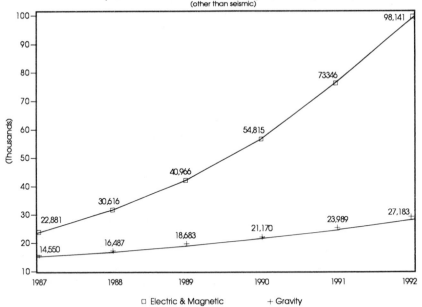

Expenditures For Geophysical Methods
(other than seismic)

□ Electric & Magnetic   + Gravity

BUSINESS ENVIRONMENT
=========================

Major Markets for Geophysical Expenditure
U.S. Dollars Spent World Wide in 1986 (in Thousands) for Geophysical Exploration

Method/Market	Petroleum	Mining	Engineering	Geothermal	Ground Water	Oceanography	Research	Total
Seismic	1,788,933	6,618	8,505	0	425	2,480	7,235	1,814,196
Magnetic & Gravity	12,934	7,849	274	164	536	303	3,264	25,223
Electromagnetic	191	9,649	70	775	91	0	788	11,564
Induced Polarization	617	1,438	234	0	65	0	22	2,376
Magnetotelluric	4,435	295	0	175	130	0	535	5,570
Resistivity	1,204	472	333	35	1,008	0	43	3,095
Other	32,500	3,298	1,300	0	0	787	1,976	39,861
Total	1,840,714	29,619	10,716	1,149	2,255	3,570	13,863	1,901,895

MAJOR COMPETITORS

Key Success factors		Weight	Self	Seismic	Gravity	Magnetic	EN	IP	MT	Res
Low–Cost vs.	Raw	4	5	2	2	2	1	1	2	2
Quality	weight		20	8	8	8	4	4	8	8
Accuracy	Raw	5	5	3	2	2	1	1	2	3
vs. Cost	weight		25	15	10	10	5	5	10	15
WEIGHTED TOTALS			45	23	18	18	9	9	18	23

KEY:
EN = Electronic   IP = Induced Polarization   MT = Magnetic   Res = Resistivity

INDUSTRY LIFE CYCLE ANALYSIS
Exploration Service Companies

Criteria	Embryonic	Growth	Mature	Aging
Growth rate			X	
Market share				X
Service line		X		
Financial				X
Competitors			X	
Market share stability			X	
Purchasing patterns		X		
Ease of entry			X	
Technology				X
Volume growth			X	
Managerial style				X
Overall stage				X

211

COMPETITOR PROFILE

Survey Type	Sales (000)	Growth Rate	Degree Integration	Strengths and Weaknesses
Seismic	$2,497,999	−7.6%	Low	Fair to Good structural data but can't locate prospective reservoirs consistently or cost effectively.
E-M	3,623	11.0%	Low	Electromagnetic gives fair data for high cost
IP	5,065	4.0%	Low	Induced Polarization can yield fair to good data but at a very high cost with limited applications
M-T	4,353	11.0%	Low	Magnetotellurics works in areas where seismic can't; slow and costly to use. Can't define reservoirs
Resistivity	3,615	4.0%	Low	Surface resistivity is mainly used for mining; Hydrocarbon exploration and environmental studies. Can't define depth/ thickness of specific objectives. Not used for large surveys.

MAJOR COMPETITORS
Total sales	$ 2,514,655
Average growth rate	4.49%
Combined market share	98.58%
Whole market sales	$2,550,797

Whole Market Forecast
============

Projected Crew/Man Months

Method/Market	1987	1988	1989	1990	1991	1992	Estimated Change
Seismic	7,911	7,562	7,305	6,910	6,536	6,182	(21.85%)
All Electric & Magnetic	919	1,119	1,363	1,661	2,023	2,464	+168.13%
Gravity	496	562	637	722	818	927	+86.82%
Total	9,326	9,244	9,305	9,292	9,377	9,573	

Projected Average Cost/Crew-Man Month

Method/Market	1987	1988	1989	1990	1991	1992	Estimated Change
Seismic	255,186	249,517	243,973	238,553	233,253	228,071	(10.63%)
All Electric & Magnetic	24,898	27,356	30,057	33,024	36,285	39,867	+60.12%
Gravity	29,334	29,930	30,538	31,158	31,791	32,437	10.58%
Average Price	220,481	209,262	198,018	185,710	173,188	160,691	

Competitor Analysis

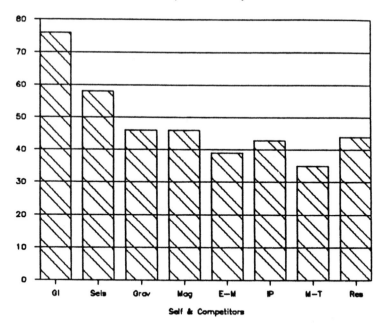

Self & Competitors

Competitive Position

A. Bases of competition		Weight	Major Competitors							
			Self	Seismic	Gravity	Magnetic	E-M	IP	M-T	Resist
Price	Raw	4	4	0	5	5	1	1	2	2
	weighted		16	0	20	20	4	4	8	8
Quality	Raw	4	4	4	1	1	3	3	2	3
	Weighted		16	16	4	4	12	12	8	12
Volume	Raw	3	3	4	5	5	3	2	1	1
	Weighted		9	12	15	15	9	6	3	3
Technology	Raw	2	5	5	1	1	2	3	3	3
	Weighted		10	10	2	2	4	6	6	6
Accuracy	Raw	5	5	4	1	1	2	3	2	3
	Weighted		25	20	5	5	10	15	10	15
Weighted totals			76	58	46	46	39	43	35	44

INFRASTRUCTURE AND OPERATIONS

The Organization

Although totally professional, the environment and managerial style of the company are informal. Taking their lead from such examples as Fred Smith of Federal Express and Tom Peters of "In Search of Excellence" fame, the company strives for the ingredients of a state of the art, modern day organization.

Management begins with intrapreneurial zeal as a foundation, the company's philosophy encompasses a generous, but, fair sharing of profits through incentive programs that acknowledge both individual effort as well as group accomplishment. Individual effort is compensated through a percentage of gross revenues attributed to each person's area of responsibility.

With only three private offices at the company headquarters, employees essentially work in an open office atmosphere. Feelings of superiority and competitiveness are rare. A basically flat salary structure -- ninety percent of personnel have same salary and equal benefits -- allows for few politicians. At Geophysics International, "Politics is the person who gets the job done." This cooperative atmosphere is the essence of productivity. Our compensation packages are tied to oil and gas industry averages as compiled by Peat, Marwick, and Mitchell.

Monthly company outings on Friday afternoons, filled with food and drink, contribute to morale. In addition, employee attendance in seminars ranging from "Excellence" to "Product development," has led to a stable, social group who, feel "on top" of what they're doing, and, most importantly, they "feel good" about it.

The Facilities

The company offices in Dallas, Texas are in a well located, high rise office building. Our lease expires in February 1991, and after seventeen months of free rent, we now pay an effective rate of $11.11 per square foot.

Other than private offices for the president, vice-president, and the manager of Satellite Imagery, all employees work in spacious, open offices.

Two Texas Instruments computers are utilized for production of Petro-Logs and are capable of servicing activity levels generating revenues of, at least, $1 million per month. We own the hardware and designed and developed the proprietary software which is copyrighted.

The accounting department presently utilizes a Texas Instruments computer. However, as funds are available, this department shall become part of a company wide computer system. We own all of our accounting hardware and software.

The Satellite Imagery Analysis lab contains two hardware systems (digital and analog) for image enhancement. The digital system includes a

Quality control — our absolute — is implemented at every level: beginning with numerous calibrations in the field, to having a second geologist and Petro-Sonde for a consensus approach, to the "in field" seasoned explorationist who reviews and guides all activities. As part of his final report to the client, both the staff geologist and the field geologist review the arrangements, the goal, and the actual field results. The report is forwarded to the chief geologist and his staff for their "imprimatur." Throughout this process there is constant communication with the client. We view client communications as the second most important thing we do, behind only the production of quality data with superior service at the lowest possible cost.

The most exacerbating element of dealing with a group of technologies in the field of exploration is the inclination to blame failure on the "other guy's technology."

By assembling a "stand alone" set of technologies, under one umbrella, to handle the largest to the smallest, we leave ourselves no opportunity to "pass the buck." This realization has focused our attention on the importance of quality control.

Typical Work Day

Our field geologists typically begin their "workday" in the evenings at the airport. Often, the client will meet with them upon arrival to review the following day's objective and plan.

The "day" begins with the field geologist being taken to several calibration points in the form of existing well bores, mine workings etc., in order for him to calibrate the equipment and assure himself and the client that the equipment is functioning properly and that the objective is achievable. Until this occurs, actual day rate charges don't begin, assuring no waste of precious exploration dollars. This feature sells more work to first time users than any other single item.

Once calibrated, work begins. This consists of making a series of logs at various points to accomplish the survey's objective. Essentially, the projects revolve around the detection, delineation, and evaluation of the objective and its environment. Customers receive eight hours work plus up to two hours calibration time per day. They pay $3,500 plus expenses within the United States and $5,000 plus expenses outside the United States.

This schedule is repeated daily until work is complete or, as is the case many times, abandoned. One of the features of our service is early abandonment by quickly being able to ascertain economic viablility of the survey. We answer the question, "Is the oil there?" before we pinpoint the entire limits of the reservoir. This often requires only a few readings instead of possibly hundreds.

Upon completion, one set of tield copies are presented to the client with a field invoice and a second set is sent or taken, whichever is quickest, to the home office for review, production of the final logs, and the report. These are sent with another copy of the invoice to the client and followed with a phone call from the staff geologist in charge. Constant communication exists between him and the client at all stages. This intensive communication continues to ingratiate us with our clients.

Each field geologist is issued his own four-wheel drive Subaru for both getting from job to job and actual work. Should even four-wheel drive be impossible, he will leave the vehicle and travel either by foot or other mode of transportation (we actually have used dog sleds, helicopters, and snowmobiles in Alaska) and merely carry a folding chair to sit on while doing his work. We also have one Nissan truck for mountainous terrain.

All personnel with access to the Petro-Sonde device and/or any other proprietary information receive a pre-employment polygraph and are routinely polygraphed to insure against theft, disclosure of operating trade secrets, and "moonlighting." This system works extremely well.

THE TEAM

With "return on assets employed" as our theme, and knowing our personnel to be our greatest asset, we create an environment in which they can grow and flourish. Our "modus operandi" is to achieve maximum productivity, hence maximum return.

By a fair and generous sharing of "profits" with all employees, we create a "bottom line" mentality throughout the company, and we attack the final villain to "return on assets employed", through variable costs such as paperclips, phone time, and so forth.

By virture of being the first with the Petro-Sonde, we now boast of a staff with three plus years' experience in the development, marketing, and operation of the Petro-Sonde technology. Administrative and field staff average between two and three years. Whenever possible, field staff, after gaining two to three years of field experience, are brought in-house. This combination of experience will ultimately become the backbone of our personnel resource as well as the hardest item to duplicate by any competitor. The interchangeability of our geologists is seen as a major strength economically as well as "morale" wise. It affords our geologists a variety of disciplines and career pursuits, without sacrificing income or seniority. We feel ultimately, all will find their niche and achieve their greatest potential, allowing Geophysics International to do likewise.

The directors, executive officers, management and technical staff of the company are listed below.

Name	Age	Position	1st Year With Company
Jerome J. Conser	43	Managing Director	1984
John Spinuzzi	58	Advisory Committee	1984
Richard L. Black	62	Advisory Committee	1984
Jack G. Elam	66	Advisory Committee	1984
Art Thompson	64	Advisory Committee	1987
Michael R. Birkos	34	President	1984
Steven W. Dickson	26	Vice-President	1984
Gary W. Jackson	40	Controller	1986
Larry E. Ferguson	33	Senior Geologist	1985
J. David Curlis	29	Manager, Satellite Imagery	1986
Robert B. Lanter	27	Staff Geologist	1985
Allan P. Hetzel	29	Staff Geologist	1987
Carolyn M. Paul	30	Staff Geologist	1988
Kevin W. Rigsby	26	Field Geologist	1984
Arnon Sugar	28	Field Geologist	1985
Jay S. King	26	Field Geologist	1987
Robert J. Schoenewe	28	Field Geologist	1987
Wendell A. Koontz	26	Field Geologist	1987
Kirk S. Gates	26	Field Geologist	1988
Dennis P. Becker	25	Field Geologist	1988
Jeff C. Hibbler	23	Field Geologist	1988

Kelli Tamsen joined Geophysics International in September 1985 as assistant bookkeeper. In 1986, she served as full charge bookkeeper and in 1987 she became the personal assistant/Executive Secretary to Mr. Conser.

Through her, Mr. Conser interfaces with all members of the Geophysics International team. Her responsibilities include handling personnel aspects of the company, such as pre-screening job applicants for support and administrative positions, and relaying company policy updates to the entire staff. She is also responsible for typing, telephoning, ordering, and filing for all Mr. Conser's business needs.

Her accomplishments since coming to Geophysics International are creating the Geophysics International's first Employee Policy Manual and coordinating the production and distribution of the company's first "Press Kit", a marketing tool distributed to potential investors and the media.

Barbara Lancaster joined Geophysics International in August 1985 as a data entry clerk in our final product division where the Petro-Log is produced on computer. She was responsible for entering, editing, and printing the Petro-Log. She also typed the geological reports which accompany all Petro-Sonde surveys. In 1986, she became manager of this department.

Mona Ginn, accounting assistant since 1986, has been responsible for preparing and processing all vendor payments, customer invoices, cash receipts, and payroll. She also runs all accounting errands and enters all data on the accounting computer.

Cindy Rawlinson joined Geophysics in September 1986 as a receptionist/secretary whose responsibilities include greeting visitors, answering and directing all incoming calls, typing letters, memos and forms, coordinating travel arrangements with travel agent, mail pick-up and drop-off, office supplies, upkeep of work and case history files, and other general office duties.

Our Senior Geologist, Larry Ferguson, and our three Staff Geologists, Robert Lanter, Allan Hetzel, and Carolyn Paul are responsible for generating client base via phone initially, followed by personal office visits, preliminary and final report writing, data interpretation, and representing Geophysics International at trade shows.

GEOLOGIST	EDUCATION	ASSIGNMENTS
Robert Lanter Texas Tech University, Lubbock, Texas	M.S., Geology	Oil and Gas Division for W. Texas, Coal Division, trade show co- ordinator, co-authored two technical papers on Petro-Sonde applications.
Larry Ferguson University of Houston, Houston, Texas	B.S., Geology	Oil & Gas Division for Oklahoma, N. Louisiana, Kansas and N.E. USA. Hydrology Division.
Allan Hetzel University of Texas at the Permian Basin, Odessa, Texas	B.S., Geology	Oil & Gas Divsion for Oklahoma and S. Texas, attends all trade shows.

Staff Geologists, Cont.

Carolyn Paul   B.S., Geology   Oil & Gas, and Coal Division,
  Edinboro University,   Rocky Mountain Region,
  Edinboro, Pennsylvania   Central Texas

FIELD GEOLOGISTS

NAME	EDUCATION	PRIMARY AREA OF EMPHASIS

Kevin Rigsby   B.S.,   Oil & Gas, resides in OK City, OK
  Geology, Oklahoma State   primarily mid-continent, Anadarko
  University, Oklahoma   Basin. Oklahoma District Office.

Arnon Sugar   M.S.,   Oil & Gas, technical presentations
  Geology, University of   Gulf Coast, Co-directed Australian
  Pennsylvania, Pennsylvania   contract, Research & Development.

Jay King   B.S.,   Oil & Gas, primarily Alabama-
  Geology, University of   Ferry Field, Arkansas, Texas
  Texas at Dallas, Texas   Louisiana.

Robert Schoenewe B.S.,   Oil & Gas, Hydrology, Anadarko
  Geology, Oklahoma State   Basin. Mid-Continent, North Texas.
  University, Oklahoma   Colorado.

Wendell Koontz   B.S.,   Coal, Oil & Gas, Engineering, West
  Geology, Hanover College   Texas, Illinois.
  Indiana

Dennis Becker   B.S.,   Oil & Gas, Mid-Continent
  Geology, Kansas State University
  Manhatten, Kansas

Kirk Gates   B.S.,   Oil & Gas, Hydrology, Texas &
  Geology, Stephen F. Austin   Oklahoma
  State U. Nacogdoches, Texas

Jeff Hibbeler   B.S.,   Oil & Gas Training
  Texas A & M University
  College Station, Texas

GEOPHYSICS INTERNATIONAL
COMPANY COMPENSATION RECAP

JOB CATEGORY	BASE PAY	YEAR END 1989	YEAR END 1990	YEAR END 1991	YEAR END 1992	YEAR END 1993
GENERAL & ADMINISTRATIVE:						
PRESIDENT	30,000	30,000	30,000	30,000	30,000	30,000
VICE PRESIDENTS:						
EXECUTIVE V/P	30,000	30,000	30,000	30,000	30,000	30,000
OIL & GAS V/P	24,000	0	24,000	24,000	24,000	24,000
MINING V/P	24,000	0	12,000	24,000	24,000	24,000
CONTROLLER	29,000	29,000	29,000	29,000	29,000	29,000
ACCOUNTANT	18,000	0	0	18,000	18,000	18,000
BOOKKEEPER	14,400	14,400	14,400	14,400	14,400	14,400
SATELLITE IMAGERY	24,000	24,000	24,000	36,000	48,000	84,000
EXECUTIVE SECRETARY	18,600	18,600	18,600	18,600	18,600	18,600
RECEPTIONIST	15,600	15,600	15,600	31,200	31,200	31,200
TOTAL G&A		161,600	197,600	255,200	267,200	303,200
MARKETING & SALES:						
VICE PRESIDENT	24,000	12,000	24,000	24,000	24,000	48,000
REGIONAL SALES MGRS	24,000	0	12,000	24,000	60,000	48,000
STAFF GEOLOGISTS	24,000	72,000	84,000	108,000	144,000	192,000
TOTAL MKTNG & SALES		84,000	120,000	156,000	228,000	288,000
TECHNICAL SUPPORT/R&D FUTURE						
R&D MANAGER	24,000	0	12,000	24,000	24,000	24,000
ELECTRONIC ENGINEER	24,000	0	0	12,000	24,000	24,000
MECHANICAL ENGINEER	24,000	0	0	12,000	24,000	24,000
ELECTRONIC ENGINEER	24,000	0	0	12,000	24,000	24,000
TOTAL TECH SUPPORT		0	12,000	60,000	96,000	96,000
FIELD OPERATIONS:						
OPERATIONS MGR	24,000	0	12,000	24,000	24,000	48,000
FIELD GEOLOGIST	24,000	240,000	288,000	336,000	408,000	480,000
OPERATION ASSISTANT	18,000	0	0	18,000	18,000	18,000
FIELD TECHNICIAN	18,000	0	0	18,000	18,000	18,000
TOTAL FIELD OPERATIONS		240,000	300,000	396,000	468,000	564,000
OTHER SUPPORT AREAS:						
PETRO LOG GENERATION	16,200	16,200	32,400	48,600	81,000	97,200
PERSONNEL DEPT	18,000	18,000	18,000	18,000	18,000	18,000
INFORMATION MGMT MGR	16,000	0	0	16,000	16,000	16,000
TOTAL OTHER SUPPORT		34,200	50,400	82,600	115,000	131,200
TOTAL ESTD BASE PAY		519,800	680,000	949,800	1,174,200	1,382,400

COMMISSIONS AND INCENTIVES:
MOST OF GEOPHYSICS INTERNATIONAL EMPLOYEES RECEIVE ADDITIONAL COMPENSATION IN THE FORM OF COMMISSIONS. THE RATES
ARE BASED ON POSITION AND SENIORITY. THE FOLLOWING TABLE PROVIDES ESTIMATED COMMISSIONS.
MR BIRKOS/PRESIDENT, AND MR DICKSON/VP HAVE STOCK OPTIONS TOTALLING 0.5% OF TOTAL STOCK EACH.

	YEAR END 1989	YEAR END 1990	YEAR END 1991	YEAR END 1992	YEAR END 1993
ESTIMATED COMMISSIONS:	165,393	271,742	433,296	582,930	784,890
TOTAL BASE + COMMISSIONS	685,193	951,742	1,383,096	1,757,130	2,167,290

"GET THE INCENTIVES RIGHT AND PRODUCTIVITY WILL FOLLOW."
TOM PETERS FROM "IN SEARCH OF EXCELLENCE".

The Proposal

(a)   General

The company is seeking $10 million. One-half ($5 million) is to be used to purchase sufficient stock from the original shareholders to make such shares available to the prospective investor. The remaining $5 million will be used by the company to expand its operations, to open new markets, for research and development, and to retire all existing company debts. The details of this "use of proceeds" are set forth later in this section.

This proposal is designed to return to the investor all or a substantial portion of his investment within three to five years, dependent upon that investor's decision in utilizing his options.

(b)   Investment in Common Stock

The company will sell and deliver 20 percent of its common stock in exchange for $6 million. The company will utilize $5 million to acquire its outstanding stock in amount sufficient to provide this 20% together with additional percentages of its common stock necessary to cover all conversion privileges/options to acquire additional common shares. The remaining $1,000,000 will be paid in capital to be utilized as hereinafter stated.

The company will commit to register the common stock (including shares acquired in the future through conversion) at any time after three years, and up to ten years, after their purchase date. The investor will also have the right to "piggy back" his shares in any registration of shares to be offered by the company provided that the number of shares to be so registered for sale by this investor shall not interfere with the company's ability to sell its own offering.

(c)   Investment in Convertible Preferred Stock and/or Convertible Debentures

The remaining $4 million may be invested in convertible preferred stock and/or convertible debentures, at the investor's option. At present the company is not authorized to issue any class of stock other than common, but such can be authorized by amendment to its Articles of Incorporation. The company prefers to utilize the preferred stock route for investment because the treatment of the investment upon the company's balance sheet would be more beneficial than the treatment of debentures. However, the accounting treatment is not as important as the desires of the prospective investor to utilize those options which would best serve his needs as to risk of capital and other personal investment decisions. In either form of investment, the rates of return, security of investment, conversion or redemption privileges are basically identical.

(i)   Repayment and Retirement of Preferred Stock/Debentures

The company will establish a sinking fund to be escrowed with a banking institution. The purpose of this fund will be to (a) first pay interest/dividends annually and (b) to retire by repurchase a percentage of the outstanding Preferred Stock/Debentures held by the prospective investor.

(a)   Annual dividends or interest shall be 8 percent of the par value of the Preferred Stock or the face value of the Debentures. Face value shall be the actual investment cost for each unit of such stock or debenture. Should there be insufficient funds to pay such interest, the interest shall cumulate. Interest shall not be paid on cumulated interest, only on principal or face value.

(b)   Redemption or repurchase of such shares or debentures shall be out of the remaining funds in the sinking fund, annually, after payment of interest.

(c)   Funding of Sinking Fund: The company shall pay, quarterly, 50 percent of its net after-tax profits into the sinking fund. The escrow bank shall hold such funds solely for the payments required above. Should the investor decide to exercise his conversion rights (converting all or a portion of his Preferred Stock or Debentures into common stock), that portion of the escrowed fund representing such purchase by conversion shall be released and transferred for the company's general business operations.

Because the company cannot accurately predict what sums will be earned and transferred into this sinking fund, the company will commit to deposit into such funds, commencing three years after this initial investment, an amount sufficient to retire not less than 20 percent annually of the then outstanding Preferred Shares/Debentures.

(d)   Conversion Rights: The prospective investor shall have the right to convert all or any part of the principal and/or accrued interest into common stock at the price of $200,000 for each 1 percent of the company's common stock - such percentage to be based upon the present outstanding common shares. Anti-dilution provisions will protect the investor's proportionate share of the outstanding stock should the company issue any additional common stock.

(e)   Redemption: The company shall have the right, in each year, to redeem up to 20 percent of the total Preferred/Debentures acquired by investor. No redemption shall be permitted unless all cumulative interest has first been paid. The company shall give 60 days notice of its intent to redeem, during which period the investor shall have the right to convert all or any part of those securities to be redeemed. However, the right of redemption shall be cumulative so that those not redeemed in any year may be redeemed at any time thereafter provided such redemption will be out of net profits. The redemption price shall be par face value.

(f)   Voting Rights: The Preferred Stock shall have no voting rights.

(g)   Liquidation Preferences: Any voluntary or involuntary liquidation, dissolution or conclusion of the company's affairs shall cause the rights of the investor to immediately mature, and such securities shall first be paid prior to any distribution to the common shareholders.

(h)   Restrictions on Borrowing: So long as these Preferred Shares/Debentures are outstanding, the company will not create nor assume any additional indebtedness not in the ordinary course of business, if, as a result, its total indebtedness will exceed 50 percent of the then value of its assets. Further, the company will not mortgage or pledge any of its property for the purpose of securing loans or other indebtedness of the company. The investor may waive any of these restrictions, in whole or in part, by written consent to any identified transaction.

Conclusion: The company believes the above format provides the prospective investor with a reasonable amount of safety for the investment made together with the investor having the opportunity to enhance his investment by exercising the options and rights available to him. At the same time, the company will be responsible in utilizing proceeds received and in setting aside a portion (50 percent) of its net profits for the benefit of that investor.

228

Use of Proceeds

Research and Development continues to be the focus of our future. In 1985, the first prototype offshore unit was built and we are presently engaged in developing its capability. Although progress is slower than anticipated, it is our goal to have it commercially available by the summer of 1989.

Efforts to replace the human ear with a field portable chart recorder have been slowed by the lack of achievement in the field of artificial intelligence. Recent progress is encouraging and we feel the time has arrived to make this our priority research and development effort. We feel that truck mounted and airborne reconnaissance will remain on the backburner until the field hard copy is achieved.

> "The force – the locomotive that pushes
> and pulls all the rest – is research"
>
> Conrad Schlumberger, circa 1940

In order to expand, either geographically or technologically, we must add personnel. Tripling staff over the next five years would be a realistic estimate.

Recognizing the volumes of data collected for each client, and that any part of this data could become necessary for day-to-day conversations between our clients and staff, the company needs an in-house computer system with terminals on every desk from sales to accounting to final product, and, to management. IBM has made the best proposal on what we believe to be the best system for this purpose. We would view this expenditure at a cost of $50,000, to be one of our very first investments out of proceeds.

The net proceeds to Geophysics International from the sale of 40 percent of its stock for $10 million are $5 million. The first $5 million is to be paid to the original stockholder for repurchase of this 40 percent to be sold. The remainder shall be applied as follows:

FUNDING SCHEDULE

CATEGORY	1988	1989	1990	1991	*1992
DEBT	47,000	–	–	–	–
MANPOWER	168,000	140,000	100,000	–	–
IRS	268,000	–	–	–	–
R&D OFFSHORE	100,000	50,000	25,000	–	–
R&D HARDCOPY	250,000	250,000	150,000	–	–
R&D MAGNETIC	50,000	25,000	–	–	–
COMPUTER SYS.	50,000	5,000	5,000	5,000	5,000
PHONE SYSTEM	20,000	–	–	–	–
SATELLITE LAB	269,000	50,000	25,000	25,000	25,000
CASE HISTORIES	100,000	110,000	110,000	110,000	110,000
G&A MISC.	125,000	240,000	125,000	500,000	210,000
PR & ADVERTIS.	120,000	180,000	240,000	300,000	360,000
TOTAL	1,567,000	1,050,000	780,000	940,000	710,000

*To be funded out of work generated revenues.

Footnote 1:

PRF	$27,000
Legal Fees– (defending patent rights)	20,000
TOTAL REPAYMENT OF DEBT	$47,000

```
                    MANPOWER MILESTONES
                Numbers of Personnel Anticipated
           ===================================
```

JOB CATEGORY	1988	1989	1990	1991	1992
GENERAL AND ADMIN.					
Presidents	1	1	1	1	1
Vice-Presidents	1	1	1	1	1
Controller	1	1	1	1	1
Accountants	0	0	1	1	1
V-P Oil & Gas Div.	0	1	1	1	1
V-P Mining Division	0	0	1	1	1
Satellite Imagery	1	1	2	4	4
Bookkeeper	1	1	1	1	1
Secty's and Recept.	2	2	3	3	3
TOTAL GEN. AND ADMIN.	7	8	12	14	14
MARKETING AND SALES					
V-P Marketing	1	1	1	2	2
Regional Account (sales) Managers	1	1	2	2	2
Staff Geologists	3	4	5	6	8
TOTAL MARKET AND SALES	5	6	8	10	12
TECHNICAL SUPPORT & R & D, FUTURE					
Research & Development Manager	0	1	1	1	1
Electronic Engineer	0	0	1	1	1
Mechanical Engineer	0	0	1	1	1
Electronic Technician	0	0	1	1	1
TOTAL TECHNICAL	0	1	4	4	4
FIELD OPERATIONS					
Operations Manager	1	1	1	1	2
Field Geologist	10	10	12	15	20
Operation Assistant	0	0	1	1	1
Field Technician	0	0	1	1	1
TOTAL FIELD OPERATIONS	11	11	15	18	24
OTHER AREAS OF SUPPORT					
Petro-Log generation	1	2	3	5	6
Personnel Department	1	1	1	1	1
Information Management Professional	0	0	1	1	1
TOTAL OTHER SUPPORT	2	3	5	7	8
TOTAL MANPOWER	25	28	44	53	62

Geophysics International will hire the very best talent to assure its expansion and profitability.

Footnote 2:

Includes finishing the Satellite Imagery Analysis Lab, Computer system throughout office, furniture (desks, etc.) as needed, and vehicles.

Fax and Telex Machine	17,000
Computer System	50,000
Nine Subarus	93,000
Office Furniture	3,000
Satellite Room Construction	4,000
Security System	2,000
TOTAL CAPITAL EQUIPMENT	269,000

Footnote 3:

Implementation of Petro-Log Hard Copy produced in the field, and initial penetration of Hydrology, Mine Engineering, Civil Engineering, and Environmental markets.

HARD COPY RESEARCH AND DEVELOPMENT

Oscilliscope	10,000
Spectrum Analyzer	35,000
Digital Recorder	2,000
Digital Filter System	10,000
Mainframe access at 3,000/day for 90/days	180,000
Technical Consulting	50,000
G.I. Staff Management and Expenses	30,000
Field Study at 10 days	35,000
Direct Drive Tuner Control	8,000
Miscellaneous	14,000
TOTAL	374,000

To penetrate hydrology, mine engineering, civil engineering, and environmental markets, it will be necessary to conduct detailed test studies for case histories and subsequent publication in the technical journals.

As a comparison, the Morton Thiokol Project is used for cost and scope estimates. Field work was conducted in ten days. Office support and data assembly was another twenty five man days.

Petro-Sonde operator at ten days	=	35,000
Consultant at twenty days		10,000
SUBTOTAL PER CASE HISTORY		45,000

We need three case histories for each division listed above from different sites with different problems.

TOTAL ALL CASE HISTORIES $540,000

Footnote 4:

PERSONNEL

Technical Staff:

2 Oil and Gas Division Geologists	= $ 80,000
1 Coal Geologist	40,000
1 Coal Mining Engineer	40,000
1 Hydrogeologist	40,000
Misc. surveying equipment	10,000
1 Civil Engineer	40,000
1 Photogeologist (10 to 15 yrs experience)	50,000
8 Field Geologists	240,000

Support Staff:

3 clerical positions	60,000
1 operations manager	24,000
TOTAL ADDITIONAL SALARIES	408,000

Because we can safely assume that the newly hired staff will not generate any significant revenues their first year with us, we can declare that their salaries will be expenses, therefore being an additional output of capital. Also, the technical staff will obviously be incurring expenses (not salary related) to get each department up and running. We estimate this at 15,000 each their first year.

15 new staff at 15,000 in expenses each first year =   225,000

TOTAL NEW PERSONNEL   633,000

As a consequence of our first major oil field discovery using the combination of our Satellite Imagery Analysis and our Petro-Sonde surveys, a joint effort by Geophysics International and a client is under way to publish and market a complete geological study of the four County area in Colorado. The project could raise as much as $1 million through the sale of the report to industry (20 reports times $50,000 each). The document would represent the largest, and most complete, data base of this entire area. We believe this project marks the beginning of our newest revenue generator. This, of course, precipitates a need for additional staff.

Finally, the company owes approximately $ 47,000 to creditors and would like to retire this debt.

SUPPORTING DATA FOR
FINANCIAL HISTORY AND PROJECTIONS

GEOPHYSICS INTERNATIONAL - DETAILED PROJECTIONS
AT MARCH 31, 1988
FISCAL YEAR - APRIL 1 TO MARCH 31

	EQUITY CAPITAL REQUIRED	$0
	CREDIT LINE REQUIREMENTS	$244,654
	NEW LONG TERM DEBT	$125,000
	TOTAL FUNDS REQUIRED	$369,654

	APRIL 1988	MAY 1988	JUNE 1988	JULY 1988	AUG 1988	SEPT 1988	OCT 1988	NOV 1988	DEC 1988	JAN 1989	FEB 1989	MARCH 1989	1ST QTR F.Y. 1989	2ND QTR F.Y. 1989	3TH QTR F.Y. 1989	4TH QTR F.Y. 1989	F.Y. 1990	F.Y. 1991	F.Y. 1992
NUMBER OF MONTHS	1	1	1	1	1	1	1	1	1	1	1	1	3	3	3	3	12	12	12
GROSS SALES ASSUMPTIONS																			
PETRO-SONDE SERVICE																			
NUMBER OF FIELD GEOLOGISTS	5	5	5	6	7	8	8	8	8	9	9	10	10	10	10	10	12	15	18
REVENUE DAYS PER MONTH	9	10	10	10	10	10	8	8	8	9	8	10	10	10	10	10	12	10	10
AVERAGE RATE PER DAY	2,250	2,500	2,500	2,500	2,500	2,500	2,500	2,500	2,500	2,500	2,500	2,500	2,500	2,500	2,750	2,750	3,000	3,250	3,500
PROJECTED SALES	101,250	125,000	125,000	150,000	175,000	200,000	200,000	160,000	160,000	180,000	180,000	250,000	750,000	750,000	825,000	825,000	4,320,000	5,850,000	7,560,000
SATELLITE IMAGERY																			
NUMBER OF GEOLOGISTS	1	1	1	1	1	1	1	1	1	1	1	1	1	1	1	1	2	4	4
REVENUE DAYS PER MONTH	5	7	7	10	10	10	10	12	12	12	12	12	18	20	20	20	20	20	20
AVERAGE RATE PER DAY	300	300	300	300	300	300	300	300	300	300	300	300	300	300	300	300	300	300	300
PROJECTED SALES	1,500	2,100	2,100	3,000	3,000	3,000	3,000	3,600	3,600	3,600	3,600	3,600	16,200	18,000	18,000	18,000	144,000	288,000	288,000
OTHER SALES-PETRO-SONDE LEASE																			
NUMBER OF INSTRUMENTS	1	1	1	2	2	2	3	3	3	4	4	4	6	6	6	6	9	12	18
NUMBER OF MONTHS	1	1	1	1	1	1	1	1	1	1	1	1	3	3	3	3	12	12	12
MONTHLY LEASE RATE	10,000	10,000	10,000	9,500	9,500	9,500	9,000	9,000	9,000	8,500	8,500	8,500	9,000	9,000	9,000	9,000	8,000	9,000	9,000
PROJECTED SALES	10,000	10,000	10,000	19,000	19,000	19,000	27,000	27,000	27,000	34,000	34,000	34,000	162,000	162,000	162,000	162,000	864,000	1,296,000	1,944,000

COST OF SALES ASSUMPTIONS	YEAR 1	YEAR 2	YEAR 2	YEAR 2	YEAR 2	YEAR 2	YEAR 2	YEAR 2	YEAR 2	YEAR 2	YEAR 3	YEAR 4	YEAR 5
SALARIES GROWTH RATE	N/A	10.0%	10.0%	10.0%	10.0%	10.0%	10.0%	10.0%	10.0%	10.0%	10.0%	10.0%	10.0%
FRINGE BENEFITS RATE - BASE SALARY													
TAXES	5.0%	5.0%	5.0%	5.0%	5.0%	5.0%	5.0%	5.0%	5.0%	5.0%	5.0%	5.0%	5.0%
PENSION	10.0%	20.0%	20.0%	20.0%	20.0%	20.0%	20.0%	20.0%	20.0%	20.0%	10.0%	10.0%	10.0%
MEDICAL, LIFE, ETC.	2.0%	5.0%	5.0%	5.0%	5.0%	5.0%	5.0%	5.0%	5.0%	5.0%	5.0%	5.0%	5.0%
	17.0%	30.0%	30.0%	30.0%	30.0%	30.0%	30.0%	30.0%	30.0%	30.0%	20.0%	20.0%	20.0%

	APRIL 1988	MAY 1988	JUNE 1988	JULY 1988	AUG 1988	SEPT 1988	OCT 1988	NOV 1988	DEC 1988	JAN 1989	FEB 1989	MARCH 1989	1ST QTR F.Y. 1989	2ND QTR F.Y. 1989	3TH QTR F.Y. 1989	4TH QTR F.Y. 1989	F.Y. 1990	F.Y. 1991	F.Y. 1992
EQUITY CAPITAL REQUIRED $0																			
CREDIT LINE REQUIREMENTS $244,654																			
NEW LONG TERM DEBT $125,000																			
TOTAL FUNDS REQUIRED $369,654																			
COST OF SALES ASSUMPTIONS (CON'T)																			
PETRO-SONDE SERVICE (ANNUAL SALARY)																			
HEAD COUNT																			
FIELD GEOLOGISTS (ABOVE) 24,000	7	7	7	8	9	10	10	10	10	11	11	12	12	12	12	12	14	17	20
STAFF GEOLOGISTS 24,000	7	0	0	0	0	0	0	0	0	0	0	0	0	0	0	0	0	0	0
OPERATION ASSISTANT 18,000	0	0	0	0	0	0	0	0	0	0	0	0	0	0	0	0	1	1	1
FIELD TECHNICIAN 18,000	0	0	0	0	0	0	0	0	0	0	0	0	0	0	0	0	0	1	1
BONUSES AND COMMISSION - PERCENT OF PETRO-SONDE SALES																			
FIELD GEOLOGISTS (ABOVE)	2.00%	2.00%	2.00%	2.00%	2.00%	2.00%	2.00%	2.00%	2.00%	2.00%	2.00%	2.00%	2.00%	2.00%	2.00%	2.00%	2.00%	2.00%	2.00%
STAFF GEOLOGISTS	0.00%	0.00%	0.00%	0.00%	0.00%	0.00%	0.00%	0.00%	0.00%	0.00%	0.00%	0.00%	0.00%	0.00%	0.00%	0.00%	0.00%	0.00%	0.00%
OPERATION ASSISTANT	0.00%	0.00%	0.00%	0.00%	0.00%	0.00%	0.00%	0.00%	0.00%	0.00%	0.00%	0.00%	0.00%	0.00%	0.00%	0.00%	0.00%	0.00%	0.00%
FIELD TECHNICIAN	0.00%	0.00%	0.00%	0.00%	0.00%	0.00%	0.00%	0.00%	0.00%	0.00%	0.00%	0.00%	0.00%	0.00%	0.90%	0.00%	0.00%	0.00%	0.00%
EXPENSES																			
SALARY AND FRINGE	16,380	16,380	16,380	18,720	21,060	23,400	23,400	23,400	23,400	25,740	25,740	28,080	102,960	102,960	102,960	102,960	514,008	709,157	906,571
UNREIMBURSED COST PER REVENUE DAY																			
FIELD GEOLOGIST	$10	$10	$10	$10	$10	$10	$10	$10	$10	$10	$10	$10	$12	$12	$12	$12	$15	$18	$21
SUPPORT GEOLOGIST	$3	$3	$3	$3	$3	$3	$3	$3	$3	$3	$3	$3	$4	$4	$4	$4	$5	$6	$7
UNREIMBURSED EXPENSES	630	700	700	800	900	1,000	1,000	800	800	880	880	1,200	4,320	4,320	4,320	4,320	25,200	36,720	50,400
BONUSES AND COMMISSIONS	2,025	2,500	2,500	3,000	3,500	4,000	4,000	3,200	3,200	3,600	3,600	5,000	15,000	15,000	16,500	16,500	86,400	117,000	151,200
PATENT PAYMENT																			
PERCENTAGE RATE	10%	10%	10%	10%	10%	10%	10%	10%	10%	10%	10%	10%	10%	10%	10%	10%	10%	10%	10%
ACTUAL PAYMENTS ARE CAPITALIZED																			
EQUIP. RENTAL	3,750	3,750	3,750	3,750	3,750	3,750	3,750	3,750	3,750	3,750	3,750	3,750	12,500	12,500	12,500	12,500	57,500	66,500	96,425
SERVICE AND MAINT.	1,500	1,500	1,500	1,500	1,500	1,500	1,500	1,500	1,500	1,500	1,500	1,500	6,000	6,000	6,000	6,000	30,000	36,000	33,000
CONTRACT LABOR	500	500	500	500	500	500	500	500	500	500	500	500	1,750	1,750	1,750	1,750	8,500	16,000	25,000
SUPPLIES	750	750	750	750	750	750	750	750	750	750	750	750	2,500	2,500	2,500	2,500	12,000	15,000	18,000
ALL OTHER	1,000	1,000	1,000	1,000	1,000	1,000	1,000	1,000	1,000	1,000	1,000	1,000	3,500	3,500	3,500	3,500	17,500	22,500	27,500
TOTAL PETRO-SERVICE	26,535	27,080	27,080	30,020	32,960	35,900	35,900	34,900	34,900	37,720	37,720	41,780	148,530	148,530	150,030	150,030	751,108	1,018,877	1,308,096

GEOPHYSICS INTERNATIONAL - DETAILED PROJECTIONS
AT MARCH 31, 1988
FISCAL YEAR - APRIL 1 TO MARCH 31

		APRIL 1988	MAY 1988	JUNE 1988	JULY 1988	AUG 1988	SEPT 1988	OCT 1988	NOV 1988	DEC 1988	JAN 1989	FEB 1989	MARCH 1989	1ST QTR F.Y. 1989	2ND QTR F.Y. 1989	3TH QTR F.Y. 1989	4TH QTR F.Y. 1989	F.Y. 1990	F.Y. 1991	F.Y. 1992
EQUITY CAPITAL REQUIRED	$0																			
CREDIT LINE REQUIREMENTS	$244,654																			
NEW LONG TERM DEBT	$125,000																			
TOTAL FUNDS REQUIRED	$369,654																			

COST OF SALES ASSUMPTIONS (CON'T)

SATELLITE IMAGERY HEAD COUNT	ANNUAL SALARY	APRIL 1988	MAY 1988	JUNE 1988	JULY 1988	AUG 1988	SEPT 1988	OCT 1988	NOV 1988	DEC 1988	JAN 1989	FEB 1989	MARCH 1989	1ST QTR	2ND QTR	3TH QTR	4TH QTR	F.Y. 1990	F.Y. 1991	F.Y. 1992
GEOLOGISTS (ABOVE)	24,000	1	1	1	1	1	1	1	1	1	1	1	1	1	1	1	1	2	4	4
SUPPORT GEOLOGISTS	18,000	0	0	0	0	0	0	0	0	0	0	0	0	1	1	1	1	1	2	2

BONUSES AND COMMISSIONS - PERCENT OF SATELLITE IMAGERY SALES

	APRIL 1988	MAY 1988	JUNE 1988	JULY 1988	AUG 1988	SEPT 1988	OCT 1988	NOV 1988	DEC 1988	JAN 1989	FEB 1989	MARCH 1989	1ST QTR	2ND QTR	3TH QTR	4TH QTR	F.Y. 1990	F.Y. 1991	F.Y. 1992
GEOLOGISTS (ABOVE)	2.00%	2.00%	2.00%	2.00%	2.00%	2.00%	2.00%	2.00%	2.00%	2.00%	2.00%	2.00%	2.00%	2.00%	2.00%	2.00%	2.00%	2.00%	2.00%
SUPPORT GEOLOGISTS	0.00%	0.00%	0.00%	0.00%	0.00%	0.00%	0.00%	0.00%	0.00%	0.00%	0.00%	0.00%	0.00%	0.00%	0.00%	0.00%	0.00%	0.00%	0.00%

EXPENSES

	APRIL 1988	MAY 1988	JUNE 1988	JULY 1988	AUG 1988	SEPT 1988	OCT 1988	NOV 1988	DEC 1988	JAN 1989	FEB 1989	MARCH 1989	1ST QTR	2ND QTR	3TH QTR	4TH QTR	F.Y. 1990	F.Y. 1991	F.Y. 1992
SALARY AND FRINGE	2,340	2,340	2,340	2,340	2,340	2,340	2,340	2,340	2,340	2,340	2,340	2,340	15,015	15,015	15,015	15,015	95,832	210,830	231,913
UNREIMBURSED COST PER REVENUE DAY																			
FIELD GEOLOGIST	$0	$0	$0	$0	$0	$0	$0	$0	$0	$0	$0	$0	$0	$0	$0	$0	$0	$0	$0
SUPPORT GEOLOGIST	$0	$0	$0	$0	$0	$0	$0	$0	$0	$0	$0	$0	$0	$0	$0	$0	$0	$0	$0
UNREIMBURSED EXPENSES																			
BONUSES AND COMMISSION	530	42	42	60	60	60	60	72	72	72	72	72	324	360	360	360	2,880	5,760	5,760
EQUIP RENTAL	1,250	1,250	1,250	1,250	1,250	1,250	1,250	1,250	1,250	1,250	1,250	1,250	6,500	6,500	6,500	6,500	30,000	40,000	50,000
SERVICE AND MAINT.	0	0	0	0	0	0	0	0	0	0	0	0	600	600	600	600	2,500	2,750	3,250
CONTRACT LABOR	0	0	0	0	0	0	0	0	0	0	0	0	0	0	0	0	0	0	0
SUPPLIES	1,000	1,000	1,000	1,000	1,000	1,000	1,000	1,000	1,000	1,000	1,000	1,000	5,000	5,000	5,000	5,000	22,500	25,000	27,500
ALL OTHER	1,200	1,200	1,200	1,200	1,200	1,200	1,200	1,200	1,200	1,200	1,200	1,200	4,000	4,000	4,000	4,000	17,500	20,000	22,500
TOTAL SATELLITE IMAGERY	6,320	5,832	5,832	5,850	5,850	5,850	5,850	5,862	5,862	5,862	5,862	5,862	31,439	31,475	31,475	31,475	171,212	304,340	340,923

238

GEOPHYSICS INTERNATIONAL - DETAILED PROJECTIONS
AT MARCH 31, 1988
FISCAL YEAR - APRIL 1 TO MARCH 31

		APRIL 1988	MAY 1988	JUNE 1988	JULY 1988	AUG 1988	SEPT 1988	OCT 1988	NOV 1988	DEC 1988	JAN 1989	FEB 1989	MARCH 1989	1ST QTR F.Y. 1989	2ND QTR F.Y. 1989	3TH QTR F.Y. 1989	4TH QTR F.Y. 1989	F.Y. 1990	F.Y. 1991	F.Y. 1992
EQUITY CAPITAL REQUIRED	$0																			
CREDIT LINE REQUIREMENTS	$244,654																			
NEW LONG TERM DEBT	$125,000																			
TOTAL FUNDS REQUIRED	$369,654																			

COST OF SALES ASSUMPTIONS (CON'T)

	ANNUAL SALARY	APRIL 1988	MAY 1988	JUNE 1988	JULY 1988	AUG 1988	SEPT 1988	OCT 1988	NOV 1988	DEC 1988	JAN 1989	FEB 1989	MARCH 1989	1ST QTR F.Y. 1989	2ND QTR F.Y. 1989	3TH QTR F.Y. 1989	4TH QTR F.Y. 1989	F.Y. 1990	F.Y. 1991	F.Y. 1992
OTHER-PETRO-SONDE LEASE																				
HEAD COUNT																				
PETRO-SONDE INSTRUMENTS	0	1	1	1	2	2	2	3	3	3	4	4	4	6	6	6	6	9	12	18
SUPPORT GEOLOGISTS	0	0	0	0	0	0	0	0	0	0	0	0	0	0	0	0	0	0	0	0
BONUSES AND COMMISSIONS																				
GEOLOGISTS (ABOVE)		0.00%	0.00%	0.00%	0.00%	0.00%	0.00%	0.00%	0.00%	0.00%	0.00%	0.00%	0.00%	0.00%	0.00%	0.00%	0.00%	0.00%	0.00%	0.00%
SUPPORT GEOLOGISTS		2.00%	2.00%	2.00%	2.00%	2.00%	2.00%	2.00%	2.00%	2.00%	2.00%	2.00%	2.00%	2.00%	2.00%	2.00%	2.00%	2.00%	2.00%	2.00%

EXPENSES

		APRIL 1988	MAY 1988	JUNE 1988	JULY 1988	AUG 1988	SEPT 1988	OCT 1988	NOV 1988	DEC 1988	JAN 1989	FEB 1989	MARCH 1989	1ST QTR F.Y. 1989	2ND QTR F.Y. 1989	3TH QTR F.Y. 1989	4TH QTR F.Y. 1989	F.Y. 1990	F.Y. 1991	F.Y. 1992
SALARY AND FRINGE																				
UNREIMBURSED COST PER REVENUE DAY		0	0	0	0	0	0	0	0	0	0	0	0	0	0	0	0	0	0	0
FIELD GEOLOGIST		$0	$0	$0	$0	$0	$0	$0	$0	$0	$0	$0	$0	$0	$0	$0	$0	$0	$0	$0
SUPPORT GEOLOGIST		$0	$0	$0	$0	$0	$0	$0	$0	$0	$0	$0	$0	$0	$0	$0	$0	$0	$0	$0
UNREIMBURSED EXPENSES		0	0	0	0	0	0	0	0	0	0	0	0	0	0	0	0	0	0	0
BONUSES AND COMMISSIONS		200	200	200	380	380	380	540	540	540	680	680	680	3,240	3,240	3,240	3,240	17,280	25,920	38,880
CUSTOMER SUPPORT		100	100	100	190	190	190	270	270	270	340	340	340	1,620	1,620	1,620	1,620	8,640	12,960	19,440
SERVICE AND MAINT.		0	0	0	0	0	0	0	0	0	0	0	0	0	0	0	0	0	0	0
CONTRACT LABOR		0	0	0	0	0	0	0	0	0	0	0	0	0	0	0	0	0	0	0
SUPPLIES		0	0	0	0	0	0	0	0	0	0	0	0	0	0	0	0	0	0	0
ALL OTHER		0	0	0	0	0	0	0	0	0	0	0	0	0	0	0	0	0	0	0
TOTAL OTHER SALES		300	300	300	570	570	570	810	810	810	1,020	1,020	1,020	4,860	4,860	4,860	4,860	25,920	38,880	58,320

EQUITY CAPITAL REQUIRED $0
CREDIT LINE REQUIREMENTS $244,654
NEW LONG TERM DEBT $125,000

	ANNUAL SALARY	APRIL 1988	MAY 1988	JUNE 1988	JULY 1988	AUG 1988	SEPT 1988	OCT 1988	NOV 1988	DEC 1988	JAN 1989	FEB 1989	MARCH 1989	1ST QTR F.Y. 1989	2ND QTR F.Y. 1989	3TH QTR F.Y. 1989	4TH QTR F.Y. 1989	F.Y. 1990	F.Y. 1991	F.Y. 1992
TOTAL FUNDS REQUIRED		$369,654																		
OPERATING EXPENSES ASSUMPTIONS																				
TECHNICAL SUPPORT																				
HEAD COUNT																				
RAD MANAGER	24,000	0	0	0	0	0	0	0	0	0	0	0	0	0	0	1	1	1	1	1
ELECTRONIC ENGINEER	24,000	0	0	0	0	0	0	0	0	0	0	0	0	0	0	0	0	1	1	1
MECHANICAL ENGINEER	24,000	0	0	0	0	0	0	0	0	0	0	0	0	0	0	0	0	1	1	1
ELECTRONIC TECHNICIAN	24,000	0	0	0	0	0	0	0	0	0	0	0	0	0	0	0	0	1	1	1
PETRO LOG TECHNICIAN	16,200	1	1	1	1	1	1	1	1	1	1	1	1	1	1	2	2	3	5	6
BONUSES AND COMMISSIONS - PERCENT OF TOTAL SALES																				
RAD MANAGER		0.00%	0.00%	0.00%	0.00%	0.00%	0.00%	0.00%	0.00%	0.00%	0.00%	0.00%	0.00%	0.00%	0.00%	0.25%	0.25%	0.25%	0.25%	0.25%
ELECTRONIC ENGINEER		0.00%	0.00%	0.00%	0.00%	0.00%	0.00%	0.00%	0.00%	0.00%	0.00%	0.00%	0.00%	0.00%	0.00%	0.00%	0.00%	0.13%	0.13%	0.13%
MECHANICAL ENGINEER		0.00%	0.00%	0.00%	0.00%	0.00%	0.00%	0.00%	0.00%	0.00%	0.00%	0.00%	0.00%	0.00%	0.00%	0.00%	0.00%	0.13%	0.13%	0.13%
ELECTRONIC TECHNICIAN		0.00%	0.00%	0.00%	0.00%	0.00%	0.00%	0.00%	0.00%	0.00%	0.00%	0.00%	0.00%	0.00%	0.00%	0.00%	0.00%	0.13%	0.13%	0.13%
PETRO LOG TECHNICIAN		0.25%	0.25%	0.25%	0.25%	0.25%	0.25%	0.25%	0.25%	0.25%	0.25%	0.25%	0.25%	0.25%	0.25%	0.25%	0.25%	0.25%	0.25%	0.25%
SALARY AND FRINGE		1,580	1,580	1,580	1,580	1,580	1,580	1,580	1,580	1,580	1,580	1,580	1,580	5,792	5,792	20,163	20,163	209,959	282,704	339,437
BONUSES AND COMMISSION		282	343	343	430	493	555	575	477	477	544	544	719	2,321	2,325	5,025	5,025	46,620	65,048	85,680
EQUIPMENT RENTAL		0	0	0	0	0	0	0	0	0	0	0	0	0	0	0	0	0	0	0
CONTRACT LABOR		0	0	0	0	0	0	0	0	0	0	0	0	0	0	0	0	0	0	0
SUPPLIES		1,000	500	500	500	500	500	500	500	500	500	500	500	1,600	1,600	1,750	1,750	9,000	12,000	16,000
ALL OTHER		750	500	500	500	500	500	500	500	500	500	500	500	1,750	1,750	1,750	1,750	8,500	10,000	12,500
TECHNICAL SUPPORT		3,611	2,922	2,922	3,010	3,072	3,135	3,155	3,056	3,056	3,124	3,124	3,299	11,462	11,467	28,688	28,688	274,079	369,752	453,617

EQUITY CAPITAL REQUIRED $0
CREDIT LINE REQUIREMENTS $244,654
NEW LONG TERM DEBT $125,000

TOTAL FUNDS REQUIRED $369,654

	APRIL 1988	MAY 1988	JUNE 1988	JULY 1988	AUG 1988	SEPT 1988	OCT 1988	NOV 1988	DEC 1988	JAN 1989	FEB 1989	MARCH 1989	1ST QTR FY 1989	2ND QTR FY 1989	3TH QTR FY 1989	4TH QTR FY 1989	FY 1990	FY 1991	FY 1992

OPERATING EXPENSE ASSUMPTIONS (CON'T)

GENERAL AND ADMIN.

HEAD COUNT	ANNUAL SALARY																		
CEO	175,000	0	0	0	0	1	1	1	1	1	1	1	1	1	1	1	1	1	1
PRESIDENT	30,000	1	1	1	1	1	1	1	1	1	1	1	1	1	1	1	1	1	1
VICE-PRESIDENT	30,000	1	1	1	1	1	1	1	1	1	1	1	1	1	1	2	3	3	3
CONTROLLER	29,000	1	1	1	1	1	1	1	1	1	1	1	1	1	1	1	1	1	1
ACCOUNTING CLERKS	16,000	1	1	1	1	1	1	1	1	1	1	1	1	1	1	1	2	2	2
OFFICE HELP	16,000	1	1	1	1	1	1	1	1	1	1	1	1	1	1	1	2	2	2
EXECUTIVE SECRETARY	18,600	1	1	1	1	1	1	1	1	1	1	1	1	1	1	1	1	1	1
PERSONNEL ADMINISTRATOR	18,000	0	0	0	0	0	1	1	1	1	1	1	1	0	0	1	1	1	1
INFORMATION MGMT MGR	16,000	0	0	0	0	0	0	0	0	0	0	0	0	0	0	0	1	1	1

BONUSES AND COMMISSIONS - PERCENT OF TOTAL SALES

		APRIL	MAY	JUNE	JULY	AUG	SEPT	OCT	NOV	DEC	JAN	FEB	MARCH	1ST QTR	2ND QTR	3TH QTR	4TH QTR	FY 1990	FY 1991	FY 1992
PRESIDENT		0.50%	0.50%	0.50%	0.50%	0.50%	0.50%	0.50%	0.50%	0.50%	0.50%	0.50%	0.50%	0.50%	0.50%	0.50%	0.50%	0.50%	0.50%	0.50%
VICE-PRESIDENT		0.50%	0.50%	0.50%	0.50%	0.50%	0.50%	0.50%	0.50%	0.50%	0.50%	0.50%	0.50%	0.50%	0.50%	0.50%	0.50%	0.50%	0.50%	0.50%
CONTROLLER		0.25%	0.25%	0.25%	0.25%	0.25%	0.25%	0.25%	0.25%	0.25%	0.25%	0.25%	0.25%	0.25%	0.25%	0.25%	0.25%	0.25%	0.25%	0.25%
ACCOUNTING CLERKS		0.13%	0.13%	0.13%	0.13%	0.13%	0.13%	0.13%	0.13%	0.13%	0.13%	0.13%	0.13%	0.13%	0.13%	0.13%	0.13%	0.13%	0.13%	0.13%
OFFICE HELP		0.13%	0.13%	0.13%	0.13%	0.13%	0.13%	0.13%	0.13%	0.13%	0.13%	0.13%	0.13%	0.13%	0.13%	0.13%	0.13%	0.13%	0.13%	0.13%
EXECUTIVE SECRETARY		0.25%	0.25%	0.25%	0.25%	0.25%	0.25%	0.25%	0.25%	0.25%	0.25%	0.25%	0.25%	0.25%	0.25%	0.25%	0.25%	0.25%	0.25%	0.25%

EXPENSES

	APRIL 1988	MAY 1988	JUNE 1988	JULY 1988	AUG 1988	SEPT 1988	OCT 1988	NOV 1988	DEC 1988	JAN 1989	FEB 1989	MARCH 1989	1ST QTR FY 1989	2ND QTR FY 1989	3TH QTR FY 1989	4TH QTR FY 1989	FY 1990	FY 1991	FY 1992
SALARY AND FRINGE	13,611	13,611	13,611	13,611	30,674	30,674	30,674	30,674	30,674	30,674	30,674	30,674	92,021	92,021	100,796	100,796	515,502	515,502	515,502
BONUSES AND COMMISSIONS	1,973	2,399	2,399	3,010	3,448	3,885	4,025	3,336	3,336	3,808	3,808	5,033	16,244	16,275	17,588	17,588	93,240	130,095	171,360
LEGAL AND PROFESSIONAL	12,500	15,000	15,000	15,000	15,000	15,000	15,000	17,500	15,000	15,000	10,000	10,000	45,000	60,000	45,000	45,000	250,000	325,000	400,000
OFFICE SPACE REQUIREMENTS (SQ. FT.)	4,199	4,199	4,199	4,199	4,199	4,199	4,199	4,199	4,199	4,199	4,199	4,199	4,199	4,199	4,199	4,199	5,000	6,000	6,000
ANNUAL RENT PER SQ. FT.	$16.20	$16.20	$16.20	$16.20	$16.20	$16.20	$16.20	$16.20	$16.20	$16.20	$16.20	$16.20	$16.20	$16.20	$16.20	$16.20	$16.20	$16.20	$16.20
OFFICE RENT EXPENSES	5,669	5,669	5,669	5,669	5,669	5,669	5,669	5,669	5,669	5,669	5,669	5,669	17,006	17,006	17,006	17,006	81,000	97,200	97,206
INSURANCE	6,250	6,250	6,250	6,250	6,250	6,250	6,250	6,250	6,250	6,250	6,250	6,250	25,000	25,000	25,000	25,000	150,000	200,000	275,000
UTILITIES	150	150	150	150	150	150	150	150	150	150	150	150	1,500	1,500	1,500	1,500	12,000	15,000	18,000
TELEPHONE	2,500	2,500	2,500	2,500	2,500	2,500	2,500	2,500	2,500	2,500	2,500	2,500	8,500	8,500	8,500	8,500	37,500	42,500	60,000
SUPPLIES	1,500	1,500	1,500	1,500	1,500	1,500	1,500	1,500	1,500	1,500	1,500	1,500	7,500	7,500	7,500	7,500	37,500	50,000	75,000
TRAVEL	1,000	1,000	1,000	1,000	1,000	1,000	1,000	3,000	3,000	1,000	1,000	1,000	4,250	4,250	4,250	4,250	25,000	35,000	50,000
OFFICE EXPENSES	6,000	6,000	6,000	6,000	6,000	6,000	6,000	6,000	6,000	6,000	6,000	6,000	27,500	27,500	27,500	27,500	165,000	250,000	375,000
EMPLOYEE BENEFITS/EDUC.	2,250	2,250	2,250	2,250	2,250	2,250	2,250	2,250	2,250	2,250	2,250	2,250	7,500	7,500	7,500	7,500	42,500	63,750	97,500
LAKEWOOD OFFICE	4,500	4,500	4,500	4,500	4,500	4,500	4,500	4,500	4,500	4,500	4,500	4,500	17,500	17,500	17,500	17,500	80,000	110,000	150,000
ALL OTHER	12,500	12,500	12,500	12,500	12,500	12,500	12,500	12,500	12,500	12,500	12,500	12,500	60,000	60,000	60,000	60,000	250,000	367,250	627,500
TOTAL GENERAL AND ADMIN.	70,403	73,329	73,329	73,940	91,440	91,877	92,017	95,828	93,328	92,850	86,800	88,025	329,520	344,551	339,639	339,639	1,739,242	2,201,297	2,912,062

241

EQUITY CAPITAL REQUIRED $0
CREDIT LINE REQUIREMENTS $244,654
NEW LONG TERM DEBT $125,000

TOTAL FUNDS REQUIRED $369,654

GEOPHYSICS INTERNATIONAL - DETAILED PROJECTIONS
AT MARCH 31, 1988
FISCAL YEAR - APRIL 1 TO MARCH 31

OPERATING EXPENSE ASSUMPTIONS (CON'T)

	ANNUAL SALARY	APRIL 1988	MAY 1988	JUNE 1988	JULY 1988	AUG 1988	SEPT 1988	OCT 1988	NOV 1988	DEC 1988	JAN 1989	FEB 1989	MARCH 1989	1ST QTR F.Y. 1989	2ND QTR F.Y. 1989	3TH QTR F.Y. 1989	4TH QTR F.Y. 1989	F.Y. 1990	F.Y. 1991	F.Y. 1992
MARKETING AND SELLING																				
HEAD COUNT																				
V.P. OF SALES	24,000	1	1	1	1	1	1	1	1	1	1	1	1	1	1	1	1	1	1	2
MGR. - PETRO-SONDE	24,000	1	0	0	0	0	0	0	0	0	1	0	0	1	1	1	1	1	1	1
MGR. - SATELLITE	24,000	0	0	0	0	0	0	0	0	0	1	0	0	1	1	1	1	1	1	1
MGR. - REGIONAL SALES	24,000	0	0	0	0	0	0	0	0	0	1	0	0	0	0	1	1	2	2	2
STAFF GEOLOGISTS	24,000	3	3	3	3	3	3	3	3	3	3	3	3	3	3	4	4	5	6	8
BONUSES AND COMMISSIONS																				
TOTAL SALES																				
V.P. OF SALES		0.25%	0.25%	0.25%	0.25%	0.25%	0.25%	0.25%	0.25%	0.25%	0.25%	0.25%	0.25%	0.25%	0.25%	0.25%	0.25%	0.25%	0.25%	0.25%
STAFF GEOLOGISTS		1.50%	1.50%	1.50%	1.50%	1.50%	1.50%	1.50%	1.50%	1.50%	1.50%	1.50%	1.50%	1.50%	1.50%	1.50%	1.50%	1.50%	1.50%	1.50%
PETRO-SONDE SALES ONLY																				
MGR. - PETRO-SONDE		0.00%	0.00%	0.00%	0.00%	0.00%	0.00%	0.00%	0.00%	0.00%	0.00%	0.00%	0.00%	0.25%	0.25%	0.25%	0.25%	0.25%	0.25%	0.25%
SATELLITE IMAGERY SALES ONLY																				
MGR. - SATELLITE IMAGERY		0.25%	0.25%	0.25%	0.25%	0.25%	0.25%	0.25%	0.25%	0.25%	0.25%	0.25%	0.25%	0.25%	0.25%	0.25%	0.25%	0.25%	0.25%	0.25%
OTHER SALES ONLY																				
MGR. - OTHER SALES		0.00%	0.00%	0.00%	0.00%	0.00%	0.00%	0.00%	0.00%	0.00%	0.00%	0.00%	0.00%	0.25%	0.25%	0.25%	0.25%	0.25%	0.25%	0.25%
EXPENSES																				
SALARY AND FRINGE		9,360	9,360	9,360	9,360	9,360	9,360	9,360	9,360	9,360	14,040	9,360	9,360	51,480	51,480	68,640	68,640	348,480	421,661	590,325
BONUSES AND COMMISSIONS																				
TOTAL SALES		1,973	2,399	2,399	3,010	3,448	3,885	4,025	3,336	3,336	3,808	3,808	5,033	16,244	16,275	17,588	17,588	93,240	130,095	171,360
PETRO-SONDE		0	0	0	0	0	0	0	0	0	0	0	0	1,875	1,875	2,063	2,063	10,800	14,625	18,900
SATELLITE IMAGERY		4	5	5	8	8	8	8	9	9	9	9	9	41	45	45	45	360	720	720
OTHER SALES		0	0	0	0	0	0	0	0	0	0	0	0	405	405	405	405	2,160	3,240	4,860
TRAVEL		3,250	4,500	4,500	4,500	4,500	4,500	4,500	4,500	4,500	4,500	4,500	4,500	9,000	9,000	9,000	9,000	36,000	40,000	45,000
TRADE SHOWS		0	0	0	0	0	0	0	0	0	0	0	0	2,500	2,500	2,500	2,500	12,500	15,500	20,000
ADVERTISING		1,250	2,000	2,000	2,000	2,000	2,000	2,000	2,000	2,000	2,000	2,000	2,000	9,000	9,000	9,000	9,000	54,000	85,000	125,000
TELEPHONE		2,750	3,000	3,000	3,000	3,000	3,000	3,000	3,000	3,000	3,000	3,000	3,000	10,000	10,000	10,000	10,000	50,000	65,000	80,000
ALL OTHER		3,250	3,250	3,250	3,250	3,250	3,250	3,250	3,250	3,250	3,250	3,250	3,250	9,000	9,000	9,000	9,000	45,000	60,000	80,000
TOTAL MARKETING AND SELLING EXPENSES		21,837	24,515	24,515	25,128	25,565	26,003	26,143	25,455	25,455	30,607	25,927	27,152	109,544	109,580	128,240	128,240	652,540	835,841	1,136,165

GEOPHYSICS INTERNATIONAL - DETAILED PROJECTIONS
AT MARCH 31, 1988
FISCAL YEAR - APRIL 1 TO MARCH 31

EQUITY CAPITAL REQUIRED $0
CREDIT LINE REQUIREMENTS $244,654
NEW LONG TERM DEBT $125,000

TOTAL FUNDS REQUIRED $369,654

	APRIL 1988	MAY 1988	JUNE 1988	JULY 1988	AUG 1988	SEPT 1988	OCT 1988	NOV 1988	DEC 1988	JAN 1989	FEB 1989	MARCH 1989	1ST QTR F.Y. 1989	2ND QTR F.Y. 1989	3TH QTR F.Y. 1989	4TH QTR F.Y. 1989	F.Y. 1990	F.Y. 1991	F.Y. 1992
FIXED ASSETS AQUISITION ASSUMPTIONS																			
NEW FIXED ASSETS																			
OFFICE EQUIPMENT	0	0	0	0	0	0	0	0	0	0	0	0	0	0	0	100,000	100,000	150,000	200,000
COMPUTER SYSTEM	0	0	0	0	0	0	0	0	0	0	0	0	0	75,000	0	0	0	0	0
TOTAL NEW FIXED ASSETS	0	0	0	0	0	0	0	0	0	0	0	0	0	75,000	0	100,000	100,000	150,000	200,000
DEPRECIATION RATES - STRAIGHT LINE																			
NEW FIXED ASSETS	5	5	5	5	5	5	5	5	5	5	5	5	5	5	5	5	5	5	5
BALANCE SHEET ASSUMPTIONS																			
OPERATING CASH BALANCES	25,000	25,000	25,000	25,000	25,000	25,000	25,000	25,000	25,000	25,000	25,000	25,000	25,000	50,000	50,000	50,000	50,000	50,000	50,006
ACCOUNT RECEIVABLE DAYS(GROSS SALES)	30	30	30	30	30	30	30	30	30	30	30	30	30	30	30	30	45	60	60
OTHER C/A INCREASE/(DECREASE)	2,012	0	0	0	0	0	0	0	0	0	0	0	(6,773)	0	0	0	0	0	0
EXISTING ASSET DEPRECIATION	2,650	2,650	2,650	2,650	2,650	2,650	2,650	2,650	2,650	2,650	2,650	2,650	7,950	7,950	7,950	7,950	31,800	31,800	18,510
OTHER ASSETS INCREASE/(DECREASE)	11,125	13,500	13,500	16,900	19,400	21,900	22,700	18,700	18,700	21,400	21,400	28,400	91,200	91,200	98,700	98,700	518,400	714,600	950,400
ACCOUNT PAYABLE - % OF MONTHLY SALES	20%	20%	20%	20%	20%	20%	20%	20%	20%	20%	20%	20%	25%	25%	25%	25%	33%	50%	50%
OTHER LIAB. INCREASE/(DECREASE)	(1,500)	(1,500)	(1,500)	(1,500)	(1,500)	(1,500)	(1,500)	(1,500)	(1,500)	(1,500)	(1,500)	(1,500)	(7,267)	0	0	0	0	0	0
NEW N/P L/T LOANS	0	0	0	0	0	0	0	125,000	0	0	0	0	0	0	0	0	0	0	0
N/P L/T PRINC. PAYMENTS	7,850	7,850	7,850	7,850	7,850	7,850	7,850	7,850	7,850	7,850	107,850	7,850	32,850	27,300	20,850	20,850	83,400	73,094	
CHANGES IN N/P L/T - DRAWS/(PRINC.PAY.)	(7,850)	(7,850)	(7,850)	(7,850)	(7,850)	(7,850)	(7,850)	117,150	(7,850)	(7,850)	(107,850)	(7,850)	(32,850)	(27,300)	(20,850)	(20,850)	(83,400)	(73,094)	
CAPITAL STOCK INCREASE/(DECREASE)	0	0	0	0	0	0	0	0	0	0	0	0	0	0	0	0	0	0	0
PAID IN CAPITAL INCREASE/(DECREASE)	0	0	0	0	0	0	0	0	0	0	0	0	0	0	0	0	0	0	0
TREASURY STOCK (PURCHASE)/SALE	0	0	0	0	0	0	0	0	0	0	0	0	0	0	0	0	0	0	0
INTEREST RATE - CASH EQUIVALENTS	5.00%	5.00%	5.00%	5.00%	5.00%	5.00%	5.00%	5.00%	5.00%	5.00%	5.00%	5.00%	5.00%	5.00%	5.00%	5.00%	5.00%	5.00%	5.00%
INTEREST RATE - SHORT TERM	12.00%	12.00%	12.00%	12.00%	12.00%	12.00%	12.00%	12.00%	12.00%	12.00%	12.00%	12.00%	12.00%	12.00%	12.00%	12.00%	12.00%	12.00%	12.00%
INTEREST RATE - LONG TERM	13.50%	13.50%	13.50%	13.50%	13.50%	13.50%	13.50%	13.50%	13.50%	13.50%	13.50%	13.50%	13.50%	13.50%	13.50%	13.50%	13.50%	13.50%	13.50%
EFFECTIVE TAX RATE	34%	34%	34%	34%	34%	34%	34%	34%	34%	30%	34%	34%	34%	34%	34%	30%	34%	34%	34%
NET OPERATING LOSS CARRYFORWARD	0	N/A	N/A	N/A	N/A	N/A	N/A	N/A	N/A	N/A	N/A	N/A	N/A	N/A	N/A	N/A	N/A	N/A	N/A

EQUITY CAPITAL REQUIRED		$0
CREDIT LINE REQUIREMENTS		$244,654
NEW LONG TERM DEBT		$125,000
TOTAL FUNDS REQUIRED		$369,654

	APRIL 1988	MAY 1988	JUNE 1988	JULY 1988	AUG 1988	SEPT 1988	OCT 1988	NOV 1988	DEC 1988	JAN 1989	FEB 1989	MARCH 1989	1ST QTR F.Y. 1989	2ND QTR F.Y. 1989	3TH QTR F.Y. 1989	4TH QTR F.Y. 1989	F.Y. 1990	F.Y. 1991	F.Y. 1992
PROJECTED INCOME STATEMENT																			
GROSS SALES																			
PETRO-SONDE	101,250	125,000	125,000	150,000	175,000	200,000	200,000	160,000	160,000	180,000	180,000	250,000	750,000	750,000	825,000	825,000	4,320,000	5,850,000	7,560,000
SATELLITE IMAGERY	1,500	2,100	2,100	3,000	3,000	3,000	3,000	3,600	3,600	3,600	3,600	3,600	16,200	18,000	18,000	18,000	144,000	288,000	288,000
OTHER SALES	10,000	10,000	10,000	19,000	19,000	19,000	27,000	27,000	27,000	34,000	34,000	34,000	162,000	162,000	162,000	162,000	864,000	1,296,000	1,944,000
TOTAL GROSS SALES	112,750	137,100	137,100	172,000	197,000	222,000	230,000	190,600	190,600	217,600	217,600	287,600	928,200	930,000	1,005,000	1,005,000	5,328,000	7,434,000	9,792,000
COST OF GOODS SOLD																			
PETRO-SONDE	26,535	27,080	27,080	30,020	32,960	35,900	35,900	34,900	34,900	37,720	37,720	41,780	148,530	148,530	150,030	150,030	751,108	1,018,877	1,308,096
SATELLITE IMAGERY	6,320	5,832	5,832	5,850	5,850	5,850	5,850	5,862	5,862	5,862	5,862	5,862	31,439	31,475	31,475	31,475	171,212	304,340	340,923
OTHER SALES	300	300	300	570	570	570	810	810	810	1,020	1,020	1,020	4,860	4,860	4,860	4,860	25,920	38,880	58,320
TOTAL C.O.G.S.	33,155	33,212	33,212	36,440	39,380	42,320	42,560	41,572	41,572	44,602	44,602	48,662	184,829	184,865	186,365	186,365	948,240	1,362,097	1,707,339
GROSS PROFIT	79,595	103,888	103,888	135,560	157,620	179,680	187,440	149,028	149,028	172,998	172,998	238,938	743,371	745,135	818,635	818,635	4,379,760	6,071,903	8,084,661
OPERATING EXPENSES																			
TECHNICAL SUPPORT	3,611	2,922	2,922	3,010	3,072	3,135	3,155	3,056	3,056	3,124	3,124	3,299	11,462	11,467	28,688	28,688	274,079	369,752	453,617
GENERAL AND ADMIN.	70,403	73,329	73,329	73,940	91,440	91,877	92,017	95,828	93,328	92,850	86,800	88,025	329,520	344,551	339,639	339,639	1,739,242	2,201,297	2,912,062
MARKETING AND SELLING	21,837	24,515	24,515	25,128	25,565	26,003	26,143	25,455	25,455	30,607	25,927	27,152	109,544	109,580	128,240	128,240	652,540	835,841	1,136,165
TOTAL OPERATING EXPENSES	95,851	100,766	100,766	102,077	120,077	121,014	121,314	124,338	121,838	126,581	115,851	118,476	450,526	465,598	496,567	496,567	2,665,861	3,406,890	4,501,844
OPERATING PROFIT	(16,256)	3,122	3,122	33,483	37,543	58,666	66,126	24,690	27,190	46,417	57,147	120,462	292,845	279,537	322,068	322,068	1,713,899	2,665,013	3,582,817
OTHER EXPENSES/(INCOME)																			
DEPRECIATION - NEW FIXED ASSETS	2,012	0	0	0	0	0	0	0	0	0	0	0	0	3,750	3,750	8,750	55,000	85,000	125,000
DEPRECIATION - EXISTING ASSETS	2,650	2,650	2,650	2,650	2,650	2,650	2,650	2,650	2,650	2,650	2,650	2,650	7,950	7,950	7,950	7,950	31,800	31,800	18,510
INTEREST INCOME	0	0	0	0	0	0	0	0	0	0	0	0	0	0	0	0	0	(5,376)	(27,948)
INTEREST EXPENSE - SHORT TERM	0	0	0	0	0	0	1,453	2,159	686	745	855	1,635	5,029	3,206	4,326	2,190	8,107	0	0
INTEREST EXPENSE - LONG TERM	1,798	1,754	1,710	1,666	3,420	1,577	3,332	3,726	4,340	4,252	3,601	2,951	8,165	7,150	6,337	5,634	15,497	4,934	0
NET PROFIT/(LOSS) BEFORE TAXES	(20,066)	(1,282)	(1,238)	29,168	31,473	54,438	58,691	16,155	19,513	38,770	50,041	113,227	271,701	257,481	299,705	297,545	1,603,495	2,548,655	3,467,255
INCOME TAXES PAYABLE	0	0	0	0	0	0	0	0	0	0	0	26,243	92,378	87,543	101,900	89,263	545,188	866,543	1,178,867
NET PROFIT/(LOSS) AFTER TAXES	(20,066)	(1,282)	(1,238)	29,168	31,473	54,438	58,691	16,155	19,513	38,770	50,041	86,983	179,323	169,937	197,805	208,281	1,058,306	1,682,112	2,288,388
NET PROFIT/(LOSS) ON GROSS SALES	-17.8%	-0.9%	-0.9%	17.0%	16.0%	24.5%	25.5%	8.5%	10.2%	17.8%	23.0%	30.2%	19.3%	18.3%	19.7%	20.7%	19.9%	22.6%	23.4%

GEOPHYSICS INTERNATIONAL - DETAILED PROJECTIONS
AT MARCH 31, 1988
FISCAL YEAR - APRIL 1 TO MARCH 31

EQUITY CAPITAL REQUIRED	$0
CREDIT LINE REQUIREMENTS	$244,654
NEW LONG TERM DEBT	$125,000
TOTAL FUNDS REQUIRED	$369,654

	04/01/88	APRIL 1988	MAY 1988	JUNE 1988	JULY 1988	AUG 1988	SEPT 1988	OCT 1988	NOV 1988	DEC 1988	JAN 1989	FEB 1989	MARCH 1989	1ST QTR F.Y. 1989	2ND QTR F.Y. 1989	3TH QTR F.Y. 1989	4TH QTR F.Y. 1989	F.Y. 1990	F.Y. 1991	F.Y. 1992
PROJECTED BALANCE SHEET																				
ASSETS																				
CASH -OPERATING ACCOUNT	16,367	25,000	25,000	25,000	25,000	25,000	25,000	25,000	25,000	25,000	25,000	25,000	25,000	25,000	50,000	50,000	50,000	50,000	50,000	50,000
MARKETABLE SECURITIES	0	0	0	0	0	0	0	0	0	0	0	0	0	0	0	0	0	107,518	558,966	1,545,714
ACCOUNTS RECEIVABLES	166,240	112,750	137,100	137,100	172,000	197,000	222,000	230,000	190,600	190,600	217,600	217,600	287,600	309,400	310,000	335,000	335,000	666,000	1,239,000	1,632,000
OTHER C/A	6,773	6,773	6,773	6,773	6,773	6,773	6,773	6,773	6,773	6,773	6,773	6,773	6,773	0	0	0	0	0	0	0
TOTAL CURRENT ASSETS	189,380	144,523	168,873	168,873	203,773	228,773	253,773	261,773	222,373	222,373	249,373	249,373	319,373	334,400	360,000	385,000	385,000	823,518	1,847,966	3,227,714
FIXED ASSETS																				
NEW P.P.+E.	0	0	0	0	0	0	0	0	0	0	0	0	0	0	75,000	75,000	175,000	275,000	425,000	625,000
LESS ACCUM. DEPREC.	0	0	0	0	0	0	0	0	0	0	0	0	0	0	(3,750)	(7,500)	(16,250)	(71,250)	(156,250)	(281,250)
EXISTING P.P.+E.	223,071	223,071	223,071	223,071	223,071	223,071	223,071	223,071	223,071	223,071	223,071	223,071	223,071	223,071	223,071	223,071	223,071	223,071	223,071	223,071
LESS ACCUM. DEPREC.	(77,999)	(80,011)	(82,661)	(85,311)	(87,961)	(90,611)	(93,261)	(95,911)	(98,561)	(101,211)	(103,861)	(106,511)	(109,161)	(117,111)	(125,061)	(133,011)	(140,961)	(172,761)	(204,561)	(223,071)
TOTAL FIXED ASSETS	145,072	143,060	140,410	137,760	135,110	132,460	129,810	127,160	124,510	121,860	119,210	116,560	113,910	105,960	169,260	157,560	240,860	254,060	287,260	343,750
OTHER ASSETS-PATENTS	913,330	924,455	937,955	951,455	968,355	987,755	1,009,655	1,032,355	1,051,055	1,069,755	1,091,155	1,112,555	1,140,955	1,232,155	1,323,355	1,422,055	1,520,755	2,039,155	2,753,755	3,704,155
TOTAL ASSETS	1,247,782	1,212,038	1,247,238	1,258,088	1,307,238	1,348,988	1,393,238	1,421,288	1,397,938	1,413,988	1,459,738	1,478,488	1,574,238	1,672,515	1,852,615	1,964,615	2,146,615	3,116,733	4,888,981	7,275,619
CURRENT LIABILITIES																				
ACCOUNT PAYABLE	183,503	22,550	27,420	27,420	34,400	39,400	44,400	46,000	38,120	38,120	43,520	43,520	57,520	77,350	77,500	83,750	83,750	146,520	309,750	408,000
CREDIT LINE	0	145,275	187,237	208,675	231,027	244,654	239,815	215,924	68,649	74,536	85,466	163,525	167,641	106,883	144,195	72,990	67,559	0	0	0
OTHER LIABILITIES	23,767	23,767	22,267	20,767	19,267	17,767	16,267	14,767	13,267	11,767	10,267	8,767	7,267	0	0	0	0	0	0	0
TOTAL CURR. LIAB.	207,270	191,592	236,924	256,862	284,694	301,821	300,482	276,691	120,036	124,423	139,253	215,812	232,428	184,233	221,695	156,740	151,309	146,520	309,750	408,000
LONG TERM DEBT																				
NOTES PAYABLE	319,694	319,694	311,844	303,994	296,144	288,294	280,444	272,594	389,744	381,894	374,044	266,194	258,344	225,494	198,194	177,344	156,494	73,094	0	0
TOTAL LONG TERM DEBT	319,694	319,694	311,844	303,994	296,144	288,294	280,444	272,594	389,744	381,894	374,044	266,194	258,344	225,494	198,194	177,344	156,494	73,094	0	0
TOTAL LIABILITIES	526,964	511,286	548,768	560,856	580,838	590,115	580,926	549,285	509,780	506,317	513,297	482,006	490,772	409,727	419,889	334,084	307,803	219,614	309,750	408,000
STOCKHOLDER'S EQUITY																				
CAPITAL STOCK	1,000	1,000	1,000	1,000	1,000	1,000	1,000	1,000	1,000	1,000	1,000	1,000	1,000	1,000	1,000	1,000	1,000	1,000	1,000	1,000
ADD. PAID IN CAPITAL	719,818	699,752	697,470	696,232	725,400	757,873	811,312	871,003	887,158	906,671	945,441	995,482	1,082,466	1,261,788	1,431,726	1,629,531	1,837,812	2,896,119	4,578,231	6,866,619
RETAINED EARNINGS	0	0	0	0	0	0	0	0	0	0	0	0	0	0	0	0	0	0	0	0
LESS TREASURY	0	0	0	0	0	0	0	0	0	0	0	0	0	0	0	0	0	0	0	0
TOTAL EQUITY	720,818	700,752	698,470	697,232	726,400	758,873	812,312	872,003	888,158	907,671	946,441	996,482	1,083,466	1,262,788	1,432,726	1,630,531	1,838,812	2,897,119	4,579,231	6,867,619
TOTAL EQUITY AND LIAB.	1,247,782	1,212,038	1,247,238	1,258,088	1,307,238	1,348,988	1,393,238	1,421,288	1,397,938	1,413,988	1,459,738	1,478,488	1,574,238	1,672,515	1,852,615	1,964,615	2,146,615	3,116,733	4,888,981	7,275,619

GEOPHYSICS INTERNATIONAL - DETAILED PROJECTIONS
AT MARCH 31, 1988
FISCAL YEAR - APRIL 1 TO MARCH 31

EQUITY CAPITAL REQUIRED	$0
CREDIT LINE REQUIREMENTS	$244,654
NEW LONG TERM DEBT	$125,000
TOTAL FUNDS REQUIRED	**$369,654**

	APRIL 1988	MAY 1988	JUNE 1988	JULY 1988	AUG 1988	SEPT 1988	OCT 1988	NOV 1988	DEC 1988	JAN 1989	FEB 1989	MARCH 1989	1ST QTR F.Y. 1989	2ND QTR F.Y. 1989	3RD QTR F.Y. 1989	4TH QTR F.Y. 1989	F.Y. 1990	F.Y. 1991	F.Y. 1992
CASH FLOW PROJECTION																			
BEGINNING MARKETABLE SECURITIES BALANCE	0	0	0	0	0	0	0	0	0	0	0	0	0	0	0	0	0	107,518	558,966
NET PROFIT OR LOSS	(20,066)	(1,282)	(1,238)	29,168	31,473	54,438	58,691	16,155	19,513	38,770	50,041	86,983	179,323	169,937	197,805	208,281	1,058,306	1,682,112	2,288,388
ADD BACK DEPRECIATION	2,012	2,650	2,650	2,650	2,650	2,650	2,650	2,650	2,650	2,650	2,650	2,650	7,950	11,700	11,700	16,700	86,800	116,800	143,510
CHANGES IN WORKING CAPITAL ACCOUNTS																			
SOURCE/(USE) OF CASH																			
CURRENT ASSETS																			
CASH - OPERATING ACCOUNT	(8,633)	0	0	0	0	0	0	0	0	0	0	0	0	0	0	0	0	0	0
ACCOUNTS RECEIVABLES	53,490	(24,350)	0	(34,900)	(25,000)	(25,000)	(8,000)	39,400	0	(27,000)	0	(70,000)	(21,800)	(25,000)	(25,000)	0	(331,000)	(573,000)	(393,000)
OTHER C/A & PATENTS	(11,125)	(13,500)	(13,500)	(16,900)	(19,400)	(21,900)	(22,700)	(18,700)	(18,700)	(21,400)	(21,400)	(28,400)	(84,427)	(91,200)	(98,700)	(98,700)	(518,400)	(714,600)	(950,400)
CURRENT LIABILITIES																			
ACCOUNT PAYABLE	(160,953)	4,870	0	6,980	5,000	5,000	1,600	(7,880)	0	5,400	0	14,000	19,830	150	6,250	0	62,770	163,230	98,250
OTHER LIABILITIES	0	(1,500)	(1,500)	(1,500)	(1,500)	(1,500)	(1,500)	(1,500)	(1,500)	(1,500)	(1,500)	(1,500)	(7,267)	(600)	0	0	0	0	0
TOTAL WORKING CAPITAL CHANGES	(127,221)	(34,480)	(15,000)	(46,320)	(40,900)	(43,400)	(30,600)	11,320	(20,200)	(44,500)	(22,900)	(85,900)	(93,664)	(116,650)	(117,450)	(98,700)	(786,630)	(1,124,370)	(1,245,150)
FIXED ASSETS																			
NEW P.P. +E.	0	0	0	0	0	0	0	0	0	0	0	0	0	(75,000)	0	0	(100,000)	(150,000)	(200,000)
EXISTING STORE P.P. +E.	0	0	0	0	0	0	0	0	0	0	0	0	0	0	0	(100,000)	0	0	0
CHANGES IN LONG TERM DEBT POSITION																			
NOTES PAYABLE	0	(7,850)	(7,850)	(7,850)	(7,850)	(7,850)	(7,850)	117,150	(7,850)	(7,850)	(107,850)	(7,850)	(32,850)	(27,300)	(20,850)	(20,850)	(83,400)	(73,094)	0
CHANGES IN STOCKHOLDER'S EQUITY																			
CAPITAL STOCK	0	(1,000)	0	0	1,000	(1,000)	1,000	0	0	0	0	0	0	0	0	0	0	0	0
ADD. PAID IN CAPITAL	0	0	0	0	0	0	0	0	0	0	0	0	0	0	0	0	0	0	0
LESS TREASURY	0	0	0	0	0	0	0	0	0	0	0	0	0	0	0	0	0	0	0
CASH BALANCE BEFORE CREDIT LINE	(145,275)	(41,962)	(21,438)	(22,352)	(13,627)	4,838	23,891	147,275	(5,887)	(10,930)	(78,059)	(4,117)	60,759	(37,313)	71,205	5,431	175,076	451,448	986,748
CREDIT LINE																			
BEGINNING BALANCE	0	145,275	187,237	208,675	231,027	244,654	239,815	215,924	68,649	74,536	85,466	163,525	167,641	106,882	144,195	72,990	67,559	0	0
PERIOD DRAWS	145,275	41,962	21,438	22,352	13,627	0	0	0	5,887	10,930	78,059	4,117	0	37,313	0	0	0	0	0
REPAYMENTS	0	0	0	0	0	4,838	23,891	147,275	0	0	0	0	60,759	0	71,205	5,431	67,559	0	0
ENDING C/L BALANCE	145,275	187,237	208,675	231,027	244,654	239,815	215,924	68,649	74,536	85,466	163,525	167,641	106,882	144,195	72,990	67,559	0	0	0
ENDING MARKETABLE SECURITIES BALANCE	0	0	0	0	0	0	0	0	0	0	0	0	0	0	0	0	107,518	558,966	1,545,714

EQUITY CAPITAL REQUIRED $0
CREDIT LINE REQUIREMENTS $244,654
NEW LONG TERM DEBT $125,000

TOTAL FUNDS REQUIRED $369,654

GEOPHYSICS INTERNATIONAL - DETAILED PROJECTIONS
AT MARCH 31, 1988
FISCAL YEAR - APRIL 1 TO MARCH 31

MARGIN ANALYSIS - INCOME STATEMENT

	APRIL 1988	MAY 1988	JUNE 1988	JULY 1988	AUG 1988	SEPT 1988	OCT 1988	NOV 1988	DEC 1988	JAN 1989	FEB 1989	MARCH 1989	1ST QTR F.Y.1989	2ND QTR F.Y.1989	3TH QTR F.Y.1989	4TH QTR F.Y.1989	F.Y. 1990	F.Y. 1991	F.Y. 1992
GROSS SALES																			
PETRO-SONDE	89.8%	91.2%	91.2%	87.2%	88.8%	90.1%	87.0%	83.9%	83.9%	82.7%	82.7%	86.9%	80.8%	80.6%	82.1%	82.1%	81.1%	78.7%	77.2%
SATELLITE IMAGERY	1.3%	1.5%	1.5%	1.7%	1.5%	1.4%	1.3%	1.9%	1.9%	1.7%	1.7%	1.3%	1.7%	1.9%	1.8%	1.8%	2.7%	3.9%	2.9%
OTHER SALES	8.9%	7.3%	7.3%	11.0%	9.6%	8.6%	11.7%	14.2%	14.2%	15.6%	15.6%	11.8%	17.5%	17.4%	16.1%	16.1%	16.2%	17.4%	19.9%
TOTAL GROSS SALES	100.0%	100.0%	100.0%	100.0%	100.0%	100.0%	100.0%	100.0%	100.0%	100.0%	100.0%	100.0%	100.0%	100.0%	100.0%	100.0%	100.0%	100.0%	100.0%
COST OF GOODS SOLD																			
PETRO-SONDE	23.5%	19.8%	19.8%	17.5%	16.7%	16.2%	15.6%	18.3%	18.3%	17.3%	17.3%	14.5%	16.0%	16.0%	14.9%	14.9%	14.1%	13.7%	13.4%
SATELLITE IMAGERY	5.6%	4.3%	4.3%	3.4%	3.0%	2.6%	2.5%	3.1%	3.1%	2.7%	2.7%	2.0%	3.4%	3.4%	3.1%	3.1%	3.2%	4.1%	3.5%
OTHER SALES	0.3%	0.2%	0.2%	0.3%	0.3%	0.3%	0.4%	0.4%	0.4%	0.5%	0.5%	0.4%	0.5%	0.5%	0.5%	0.5%	0.5%	0.5%	0.6%
TOTAL C.O.G.S.	29.4%	24.2%	24.2%	21.2%	20.0%	19.1%	18.5%	21.8%	21.8%	20.5%	20.5%	16.9%	19.9%	19.9%	18.5%	18.5%	17.8%	18.3%	17.4%
GROSS PROFIT	70.6%	75.8%	75.8%	78.8%	80.0%	80.9%	81.5%	78.2%	78.2%	79.5%	79.5%	83.1%	80.1%	80.1%	81.5%	81.5%	82.2%	81.7%	82.6%
OPERATING EXPENSES																			
TECHNICAL SUPPORT	3.2%	2.1%	2.1%	1.7%	1.6%	1.4%	1.4%	1.6%	1.6%	1.4%	1.4%	1.1%	1.2%	1.2%	2.9%	2.9%	5.1%	5.0%	4.6%
GENERAL AND ADMIN.	62.4%	53.5%	53.5%	43.0%	46.4%	41.4%	40.0%	50.3%	49.0%	42.7%	39.9%	30.6%	35.5%	37.0%	33.8%	33.8%	32.6%	29.6%	29.7%
MARKETING AND SELLING	19.4%	17.9%	17.9%	14.6%	13.0%	11.7%	11.4%	13.4%	13.4%	14.1%	11.9%	9.4%	11.8%	11.8%	12.8%	12.8%	12.2%	11.2%	11.6%
TOTAL OPERATING EXPENSES	85.0%	73.5%	73.5%	59.3%	61.0%	54.5%	52.7%	65.2%	63.9%	58.2%	53.2%	41.2%	48.5%	50.1%	49.4%	49.4%	50.0%	45.8%	46.0%
OPERATING PROFIT	-14.4%	2.3%	2.3%	19.5%	19.1%	26.4%	28.8%	13.0%	14.3%	21.3%	26.3%	41.9%	31.5%	30.1%	32.0%	32.0%	32.2%	35.8%	36.6%
OTHER EXPENSES/(INCOME)																			
DEPRECIATION - NEW FIXED ASSETS	0.0%	0.0%	0.0%	0.0%	0.0%	0.0%	0.0%	0.0%	0.0%	0.0%	0.0%	0.0%	0.0%	0.4%	0.4%	0.9%	1.0%	1.1%	1.3%
DEPRECIATION - EXISTING ASSETS	1.8%	1.9%	1.9%	1.5%	1.3%	1.2%	1.2%	1.4%	1.4%	1.2%	1.2%	0.9%	0.9%	0.9%	0.8%	0.8%	0.6%	0.4%	0.2%
INTEREST INCOME	0.0%	0.0%	0.0%	0.0%	0.0%	0.0%	0.0%	0.0%	0.0%	0.0%	0.0%	0.0%	0.0%	0.0%	0.0%	0.0%	0.0%	-0.1%	-0.3%
INTEREST EXPENSE - SHORT TERM	0.0%	0.0%	0.0%	0.0%	0.0%	0.0%	0.6%	1.1%	0.4%	0.3%	0.4%	0.6%	0.5%	0.3%	0.4%	0.2%	0.2%	0.0%	0.0%
INTEREST EXPENSE - LONG TERM	1.6%	1.3%	1.3%	1.0%	1.7%	0.7%	1.4%	2.0%	2.3%	2.0%	1.7%	1.0%	0.9%	0.8%	0.6%	0.6%	0.3%	0.1%	0.0%
NET PROFIT/(LOSS) BEFORE TAXES	-17.8%	-0.9%	-0.9%	17.0%	16.0%	24.5%	25.5%	8.5%	10.2%	17.8%	23.0%	39.4%	29.3%	27.7%	29.8%	29.6%	30.1%	34.3%	35.4%
INCOME TAXES PAYABLE	0.0%	0.0%	0.0%	0.0%	0.0%	0.0%	0.0%	0.0%	0.0%	0.0%	0.0%	9.1%	10.0%	9.4%	10.1%	8.9%	10.2%	11.7%	12.0%
NET PROFIT/(LOSS) AFTER TAXES	-17.8%	-0.9%	-0.9%	17.0%	16.0%	24.5%	25.5%	8.5%	10.2%	17.8%	23.0%	30.2%	19.3%	18.3%	19.7%	20.7%	19.9%	22.6%	23.4%

COMPANY ANALYSIS

FUNCTION	STRONG	AVERAGE	WEAK	RESOURCES AND COMMENTS
General/admin		X		Need more experienced management
Marketing			X	Need full time Public Relations/ marketing firm
Finance			X	Need a capital infusion
Human Resources		X		Company is in a hiring mode.
Engineering			X	Require own R & D and inhouse engineering
Operations	X			Extremely efficient
Resource Utilization			X	Our field and lab resources are under utilized in terms of revenue generation potential
Client Relations		X		We are identifying clients' needs and responding to them
Areas served			X	We need to be better prepared to shift resources on a seasonal basis
International		X		A continuing effort to obtain international contracts is under way

The company is in the process of identifying and correcting certain deficiencies found in the corporate structure or operating procedures. We have revised our marketing and sales strategy to reflect the technical nature of the company. We are currently seeking experienced companies and individuals to work with to facilitate our expansion internationally. We are permanently moving our field personnel to the part of the country they are most often assigned to work in. This reduces field expense and allows an individual geologist to become thoroughly familiar with the geology in one specific region. An effort is under way to recruit the best talent to fill key positions in the company that cannot be filled internally while continuing to search for Geologists and support personnel who can meet our high standards of "excellence."

RISK ANALYSIS TABLE

		RATINGS	
ELEMENT	Low	Medium	High
Industry		XX	
Market		XX	
Competitive position	XX		
Strategy		XX	
Assumptions		XX	
Financial performance		XX	
Management performance			XX
Future performance		XX	
Technological development			XX
OVERALL RISK		XX	

The following assumptions were made for the Risk Analysis:

- A moderately stable market with few disruptions
- No direct competition is anticipated in the near future. Our technology is patented in U.S. and Canada and is difficult to copy.
- Our R & D efforts will keep us ahead of the competition when there is competition.
- The management of Geophysics International is not risk adverse.
- Geophysics International will diversify its markets, locations of operation, and its services.
- The company can make a profit without outside investment but expansion will come about in less time with outside investment.
- Geophysics International will form partnerships with those companies who will facilitate expansion into areas where it lacks contacts or expertise.
- Geophysics International has a strong organization and is well positioned for the future.

Areas of Concern

Areas of concern to Geophysics International are: tax legislation affecting the petroleum and mining industries; the price of crude, gas, and raw materials; and the economic health of the industrialized world. A major change in any one of those areas can cause the company to rethink its future plans. Present planning stresses flexibility. We are trying to limit the impact of a downturn in any one of them. We are expanding geographically using the same concept of diversification to limit potential disruptions in cash flow. We believe we have been successful in following this strategy.

Regarding the generation of geologic reports, our major concerns are a lack of personnel and "perceived" conflicts of interest. We can effectively deal with both concerns.

While government regulation and economic or political turmoil may impact our clients, we are affected only indirectly. We anticipate a very friendly relationship with all governments of the world by:

- proving our technology superior in locating, delineating and evaluating old mine workings;
- having the Department of Interior utilize our service to detect dam site problems;
- having the EPA enthused about our ability to trace underground contaminants;
- and by the fact that at no time does our technology ever represent a threat to the environment, above or below the earth's surface.

In summary, our product is unique, well-integrated with nature, industry, government, and society, and represents enormous economic potential with very little risk.

In July 1985, Geophysics International published its first five year business plan. The following is a summary of where we are today versus where we thought we were going. I believe the record bodes well for our present plan.

There were six major goals identified in the 1985 plan which were as follows:

1) Penetrate the market of China
2) Penetrate the market of Australia
3) Penetrate the market of Canada
4) Add Satellite Imagery Analysis capabilities (Landsat)
5) Add Ground Penetrating Radar capabilities
6) Achieve $2.5 million gross revenues in 1986/87 fiscal year.

The first four goals were accomplished far sooner and better than our wildest dreams. Ground penetrating radar is still in the development stage and it may be years before problems are resolved. The price collapse of oil prevented us from achieving our $2.5 million in revenues, but, we still managed a small profit. However, this in turn caused us to streamline our operations to the "bare bone," and has shown us our true level of productivity, which has become our yardstick for the future. Simultaneously, diversification became our byword, and that too became a competitive advantage!

COMPANY MISSION

Geophysics International is successful because the company: competes on perceived value, not on price; provides unparalleled service and product quality; builds strong relationships with our customers; listens to their needs and responds quickly.

We are innovative and unique from our competitors. Above all, we are successful because of our people. We take pride in being an organization where "you make the difference."

Geophysics is pledged to provide a worldwide exploration service low in cost and high in results. We are in the business of locating earth's natural resources for our clients, and for the advancement of industry in general. We supply pertinent information to the clients about the subsurface of an area, before drilling, mining or engineering begins, and during the development phase.

We satisfy our client's needs by supplying low-cost geologic information that greatly increases the chance of discovering a new economic deposit beneath the earth's surface. The technology is the most advanced in the world. Our exploration instrument is called the Petro-Sonde and the principle behind it is called electrotellurics. Together, with our Satellite Imagery Analysis, we provide the most accurate resource exploration and engineering services in the world.

We will continue to provide the best service technically achievable through continued research and development. The company is a strong believer in research as a vehicle for expanded growth and profitability. We will continue to identify new applications which can successfully employ the Petro-Sonde method and/or our Satellite Imagery Analysis capability.

Those who invest with us, and all of Geophysics International's employees, can feel that they are making a major contribution to meeting the world's needs for natural resources. To our investors, we will provide above average returns on investments. To our employees, we will provide highly competitive salaries, benefits, and bonuses.

We will generate profits by hard work, aggressive marketing, strong research and development programs, excellent training programs, accurate Petro-Sonde field surveys, quality Satellite Imagery, and responsible fiscal management.

COMPANY PHILOSOPHY

We pledge to:

Provide the best exploration and engineering services possible for the least cost.

Have all management lead by example. To have management act in a manner in which they would want all employees to act.

Treat all employees like we ourselves would want to be treated.

Adhere to reasonable fiscal control. To spend money on those areas where we can expect a reasonable return in capital or human resources.

Create a working atmosphere which provides a good place for people to work; a good company in which to invest; and a good company from which to buy.

Observe these codes of conduct:
   Honesty
   Integrity
   Leadership
   Teamwork
   Development of employees
   Open opportunities for employees
   Be a good citizen
   Preserve private enterprise system
   Duty and loyalty
   Religious devotion

BENEFITS TO SOCIETY

Through our resource technology we hope to improve the lives of every man, woman, and child in the world. This may sound like a tall order but, just think what new fresh water discoveries would mean to millions of people who face starvation and drought in Africa.

In a capitalistic society, profit measures the rate of achievement towards your goals. The more worthwhile the goals, the more worthwhile it is to strive for that profit, and the more value that profit will have to society as a whole.

COMPANY CONCEPT OF SELF

We provide a low cost method of exploring for natural resources. The discovery and distribution of these resources on a planetary scale, can reduce the threat of war, while removing governments from the money markets, thereby allowing capital to be distributed in endeavors that will be of direct benefit to mankind.

The employees of Geophysics International are selected, not only for their professional abilities, but for their sense of commitment and appreciation of our ultimate goals. They communicate our values to outsiders, by their conduct and professionalism.

Those people who are associated with Geophysics International, either as employees or investors, will be part of the greater social impact that the company will make.

A Note From Jerome J. Conser, Founder and Managing Director:

In closing, let me interject a personal note. A strong belief in the Diety has guided me throughout my life. I believe in honesty and integrity. These are the principles that all employees of Geophysics International, as well as all people, should strive to follow, whether carrying on company business or living their personal lives. This is the image I want this company to project to all persons who come in contact with us. Only then can we assure long term growth and profitability.

APPLICATIONS OF THE *PETRO-SONDE*® TECHNOLOGY

SUBSURFACE EXPLORATION	OIL & GAS	COAL	NON-METALLIC MINERALS	ARCHAEOLOGY	CIVIL ENGINEERING	ENVIRONMENTAL GEOLOGY	HYDROLOGY		
RECONNAISSANCE									
Detect lithological changes	*	*	*		*	*	*		
Detect potential resource anomalies	*	*	*		*	*	*		
Define & correlate structural features	*	*	*		*	*	*		
Define drilling prospects	*	*	*		*	*	*		
EVALUATION									
Determine depth of resource	*	*	*		*	*	*		
Determine thickness	*	*	*		*	*	*		
Estimate volume & tonnage	*	*	*			*	*		
Evaluate resource quality & distribution	*	*	*		*	*	*		
Correlate stratigraphic units	*	*	*	*	*	*	*		
Define voids, abandoned mines, karst topography & soft beds		*	*	*	*	*			
Foundation & tunnel studies				*	*	*			
DEVELOPMENT									
Well planning	*	*	*		*	*	*		
Relative porosity	*	*	*		*	*	*		
Define ore limits, lenses, unproductive zones	*	*	*			*	*		
Detect hazardous conditions		*	*		*	*			
Mine planning		*	*						

Geophysics International strives to provide low cost, highly accurate exploration services to our clients. Use of advanced technology and excellent personnel, with the support of aggressive research and development programs, allows provision of an outstanding natural resource exploration service.

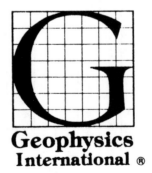

Appendix V

INGREDIENTS OF A REAL ESTATE LOAN SUBMISSION

  I. LOAN APPLICATION SUMMARY
    A. Amount requested
    B. Interest rate of loan
    C. Term of loan
    D. Key indicators and ratios
       1. Loan to value ratio
       2. Debt service coverage
       3. Break-even point
    E. Narrative summary of project

 II. PHYSICAL DESCRIPTION OF PROJECT
    A. Project description (narrative)
    B. Neighborhood and vicinity description
       1. City location map (street map) showing subject property and competition
       2. Vicinity map of immediate neighborhood
       3. Aerial photograph of site
    C. Plot plan
       1. Subject property outlined in red
       2. Square footage of land area indicated
    D. General and economic information on the area
    E. Plans and specifications
       1. Floor plan
       2. Elevations
       3. Layout of site including parking
    F. Cost breakdown of project
       1. Direct building costs
       2. Land acquisition costs and date of acquisition
       3. Site preparation

    4. Consultants (architects, engineer, attorney, realtor)
    5. Construction period interest and taxes
    6. Marketing costs and leasing costs
    7. Loan fees
    8. Overhead items
    9. Projected profit
  G. Schedule of construction, leasing, and loan closing
  H. Appraisal of project including land
  I. Photographs

III. PRINCIPALS
  A. Background and experience of principals
    1. Experience in similar projects
    2. Other projects of principals
  B. Financial statement of principals
  C. Additional financial information
    1. Credit report
    2. Bank references
    3. Taxpayer ID number
    4. Tax returns for two previous years

IV. FINANCIAL DESCRIPTION OF PROJECT
  A. Pro forma income and expense statement
  B. Actual operating history for past three years (if available)
  C. Source of equity capital

V. PROJECT LEASE INFORMATION
  A. Summary of leases or letters of intent
    1. Name of lessee
    2. Gross leaseable area
    3. Rent
      a. Gross annual rent
      b. Rent per square foot
      c. Rental escalators
      d. Percentage rentals
    4. Expenses borne by lessee as part of rent
      a. Taxes
      b. Insurance
      c. Maintenance
      d. Utilities and other
      e. Common area charges
    5. Terms of lease
    6. Options for renewal
    7. Estimated sales and income of tenant

      8. Status of lease execution
- B. Copies of tenant leases
- C. Credit information on tenant

VI. LEGAL DATA CONCERNING PROJECT
- A. Legal description
- B. Title report
- C. Survey
- D. Zoning and land use information
  1. Building restrictions
  2. Parking requirements to meet ordinances
- E. Building Permit
- F. Construction Contracts
- G. Declaration of Conditions, Covenants, and Restrictions (CC&R)

Index